THE IMAGINATIVE VISION OF ABDILATIF ABDALLA'S *VOICE OF AGONY*

African Perspectives
Kelly Askew, Laura Fair, and Pamila Gupta
Series Editors

The Imaginative Vision of Abdilatif Abdalla's Voice of Agony
Abdilatif Abdalla, edited by Annmarie Drury

Congo Style: From Belgian Art Nouveau to African Independence
Ruth Sacks

Writing on the Soil: Land and Landscape in Literature
from Eastern and Southern Africa
Ng'ang'a Wahu-Mũchiri

Lagos Never Spoils: Nollywood and Nigerian City Life
Connor Ryan

Continuous Pasts: Frictions of Memory in Postcolonial Africa
Sakiru Adebayo

Power / Knowledge / Land: Contested Ontologies of Land
and Its Governance in Africa
Laura A. German

In Search of Tunga: *Prosperity, Almighty God,*
and Lives in Motion in a Malian Provincial Town
André Chappatte

The Infrastructures of Security: Technologies of Risk
Management in Johannesburg
Martin J. Murray

There Used to Be Order: Life on the Copperbelt after the Privatisation
of the Zambia Consolidated Copper Mines
Patience Mususa

Animated by Uncertainty: Rugby and the Performance
of History in South Africa
Joshua D. Rubin

A complete list of titles in the series can be found at
www.press.umich.edu

The Imaginative Vision of Abdilatif Abdalla's *Voice of Agony*

Abdilatif Abdalla

POEMS TRANSLATED BY KEN WALIBORA WALIAULA

EDITED BY ANNMARIE DRURY

University of Michigan Press
Ann Arbor

Copyright © 2024 by Abdilatif Abdalla

All rights reserved

For questions or permissions, please contact um.press.perms@umich.edu

Published in the United States of America by the University of Michigan Press
Manufactured in the United States of America
Printed on acid-free paper
First published January 2024

A CIP catalog record for this book is available from the British Library.
Library of Congress Cataloging-in-Publication data has been applied for.

ISBN 978-0-472-07661-1 (hardcover : alk. paper)
ISBN 978-0-472-05661-3 (paper : alk. paper)
ISBN 978-0-472-22146-2 (e-book)

Cover art and design by Khalid Khamis Mwajambia.

Published in Africa by Mkuki na Nyota Publishers Ltd., Dar es Salaam, Tanzania

CONTENTS

Editor's Introduction
  Annmarie Drury   ix

Preface to the Translation
  Ngũgĩ wa Thiong'o   xix

Translator's Introduction
  Ken Walibora Waliaula   xxiii

Voice of Agony | *Sauti ya Dhiki* | Translated by Ken Walibora Waliaula

I Won't Compromise | *N'shishiyelo ni Lilo*   5
Go and Console Him | *Kamliwaze*   13
Worry Not | *Tuza Moyo*   15
The Boil | *Jipu*   17
I'll Never Let Go | *Siwati*   21
Crocodile | *Mamba*   23
I Remember You | *Nakukumbuka*   25
Human Perfection | *Ukamilifu wa Mja*   27
What Has Offended You? | *Lilokuudhi ni Lipi?*   33
Coconut Palm: A Tug-of-War | *Mnazi: Vuta N'kuvute*   39
This Speaking Out | *Kuno Kunena*   57
Slipperiness | *Telezi*   59
Speak Out, You Who Dare | *Semani Wenye Kusema*   63
Even a Clever Guy Can't Shave His Own Head |
   Muwerevu Hajinyowi   65
It Will End | *Yatakoma*   67
Alas, My Friend! | *Ah! Mwenzangu*   69
Be Gone, Anxiety | *Wasiwasi Enda Zako*   75
What a Bad Fellow! | *Mja si Mwema*   79
What Will Happen? | *Lipi Litakalokuwa?*   83

vi • Contents

Our Mother Africa | *Mamaetu Afrika*	85
Yesterday and Today and Tomorrow | *Jana na Leo na Kesho*	101
A Precious Thing Can't Last | *Chema Hakidumu*	113
Be Patient, My Heart | *Moyo Iwa na Subira*	115
Don't Kill Me! | *Usiniuwe!*	121
Things Have Their Own Ways | *Mambo Yana Mambo Yake*	133
Don't Listen to Them | *Watiliye Pamba*	147
Pampering | *Tendekezo*	149
I Wouldn't Be Here Today | *Leo N'singekuwako*	151
Cockadoodle-do! | *Kokoiko!*	153
Don't Cling to Silence | *'Sikakawane na Kimya*	155
Travelers, Let's Wake Up | *Wasafiri Tuamkeni*	159
Come to Your Senses | *Zindukani*	165
Goodbye | *Kwa Heri*	175
The Town Cockerel and the Country One | *La Mjini na la Shamba*	177
Wash Him | *Muosheni*	179
I'm Coming | *Naja*	183
Crossroads | *Ndiya Panda*	189
A Thing Can't Be Human | *Kichu Hakiwi ni Uchu*	197
Tit for Tat | *Kutendana*	215
I'm Back | *N'sharudi*	285

Critical Perspectives

Sauti ya Dhiki: Its Place in Swahili Literature and East African Literature	
Ann Biersteker	289
Abdilatif and I: Reflections on Comparative Experiences	
Alamin Mazrui	301
Rhymed, Metrical Translations of Four Poems	
Meg Arenberg	313
This is What I Hold Fast | *N'shishiyelo ni Lilo*	313
Crocodile | *Mamba*	317
I Remember You | *Nakukumbuka*	318
Which Will It Be? | *Lipi Litakalokuwa?*	319

Contents • vii

Textual Backgrounds: *Voice of Agony* in Its Historical Moment

Kenya: Twendapi? | Kenya: Where Are We Heading?
  Abdilatif Abdalla, Translated by Kai Kresse   323
Introduction to the 1973 Edition
  Shihabuddin Chiraghdin, Translated by Ann Biersteker   331
Author's Preface to the 1973 Edition
  Abdilatif Abdalla, Translated by Ann Biersteker   337

Bibliography   339

Contributors   343

EDITOR'S INTRODUCTION: ON THE IMAGINATIVE VISION

Annmarie Drury

Sauti ya Dhiki, in English translation *Voice of Agony*, is an extraordinary collection of poetry. Abdilatif Abdalla wrote 39 of its 40 poems while he was held as a political prisoner in Kenya from 1969 to 1972; only the final poem, "N'sharudi" ("I'm Back"), was composed after his release. While the eminence of the collection within Swahili literature might suggest otherwise, these are poems of a young man. When he was arrested in December 1968, for his authorship of a pamphlet sharply critical of the autocratic and repressive government of Jomo Kenyatta, the first president of independent Kenya, Abdalla was 22 years old. He turned 23 shortly after presenting his own legal defense in court in Mombasa, having found no lawyer willing to represent him. He successfully defended himself against the charge, conspiracy to overthrow the government by force of arms, that carried a death penalty, the possibility of which haunted him throughout his trial; but he was sentenced to 18 months in prison on three charges of sedition. On the government's appeal, in May 1969, the court doubled his sentence to three years in solitary confinement. Such was the traumatic experience behind Abdalla and the grim prospect he faced when he wrote, on toilet paper, the first poem in this collection, "N'shishiyelo ni Lilo" ("I Won't Compromise"). Its first word, if partly a plea, is also an instruction, and an authoritative wielding of a traditional poetic opening in Swahili: *Nipulikiza*: Listen to me.

Thus Abdalla's earliest poem from prison articulates his recommitment to the political stance, the challenge to authoritarianism, that had brought him profound hardship. An important term in the pamphlet that motivated his arrest, *Kenya: Where Are We Heading?* (*Kenya: Twendapi?*), as the scholar Kai Kresse has remarked, is "wasiotosheka," which appears there in capital letters—in English translation, THE DISCONTENTED.[1] In defending

---

1. Kai Kresse, "*Kenya: Twendapi?*: Re-Reading Abdilatif Abdalla's Pamphlet Fifty Years after Independence," *Africa* 86, no. 1 (February 2016): 8. Kresse's English translation of the pamphlet appears in this volume.

x • *Editor's Introduction: On the Imaginative Vision*

himself in court, Abdalla resolutely insisted on his commitment to justice in Kenya, which had gained independence five years before he published his pamphlet. Of his giving evidence at trial, a newspaper reports:

> Explaining what he said was his intention when he wrote the pamphlet, Abdul latif [*sic*] said that first he was made to write it by the belief he held.

> He believed that in Kenya should exist an atmosphere in which every citizen shared the responsibility for every wrong and injustice done in the country. He also believed that it was the duty of every Kenyan to see that any wrong or injustice was not committed.[2]

Alone in his cell in Kenya's infamous Kamiti Maximum Security Prison, where he was held for most of his sentence, Abdalla remained discontented with political conditions in his country, and poetry became his primary vehicle of communication. One way of reading the poems in this collection, each of which carries the date of its composition, is as an extension and transformation of the pamphleteering for which Abdalla paid a high price. Raised in a community and family that shared in a lively poetic tradition, he had absorbed and pondered poems from his childhood. Alone in prison, writing with pencil stubs provided him by sympathetic guards, he transferred his engagements—political, literary, emotional—fully into the poetic genre, his métier.

Those engagements are complex. Composed in an array of rhymed, metrical forms—some established Swahili verse forms and some of Abdalla's own subtle invention—the poems in *Voice of Agony* undertake many tasks. They reiterate and develop Abdalla's political stance, philosophize, lament bodily suffering (such as in "Jipu," "The Boil"), elegize the dead (Abdalla's grandmother and infant son poignantly in "Chema Hakidumu," "A Precious Thing Can't Last," for example), wrestle with loneliness, self-console, enact mini-dramas between men and women (as in "Kutendana," "Tit for Tat"), and meditate on the choices and betrayals that brought Abdalla to prison (as in "Telezi," "Slipperiness," and "Mja Si Mwema," "What a Bad Fellow!"). Many

---

2. "Lawyers Refuse to Defend, Says Accused," *The Standard*, Thursday 6 March 1969. Additional reporting from Mombasa on the trial and sentencing includes "Two in Kenya Deny Sedition," *The Standard*, Tuesday 4 March 1969; "Writer Denies Incitement," *The Standard*, Friday 7 March 1969; "18 Months Jail for Sedition," *The Standard*, Thursday 20 March 1969; "Judge Doubles Sedition Sentence," *The Standard*, Friday 9 May 1969.

poems engage in more than one of these endeavors, of course. Encountering the evocative depiction of somatic experience in "Jipu" ("The Boil"), a reader may sense that the "boil" has a metaphorical register—that Abdalla describes bodily experience to communicate about other sorts of painful conditions, political ones, from which people seek release.

Abdalla writes primarily in the Swahili of Mombasa, the dialect called Kimvita, except where he experiments with other Swahili dialects. Since the term "dialect," *lahaja* in Swahili, circulates throughout this volume and is crucial for an understanding of Abdalla's place in Swahili literature, it will be helpful to clarify its significance for readers unfamiliar with the Swahiliphone world. The Swahili language has a dozen or so regional variants, or dialects, largely mutually intelligible but distinguished by significant differences in morphology, vocabulary, and thus, at the auditory level, sound patterns. (In writing, whether in the Roman alphabet or in a modified version of the Arabic alphabet, these register as different spellings.) The "Standard Swahili" established under British rule from the late 1920s is based on the dialect of Zanzibar, Kiunguja. Kimvita, a more northerly dialect than Kiunguja, differs from Standard Swahili, and differs again from, for example, the still more northerly dialect of Lamu, Kiamu. Historically, the northern dialects of Swahili, especially Kiamu and Kimvita, served as repositories of the poetic tradition, and so the language standardization of the British colonial era functioned to sideline texts in that tradition.[3] Abdalla's choice of Kimvita—the language of his home and community, as opposed to an imposed standard—thus forms part of his political stance.

His poems also join a tradition of Swahili poetry in Kimvita. The celebrated nineteenth-century Mombasan poet Muyaka bin Haji (1776–1840), from whom Abdalla takes the epigraph to his volume, and who was himself politically engaged, is the most significant predecessor informing Abdalla's original and learned collection.[4] Yet the Kimvita of Abdalla's poems is not Muyaka's nineteenth-century language. Rather, Abdalla forges a poetic Kimvita for and of the latter twentieth century, an accomplishment that the celebrated Swahili scholar Shihabuddin Chiraghdin, in his

---

3. On the standardization of Swahili and its significance for Swahili literature, see Serena Talento, "Consecration, Deconsecration, and Reconsecration: The Shifting Role of Literary Translation into Swahili," in *Translators Have Their Say?: Translation and the Power of Agency*, edited by Abdel-Wahab Khalifa (Zürich: LIT, 2014), 52–57.

4. The best English-language source on Muyaka and his poems remains Mohamed H. Abdulaziz, *Muyaka: 19th century Swahili Popular Poetry* (Nairobi: Kenya Literature Bureau, 1979).

xii • *Editor's Introduction: On the Imaginative Vision*

original introduction to the collection, recognized. Writing in an era of lively intellectual debate over Swahili language and literature, when the very term *for* "literature" in Swahili was up for discussion,[5] Chiraghdin saw in Abdalla's poetry a model for how the diverse literary languages of Swahili might be cultivated—how Swahili might, in effect, be de-standardized through the nurturing of writers in each dialect of the language.[6] Although Abdalla's poems play with dialectical variation more than Chiraghdin acknowledges, Chiraghdin's perspective illuminates the significance of Abdalla's Kimvita at the moment when his poems entered the world—how their language in itself constituted a statement of independence, possibility, and dissent.

Yet that statement is not bald, and Abdalla's poems resonate with a distinctive subtlety and complexity in language. The role that Swahili dialectal variation has in this will remain largely hidden to readers in English, but with a little guidance it is possible to discern something about it. The most notable experimentation with dialect in the collection occurs with the Kigunya dialect in "Kichu Hakiwi ni Uchu" ("A Thing Can't be Human").[7] For a reader of Swahili, the dialectical shift presents itself from the start, in the poem's title (where Standard Swahili would have "Kitu Hakiwi ni Utu"); but a non-Swahili speaker can locate the movement between dialects at stanza 13 and can then grasp the sound profile of Kigunya, with the prominence of "ch" and "dh" (instead of "t" and "z"), by sight-reading, so to speak, the Swahili text up

---

5. Joshua Madumulla, Elena Bertoncini, and Jan Blommaert, "Politics, Ideology and Poetic Form: the Literary Debate in Tanzania," in *Language Ideological Debates*, edited by Jan Blommaert (New York: Mouton de Gruyter 1999), 316.

6. As part of his argument against colonial hierarchization of varieties of Swahili, Chiraghdin advocates use of the Swahili term *lahaja*, "dialects," instead of *vilugha*, "lesser languages," at a moment when *lahaja* was not yet fully in use; see Ann Biersteker's English translation of his introduction in this volume. Recent scholarship argues for the value of understanding Swahili dialects on a "continuum" and considers the poetic action of dialectical multiplicity: see Alena Rettová, "Swahili and Swahili Poetry in Lubumbashi: The Language and Lyrics of Sando Marteau," *Archiv Orientální* 86, no. 3 (2018): 333–362, from which I take the term "continuum" (334). For an account of ideologies shaping approaches to historical linguistics of African languages, including Swahili, before the 1960s, and of transformations in contemporary approaches, see Augustine Agweule, "Practice of Historical Linguistics and Language Codification in Africa," *History Compass* 6, no. 1 (2008): 1–24.

7. The Kigunya dialect is also known as Kitikuu. It is worth noting the impossibility of adequately translating the title phrase, which draws meaning from the Swahili noun-class system (specifically, the distinction between nouns of the "ki/vi" class, sometimes called the "useful objects" class, on one hand, and of the "u" class, sometimes called the "abstract concepts" class, on the other) and so links philosophy with grammar.

Editor's Introduction: On the Imaginative Vision • xiii

to that point in the poem. Even as he enacts his dialectical shift in the 13th stanza, out of Kigunya and into Kimvita, Abdalla remarks that communicating in Kigunya is a bit arduous:

> Kiswahili cha Kigunya, kwacho 'kiwazungumza
> 'Mejaribu kubambanya, kiyasi n'livyoweza

> The Kiswahili I've been speaking is the Kigunya dialect
> I've only tried to fumble as far as I could

Perhaps the adeptness of these lines belies their assertions. Even so, a change in pacing and voice emerges in subsequent stanzas, after Abdalla has moved into his own Kimvita. He remarks on the difference in his relationship with these dialects. Of Kimvita, now writing *in* Kimvita, he says:

> Sikwenda kukitafuta, n'likikuta nyumbani
> Mi nacho ni kama pata, twendapo hatuwatani
> Na tangu kwinukiyani, hicho ndicho hutumiya

> I never went looking for it, I found it at home
> Kimvita and I are like twins, together wherever we go
> In all my growing up, this is what I've used

The lines bear witness to the conjunction of language and self.[8] Abdalla's testament of devotion to language here, especially to Kimvita, the Swahili of his home, emerges implicitly and explicitly throughout *Voice of Agony*.

If one reads *Voice of Agony* by attending to the order of the poems, thinking about the collection as itself poetical in construction, the volume reveals how lyrical and socio-political interests create and re-create one another in Abdalla's poetic practice. Take, for example, a poem at the center of the collection, "A Precious Thing Can't Last" ("Chema Hakidumu"). The lack of attention to this poem in critical discussion suggests it is usually understood to be separate from the overtly political poems of *Voice of Agony*, but the lyric presence it fashions has an intrinsic role in the political project of the book. The lyrical and the socio-political are deeply intertwined in Abdalla's volume,

---

8. Clarissa Vierke, in an excellent discussion of this poem, refers to Abdalla's "incomparable familiarity" with Kimvita: "'What Is There in My Speaking': Re-Explorations of Language in Abdilatif Abdalla's Anthology of Prison Poetry, *Sauti Ya Dhiki*," *Research in African Literatures* 48, no. 1 (2017): 140.

xiv • *Editor's Introduction: On the Imaginative Vision*

and interchange between them operates as an engine of *Voice of Agony*. The poems make and re-make lyric subjectivities as they, and so that they may, communicate political dissent and social commentary.

In the Swahili of "A Precious Thing Can't Last" ("Chema Hakidumu"), each stanza opens with "chema," a good or precious thing; thus the poem insists on its endurance for the life of the poem—a precious thing may not last always, but in repetition it will endure here—and enacts, with its own ending, the transience it laments. The poem's central stanza, the third of five, enters a striking mode of questioning:

> Chema mara ngapi, kinniondoka!
> Mwanangu yu wapi? Hakukaa mwaka
> Kwa muda mfupi, aliwatilika
> Ningefanya lipi, ela kumzika?

> How many times has a precious thing gone!
> Where is my child? He didn't live beyond a year
> For just a brief moment—before he died, it wasn't long
> What could I do but bury him?

Poetic questions such as these have no simple answers. The final stanza mingles consolation with loss. Its two middle lines intimate a challenge to the argument of the poem until now, the assertion that "a precious thing can't last," for they dwell on the presence in emotional experience of the poet's grandmother, Poni, rather than on her absence:

> Hadi siku hini, yu moyoni mwangu
> Yu moyoni ndani, hadi kufa kwangu

> Until today she remains in my heart
> She is in my heart until the day I die

In the Swahili, rhyme in these two lines enhances concentration on the interior life and develops a sense of self-possession: rhyme on the possessive adjective "-angu," "my," at the end of lines and, medially, on "ni," a syllable that links sonically to the first-person singular in Swahili (as a subject prefix) and to interiority (which it can denote as a suffix). For and within the poet, in these lines, the beloved grandmother remains present.

Abdalla wrote "A Precious Thing Can't Last" after the sudden death of a senior superintendent in the prison where he was held in solitary confinement,[9] and here we find a pattern characteristic of the collection, a movement in emotional line from an immediate occasion within the prison walls—here, of grief—outward to events across the poet's life. The superintendent, named Haji, had shown compassion and kindness towards Abdalla, coming to talk with him and letting him out of his solitary cell. He held this position only for about three months before his death, which was a blow to Abdalla. Conversation and time outdoors ended, changing Abdalla's days for the worse. Impelled by this grief, the poem visits a series of scarcely ponderable losses; the sorrows connect. The articulation of such relation contributes to *Voice of Agony*'s meditative and philosophical quality. That in turn enriches its political stance. Experientially, "A Precious Thing Can't Last" connects to "Wash Him" ("Muosheni"), with its depiction of an elegiac Islamic ritual, the washing of a body to prepare it for burial. Unable to participate in this ritual for the departed Haji, the poet evokes it in imagination: "Wash him so we can hoist him on our shoulders/ Wash him so we can go and bury him" ("Muosheni, mabegani tujitweke/ Muosheni, twenende tukamzike"). Poetic evocation of ritual joins the world inside Kamiti Prison with the world outside, threading together experiences in the poet's own psyche and lending a holistic quality to his political philosophy.

The poems of *Voice of Agony* are often sociable, invoking their audience, and sometimes resonantly playful. "Tit for Tat" ("Kutendana"), the longest poem of the book, which Abdalla wrote late in his imprisonment, displays these qualities. While Abdalla suggested to his editor at Oxford that this poem might be published separately from the rest of the manuscript, given its length and dramatic mode, the editor's insistence that it be included in *Voice of Agony*—because, like the other poems, it was composed during Abdalla's imprisonment—seems astute.[10] This animated poem reveals an imaginative phase late in Abdalla's incarceration, one in which, as the poet imagines the interior life of the man and two women at its center, he engages with them as commentator and interlocutor, witnessing their romantic drama and discussing it with readers. The Swahili phrase *moyoni akatamka*, "he thought in his heart," or "she said [to herself] in her heart," or simply "she said to herself,"

---

9. My source on the circumstances surrounding this poem is conversation with Abdilatif Abdalla, November 2018.

10. My source on the editorial background is conversation with Abdilatif Abdalla, March 2021.

xvi • *Editor's Introduction: On the Imaginative Vision*

which recurs in this poem, suggests the poet's quest to engage with the interiority of others. In this poem, we find the poet creating a small society for himself—and for us, now.

After he was released from prison, Abdalla's life had many phases. He left Kenya for Tanzania, where he worked at the University of Dar es Salaam. He left East Africa for London, where he worked in radio and print journalism while contributing significantly to the Committee for the Release of Political Prisoners in Kenya, and later moved to Germany, where he taught at the University of Leipzig. In Swahili literature, he has translated and edited extensively, creating a Swahili translation of Ayi Kwei Armah's *The Beautyful Ones Are Not Yet Born* and, as co-translator, a Swahili version of Vaclav Havel's *Vernisáž* (in English, *Unveiling* or *Private View*), and editing many volumes of poetry, from nineteenth-century poetry of Pemba to collections of contemporary poetry such as Said Ahmed Mohamed's *'Sikate Tamaa*.[11] He also collaborated on the first comprehensive English translation of poems attributed to the Swahili poet-hero Fumo Liyongo.[12] His political commitments have endured. They include his dedication to explaining and fulfilling his understanding of the social responsibility of the writer, an interest that early emerged in two eloquent talks delivered at the University of Dar es Salaam in the late 1970s, "Wajibu wa Mshairi katika Jamii Yake" ("The Obligations of a Poet within His/Her Society") and "Matatizo ya Mwandishi wa Jamii katika Afrika Huru" ("Problems of a People's Writer in Independent Africa").[13]

There is always a case for reading a book of poems in translation on its own, as a collection of poems that lend context to one another, a world in

---

11. The translations are Ayi Kwei Armah, *Wema Hawajazaliwa*, translated by A. Abdalla (Nairobi: Heinemann, 1975) and Vaclav Havel, *Uzinduzi*, translated by Abdilatif Abdalla and Alena Rettová (Prague: Zdeněk Susa, 2005); the collection of poems from Pemba is Abdurrahman Saggaf Alawy and Ali Abdalla El-Maawy, *Kale ya Washairi wa Pemba: Kamange na Sarahani*, edited by Abdilatif Abdalla (Dar es Salaam: Mkuki na Nyota, 2011); volumes of contemporary poetry edited by Abdalla include Said Ahmed Mohamed, *'Sikate Tamaa*, edited by Abdilatif Abdalla (Nairobi: Longman, 1980); K.A. Nyamaume, *Diwani ya Ustadh Nyamaume*, poems collected by S.C. Gonga, edited by Abdilatif Abdalla (Nairobi: Shungwaya Publishers, 1976); and (by Abdalla's half-brother) Ahmad Nassir (Juma Bhalo), *Taa ya Umalenga*, edited by Abdilatif Abdalla (Nairobi: Kenya Literature Bureau, 1982).

12. Gudrun Miehe, Abdilatif Abdalla and Liyongo Working Group, eds. *Liyongo Songs: Poems Attributed to Fumo Liyongo* (Cologne: Rüdiger Köppe Verlag, 2004).

13. Abdilatif Abdalla, "Wajibu wa Mshairi katika Jamii Yake" ("The Obligations of a Poet within His/Her Society"), 1976, in *Abdilatif Abdalla: Poet in Politics*, edited by Rose Marie Beck and Kai Kresse (Dar es Salaam: Mkuki na Nyota, 2016), 81–86; and "Matatizo ya Mwandishi wa Jamii katika Afrika Huru" ("Problems of a People's Writer in Independent Africa"), 1978, in *Abdilatif Abdalla: Poet in Politics*, 87–95.

themselves. It remains possible, here, to read *Voice of Agony* that way. But the supplementary materials in *Imaginative Vision* have been chosen to tell a story: of Abdalla's political activism before his imprisonment, including the pamphlet that directly motivated his arrest; of the influence of these poems throughout Swahili literature, across genres and generations; and of the persistence within the poet himself of the social and literary commitments—the belief in the power of the political and of the word—vividly evident in this collection. Ngũgĩ wa Thiong'o, in his "Preface to the Translation," writes from his decades-long friendship with Abdalla, tracing the significance of *Voice of Agony*, "the founding text of modern Kenya's prison literature" (p. xix), in his own career as a writer and activist. In his "Translator's Introduction," the late Ken Walibora Waliaula reflects on the experience of translating Abdalla's poems and situates them within African traditions of prison literature and political resistance, particularly in their use of "symbols and metaphors" that constitute "survival tactics" for the political prisoner (p. xxvi).

In the "Critical Perspectives" section, Ann Biersteker, in "*Sauti ya Dhiki*: Its Place in Swahili Literature and East African Literature," traces the influences of and upon *Voice of Agony* with rare expertise and considers the collection's affiliations with a global literature of social engagement, envisioning the constellation of texts it would join "if a history were written of socialist poetry worldwide published in 1973" (pp. 298–99). The poet, playwright, and scholar Alamin Mazrui, in "Abdilatif and I," describes how his own arrest, imprisonment, and authoring of a book of poems while he was incarcerated in Kenya intertwined with his reading and teaching of *Sauti ya Dhiki*—down to the very notes he had made, prior to his arrest, to share with his university class. He reflects on similarities and divergences between his poems and Abdalla's to illuminate Abdalla's poetic ethos and aesthetic, highlighting Abdalla's powers of creative synthesis: his unusual ability "to translate radical ideas from the West in ways that make them organic to the African body politic" (p. 309). Meg Arenberg, in "Rhymed, Metrical Translations of Four Poems," offers her translatorly reflection alongside rhymed, metrical English renderings of four poems from the collection. Here, we adopt the understanding of translation Lawrence Venuti calls "hermeneutic," which recognizes translation as "an interpretive act that varies the source text."[14] Multiplicity in

---

14. Lawrence Venuti, *Contra Instrumentalism: A Translation Polemic* (Lincoln: University of Nebraska Press, 2019), 8. In this understanding, Venuti writes, translation illuminates how "the linguistic and cultural differences constituting that text [...] are always reworked to be comprehended and affective in the translating culture" (8).

xviii • *Editor's Introduction: On the Imaginative Vision*

translation enriches reading, as Matthew Reynolds writes, "opening up the plural signifying potential of the source text and spreading it into multiple versions."[15] Arenberg's four renderings, created with a prosodic approach distinct from Ken Walibora Waliaula's in the main body of translations, give English-language readers a source of further insight into Abdalla's verbal art and into the choices and contingencies involved in bringing it into English.

In the section "Textual Backgrounds: *Voice of Agony* in Its Historical Moment," Kai Kresse provides the first English translation of the pamphlet that caused Abdalla's arrest, *Kenya Twendapi* (*Kenya: Where Are We Heading?*). Ann Biersteker's English translations of the original introduction to the 1973 edition, by Shihabuddin Chiraghdin, and of Abdalla's author's preface to that volume, show Anglophone readers, for the first time, how Abdalla's poems were heard upon their entrance into the world and reveal the terms that Abdalla used to introduce them to their first audience.

It remains to offer thanks, inadequate as these may be. The title of this book shares a phrase with two events, a panel chaired by Kai Kresse at the annual meeting of the African Literature Association in June 2017 ("The Imaginative Vision of Abdilatif Abdalla, Swahili Poet and Activist") and a roundtable of November 2017 organized by Meg Arenberg at the Princeton Institute for International and Regional Studies ("The Imaginative Vision of Abdilatif Abdalla"). I am grateful to each of them for agreeing to our use of the phrase here. We thank Cambridge University Press and the editors of *Africa* for permission to reprint Kai Kresse's English translation of *Kenya: Where Are We Heading?* An earlier version of Meg Arenberg's translation "Crocodile" appeared in *Words Without Borders*. This book benefited greatly from the knowledgeable comments of two anonymous readers; from the insights and generosity of our series editors Kelly Askew and Laura Fair, whose interventions assisted immensely at crucial moments; and from the discernment and know-how of Ellen Bauerle, formerly the executive editor of the University of Michigan Press, and of Elizabeth Demers, currently the executive editor, who made everything possible. Abdilatif Abdalla is an unfailing source of wisdom and levity and a model for a literary life; I cannot thank him enough for all he has contributed to this book, and to my understanding of poetry. In April 2020, all of us working on this volume were deeply saddened by the sudden and tragic death of Ken Walibora Waliaula, whose love for Abdalla's poetry animated this project. We remember him and thank him.

---

15. Matthew Reynolds, Introduction to *Prismatic Translation*, edited by Matthew Reynolds (Cambridge: Legenda, 2019), 3.

PREFACE TO THE TRANSLATION

Ngũgĩ wa Thiong'o

Abdilatif Abdalla is independent Kenya's first political and literary prisoner. But there were other such prisoners in pre-independence Kenya. In the colonial era, poets and singers of the Land and Freedom Army, misnamed Mau Mau by the colonial state, were hurled into prisons and concentration camps, along with thousands of other members of the anti-colonial resistance movement. These poets and writers and editors include Henry Muoria, Stanley Kagika, Gakaara Wa Wanjaũ, the latter remaining in the concentration camp for eight years. Abdalla's imprisonment in the post-colonial era thus connects him to those of the colonial era.

But it also connects him to those of the pre-colonial era, including the most famous, Fumo Liyongo, in twelfth-century Pate, an island to the north of Kenya's coast. All these fall into a category that goes beyond political prisoner. They were imprisoned for their politics, yes, but theirs was the politics inherent in their art. It was the voice of prophecy in their poetry and stories that the ruling powers wanted to silence.

But in each case their imagination broke through the walls of confinement to voice their prophecies. In other words, the ruling power could imprison the body of the poet, but not the imagination of the poet. So in prison the poets wrote back to power. They used every guise and guile to access writing material denied them. When they could not reach pen and paper, they committed their art to memory, to release it to the world whenever time and opportunity allowed.

Abdalla's *Sauti ya Dhiki* is the first major work of Kenyan and East African writers in general to survive prison and speak to the world. It is the founding text of modern Kenya's prison literature. After three years in the Kamiti Maximum Security Prison, Abdalla could come out swinging defiance left and right, with the affirmation that he still held the pro-people beliefs for which he had been incarcerated.

I personally am indebted to the writer and the text. *Sauti ya Dhiki* was published in 1973 and won the prestigious Jomo Kenyatta Prize for Literature.

xx • *Preface to the Translation*

Ironically, Jomo Kenyatta was the president who had imprisoned him—the same president who, eight years later, would put me in the same maximum-security prison that had held Abdilatif Abdalla for three years. There I found other political prisoners who immediately pointed me to the neighboring block where Abdalla had been held. Through the window of my own cell, I could see the window of his prison cell where *Sauti ya Dhiki* was written on toilet paper. It was comforting and even inspiring to me to know that another writer had survived prison and told the tale. This knowledge was important to me as I also wrote my own work on toilet paper, the work that would bear the title, *Caitaani Mũtharabainĩ* (*Devil on the Cross*), which would become the founding text of the modern Gĩkũyũ-language novel.

Thus, Abdilatif Abdalla's work connects him to another tradition: of refusing to bow down, of defiance, which produces art that embodies the aesthetic of resistance. The politician had tried to muzzle the poet; the poet came out with words that dazzled the world. Kenyans and others who could access *Sauti ya Dhiki* have always known of its centrality in the canon of Swahili literature and Kenyan literature in general. But it has not been readily available to English-language readers in and outside Africa.

This splendid translation by Ken Walibora Waliaula rectifies that situation. Through this translation Abdilatif Abdalla will now be accessible to that worldwide scholarship and readership of African Literature in English. But I hope this translation generates other translations into other languages of the earth, both African and non-African.

I also hope it will draw attention to Abdilatif Abdalla and his many-sided achievements. He has published many articles in literary magazines and chapters in several books. He has given many more papers at conferences all over the world. One of his important legacies is as a major compiler and editor of *Kamusi ya Kiswahili Sanifu*, a monolingual Kiswahili dictionary published by Oxford University Press.

He has also given platform to many writers and thinkers, especially when, from 1979 to 1986, he worked at the Kiswahili Department of the BBC World Service, Bush House, London, and when, from 1986 to 1994, he was Managing Director and Editor-in-Chief of *Africa Events*, an international current-affairs monthly magazine on Africa published in London.

Outside his writing, teaching, and editing, Abdilatif has been a great fighter for human rights. The spirit that drove him when he was a young man to write *Kenya Twendapi*, which led him to Maximum Security Prison, lives on in his political activism. He has been a leader in opposing human rights abuses in Kenya, and for many years he was a leader in the international Committee for the Release of Political Prisoners in Kenya and a central figure in the movements for democracy in Kenya.

Quite rightly, his writing and human rights activism have earned him several awards, including the Kenyatta Prize; the 2018 Fonlon-Nichols Award for Excellence in Creative Writing and Contributions to the Struggle for Human Rights and Freedom of Expression; and the 1977 Saba-Saba Literary Award (in Tanzania).

His many-sided talents are still most manifest in *Sauti ya Dhiki*. English readers will now be able to get glimpses of the soul of a great Swahili writer and thinker and a global public intellectual.

TRANSLATOR'S INTRODUCTION

Ken Walibora Waliaula

After intense and delightful study of Abdilatif Abdalla's Swahili masterpiece *Sauti ya Dhiki* in my doctoral dissertation at The Ohio State University, I found irresistible the urge to translate it into English for the non-Swahili-speaking audience. Yet it was in interactions with Abdalla himself, at conferences such as the one held in his honor at the University of Leipzig in May 2011, that the idea of translating his anthology of prison poems was crystallized. When I broached the subject, Abdalla not only readily granted me permission to translate his work, but expressed confidence in my ability to do so. Upon starting the project, I realized that the translation would be useful not only to the non-Swahili-speaking audience, but also to those with knowledge of and competence in both Swahili and English, who would profit doubly from consideration of the remarkable poetry that Abdalla has produced.

This is a poetry collection whose translation is long overdue. Indeed, the more I worked on the translation, the more profound and aesthetically complex I found Abdalla's poetry to be, in the original language and in translation. It is my ardent hope that this translation may catalyze translations of his work into other international languages as well. In addition, I hope that this translation may engender translations of more of the many Swahili literary works that remain unknown, unnamed, and unread beyond the Swahiliphone realm. This certainly is not the first translation of a major work from the Swahili literary corpus. To mention a few important early forays into Swahili-English translation, East Africa's leading Swahili playwright, Ebrahim Hussein, translated his own classic Swahili play *Kinjeketile* into English, and Kimani Njogu translated another play by Hussein, *Kwenye Ukingo wa Thim*.[1]

---

1. Ebrahim N. Hussein, *Kinjeketile* (Dar es Salaam: Oxford University Press, 1969); *Kinjeketile* [English version] (Dar es Salaam: Oxford University Press, 1970); *Kwenye Ukingo wa Thim* (Nairobi: Oxford University Press, 1988) and *At the Edge of Thim*, translated by Kimani Njogu (Oxford: Oxford University Press, 2000).

xxiv • *Translator's Introduction*

In poetry, Mohamed H. Abdulaziz's translation of the nineteenth-century Swahili poet Muyaka bin Haji is both exemplary and extraordinary.[2] Like Abdulaziz, I depart from adherence to prosodic conventions in my translations; and I have tried to retain the substance and essence of the original poems while making the work more accessible, rather than needlessly opaque.

In undertaking this translation, I rejected the notion that poetry is untranslatable, even if, as some claim, something is lost in the translation. Admittedly, something is always lost in translation—the nuances and the musicality, for example, particular to the original. Anyone who has listened to Abdalla's booming baritone as he contextualizes and recites his poems in places such as Kenya, Tanzania, Germany, and the United States, would bear witness to the deeper meaning that the sounds of his Swahili verses enable and enhance. I had the pleasure to listen to his moving performances at Leipzig in May 2011 and at Kenyatta University, Nairobi, in December 2015. Not only do Abdalla's recitations suggest what is lost in reading his poems silently, but they highlight the loss involved when translation fails, as it is wont to do, to capture the audio and musical matrix of the original. Yet, despite the shortcomings of translation, clearly something is also gained in the process—particularly, accessibility for those to whom the original language is unfamiliar. And on this accessibility for the non-Swahili-speaking world hinges the entire project of rendering into English *Sauti ya Dhiki*, a collection of poems that has invited considerable critical acclaim beyond the Swahiliphone sphere. Notable among critical analyses are Chacha Nyaigotti-Chacha's seminal work *Ushairi wa Abdilatif Abdalla: Sauti ya Utetezi* (1992) and Rose Marie Beck's and Kai Kresse's edited volume *Poet in Politics* (2016).[3]

My own critical study of Abdalla's *Sauti ya Dhiki* has resulted in two publications, the book *Narrating Prison Experience: Human Rights, Self, Society, and Political Incarceration in Africa* (2013), which deals with a range of prison narratives, and an article.[4] I believe *Sauti ya Dhiki* has to be read within a

---

2. Mohamed H. Abdulaziz, *Muyaka: 19th Century Swahili Popular Poetry* (Nairobi: Kenya Literature Bureau, 1979).

3. Chacha Nyaigotti-Chacha, *Ushairi wa Abdilatif Abdalla: Sauti ya Utetezi* (Dar es Salaam: Dar es Salaam University Press, 1992); Rose Marie Beck and Kai Kresse, eds., *Abdilatif Abdalla: Poet in Politics* (Dar es Salaam: Mkuki na Nyota, 2016).

4. Ken Walibora Waliaula, *Narrating Prison Experience: Human Rights, Self, Society, and Political Incarceration in Africa* (Champaign, IL: Common Ground, 2013); and "Prison, Poetry, and Polyphony in Abdilatif Abdalla's *Sauti ya Dhiki*," *Research in African Literatures* 40, no. 3 (2009): 129–148.

broader context of the literature of incarceration across time and space, but more particularly its upsurge in colonial and post-colonial Africa. In the past century, Africa has witnessed a tremendous increase in its numbers of incarcerated intellectuals and activists. The late Nelson Mandela remains perhaps the most famous of African prisoners of conscience, thanks to his 27-year imprisonment by the apartheid government of South Africa. But the colonial encounter in Africa produced a long list of political prisoners from the rank and file of indigenous peoples who sought to break free from the colonial yoke. The treatment of the colonized during this turbulent period underscores the excesses and abuses of empire as it clung to its illegitimate overseas sphere of influence.

Indeed, although the level of bloodshed and human rights violations in colonial Africa differed from country to country and from region to region, it was generally a tale of wanton and egregious violation of the human rights of indigenous populations. Quite a number of the founding fathers of post-independent African states met the full force of colonial tyranny, becoming prisoners themselves. Ghana's Kwame Nkrumah and Kenya's Jomo Kenyatta, who became the first presidents of their independent nations, were themselves imprisoned, becoming victims of the colonial attempt to silence opposition. Could it be said that, in a sense, Nkrumah and Kenyatta were "convicted criminals" who later became leaders of their respective nations? Was not the British colonial presence in Africa criminal in and of itself?

The devastating colonial encounter and its attendant violation of human rights sullied the spurious "civilizing mission" in Africa that empire had assigned itself. Even those Africans not included in the tens and even hundreds of thousands who were literally incarcerated were within the figurative colonial prison. What Harold Scheub has rightly suggested in his *Uncoiling Python: South African Storytellers and Resistance* regarding the use of narration as a critical survival tool for black masses in apartheid South Africa is also true of Africans across the continent recoiling under colonial abuses of human rights.[5] The figures of speech and symbols that characterized these stories were coded in ways the agents of empire could not easily decode. Their decoding would have been hazardous both to the African storyteller and his or her audience, because the stories were counter-hegemonic and critical of the unwelcome presence of empire in the African homestead or homeland.

---

5. Harold Scheub, *The Uncoiling Python: South African Storytellers and Resistance* (Athens, Ohio: Swallow Press, 2010).

xxvi • *Translator's Introduction*

I have attempted in this translation to retain the symbols and metaphors in Abdalla's work, so that the poems suggest the survival tactics necessitated by the context within which they were penned. Fear of further reprisal and victimization often motivates prison writers to deploy fascinating inventiveness and circumlocution. This explains, for instance, the absence of direct mention of Kenyatta in *Sauti ya Dhiki*, a collection of poems in which Kenyatta constitutes the object of unflinching indictment and critique.

Abdalla's *Sauti ya Dhiki* is, no doubt, the poet's valiant and artistic attempt to reclaim his humanity, to preserve himself. But in writing about his or her self, a poet reveals endless possibilities for humanity and the human spirit in general, even in the wake of inhuman and inhumane treatment. This striving to be heard through writing rather than to be silenced, this writing against the grain to be or to remain human, constitutes an integral attribute of the tradition of prison literature. In Abdalla's expression of this striving lies the signal achievement of his poems.

In undertaking this translation project, I owe a huge debt of thanks to a number of individuals without whose significant contributions this work would not have reached fruition. Time and space cannot allow me to mention all of them. But let me single out at least four: Ngũgĩ wa Thiong'o for graciously accepting to write the preface to this book, Annmarie Drury for her meticulous editorial intervention, and Abdilatif Abdalla and Alamin Mazrui for their ceaseless moral and material support. Yet, I must say, if there are errors of omission or commission, those are mine and not theirs. I wish you all the best in reading *Voice of Agony*, the English translation of *Sauti ya Dhiki*, one of the most outstanding volumes of poetry ever to have emerged from the suffering of a writer's incarceration.

Voice of Agony

Sauti ya Dhiki

Translated by Ken Walibora Waliaula

... Ngome intuumiza
Naswi tu mumo ngomeni.

... The dungeon has tormented us
And we are still languishing in it.

—Muyaka bin Haji (1776–1840)

N'shishiyelo ni Lilo

1   Nipulikiza ndu yangu, ninenayo usikiye
Yaliyo moyoni mwangu, ningependa nikwambiye
Ujuwe imani yangu, ambayo niishishiye
Siiwati ingawaye, n'shishiyelo ni lilo

2   Walinena walimwengu, wa zama zilopisiye
Kwamba kweli i utungu, kwa yule aambiwaye
Nami haya ndugu yangu, sasa niyaaminiye
Asojuwa nasikiye, apeleleze ajuwe

3   Kweli n'naifahamu, haipendwi aswilani
Kwa mja hiyo ni sumu, mbaya iso kifani
Mwenye kuitakalamu, hapendezi katwaani
Sasa n'shayaamini, ni kweli haya ni kweli

4   Kweli imenitongeya, kwa kuinena mwendani
Wale nalowaambiya, wamenitiya dhikini
Wameniona mbaya, kumshinda Firauni
Kweli, sasa naamini, si wangi waipendao

5   Kweli naliwaambiya, wakuu wa nti hini
Haeleza moya moya, kwa wanati wa ntini
Kuhusu walofanyiya, upande wa Upinzani
Sasa kuwamo tabuni, nalipwa kwa hiyo kweli

6   Kweli ilipowatoma, kama dasturi yake
Wao wakaona vyema, afadhali wanishike
Wanishike hima hima, hima ndani waniweke
Ngomeni n'adhibike, nijute kusema kweli

I Won't Compromise

1 Listen to me brother, so you can hear what I have to say
   I want to explain what's in my heart
   So you know the conviction to which I've clung
   I will never forsake it, I'm uncompromising in my stand

2 So said the people of the world, of times past
   That truth is bitter for the one being told
   As for me, my brother, I've come to believe it
   May the one who doesn't know seek to know

3 I understand truth is unpalatable
   For humans it's poisonous, dangerous beyond compare
   Whoever speaks truth gains no popularity
   Now I believe this; it's true, indeed true

4 Truth has imperiled me; for speaking it, my friend
   Those to whom I spoke subject me to anguish
   They view me as evil, more evil than Pharaoh
   Now I know truth is not loved by many

5 I spoke the truth to the leaders of this country
   I recounted one by one to the citizens of this country
   How the side of the opposition had been deprived
   Now trouble is the price I pay for that truth

6 When truth seared them, as it was wont to do
   To arrest me they deemed it fit
   To arrest me speedily, to incarcerate me speedily
   To make me suffer in the dungeon, so I might regret speaking the truth

6 • *N'shishiyelo ni Lilo*

7 Kweli yanipasha tabu, ndugu yangu niamini
  Na nyingi mno adhabu, za moyoni na mwilini
  Yote haya ni sababu, ya kunena kweli hini
  Ndipo sasa haamini, kweli i utungu kweli

8 Kweli 'menibaidisha, na huko kwetu mjini
  Pia 'menitenganisha, na walo wangu nyumbani
  Kuja kuniadhibisha, kwa kunileta ngomeni
  Yote sababu ni nini? Ni kwamba 'mesema kweli

9 Kweli 'menifunga ndani, ya chumba nde sitoki
  Kutwa kucha ni chumbani, juwa kuota ni dhiki
  Na mlinzi mlangoni, yu papo kattu ha'ndoki
  Nilindwavyo bilhaki, ni kama simba marara

10 Kweli yanilaza tini, ilo na baridi kali
  Ningawa burangetini, natetema kweli kweli
  Na maumivu mwilini, daima ni yangu hali
  Shauri ya idhilali, ya kulazwa simitini

11 Kweli japo ni ngomeni, kwenye kuta ndefu nene
  Kabisa sitangamani, na mahabusu wengine
  Na lengo kubwa nadhani, ni: nilonalo 'sinene
  Hazuwa mambo mengine, kwa kuambukiza watu

12 Kweli pia meninyima, haki zilizo ngomeni
  Wangu kuja nitizama, hilo haliwezekani
  Haya nnayoyasema, ndivyo yalivyo yakini
  Baruwa sitakikani, kwandika wala kwetewa

13 Sendi mbele 'tasimama, sikupi kwa tafswili
  Kusudi nirudi nyuma, kwa ubeti wa awali
  Ili nipate kusema, imani yangu kamili
  Ujuwe kwa jambo hili, mtima wangu ulivyo

7   Truth has caused me trouble, believe me, brother
And ceaseless anguish, emotionally and physically
Those are the consequences of speaking the truth
So now I believe truth is truly bitter

8   Truth has separated me from my hometown
And it has torn me asunder from my beloved ones at home
Confining me for punishment in the dungeon where I was brought
Why all this? Because I spoke the truth

9   Truth has me incarcerated, I'm absolutely confined
In the cell day and night, I can never bask in the sun
And the guard at the door is there all the time
Like a tiger, surely, that's how I'm guarded

10   Truth has laid me down on the chilly floor
I quake badly, despite wrapping myself in a blanket
Bodily pain has become my constant condition
Because of this degradation of lying on the concrete

11   Although we share a dungeon with tall, thick walls
I'm absolutely isolated from other inmates
And for purposes, I think, of preventing me from speaking
Creating other upheavals, infecting the rest

12   For sure I'm deprived of my rights as a prisoner
I'm denied visits from my relatives and friends
What I'm saying is precisely so
I'm not allowed to write or receive any letters

13   Let me pause for moment and give no further details
So I can return to the first verse
So I can communicate my belief in full
So you may know my stand in this matter

8 • *N'shishiyelo ni Lilo*

14   Nilipoenua kimo, kutaka niseme kweli
       Nilidhani yaliyomo, hinena sina aili
       Kanama wangu mdomo, waja fungika kauli
       Nisiseme bilkuli, kuwaeleza wanati

15   Mno wanganiadhibu, adhabu kila namna
       Na mangi yanganiswibu, ya usiku na mtana
       Hayatakuwa sababu, ya kuniasa kunena
       Kweli nitapoiyona, tanena siinyamai

16   Mateso yao yangawa, nda kuumiza mtima
       Hayatakuwa ni dawa, ya kutonipa kusema
       Ni bure wajisumbuwa, nilipo nnasimama
       Si 'mi wa kurudi nyuma, kweli ilipo 'tasonga

17   Ama hakika mwendani, kwa mwenye moyo wa sawa
       Mateso ya duniani, wakati kijaaliwa
       Hushukuru Rahamani, kajikaza kutukuwa
       Nami yangawa ya kuwa, hikaza moyo si ila

18   Mateso humbadili, aso na moyo thabiti
       Apawapo idhilali, japo ingawa katiti
       Huona ni afadhali, awate yakwe ya dhati
       Ela langu siliwati, n'shishiyelo ni lilo

19   Wengi washasumbuliwa, waneni wa kweli hiyo
       Na wengi washauliwa, kwa kutobadili nyoyo
       Na mimi nimeradhiwa, ku'yandama sera hiyo
       'Tafuwata zao nyayo, n'shishiyelo ni lilo

14 When I rose to speak the truth
I thought there was nothing wrong with saying what had to be said
I didn't know my mouth would be gagged
So I could never speak, never communicate with fellow citizens

15 However much they punish me, with punishment of every kind
Whatever hardships I undergo, by day and by night
It won't be a reason for me to stop speaking
When I see the truth, I'll speak, I won't keep quiet

16 Even if their torture is heart-wrenching
It won't prove a means of silencing me
They are wasting their time, as I'm immovable
I'm not the sort that retreats; where truth is, I go

17 A person with a steady heart, certainly, my friend
Whenever he is fated to suffer in this world
He is grateful to God, he takes it in stride
And as for me, whatever happens, I'll endure it

18 Torture changes a person whose heart is feeble
When faced with humiliation, even just a bit of it
He thinks it's better to give up what is genuinely his
But as for me I don't give up, I'm uncompromising

19 Many have been attacked, the harbingers of truth
Many others have been killed for their resolute stand
And I have chosen to follow that path
I will follow in their footsteps, I'm uncompromising

20 Atwambizile Rasuli, kipenzi cha Bwana M'ngu
Ya kwamba tuseme kweli, japokuwa i utungu
Na mimi siibadili, ni yiyo imani yangu
Nililoamini tangu, ni lilo hilo sil'ati

21 Kweli naitiya tamma, nikuage ndugu yangu
Kweli si mwenye kukoma, kuwambiya walimwengu
Kweli si'yati kusema, katika uhai wangu
Nami kwa upande wangu, hi'yambiwa 'takubali

—*Septemba 1969*

20   As the Prophet told us, God's beloved creature
We have to speak the truth even if it's bitter
And I won't change, that's my conviction
That's what I believe, and I'm not giving in

21   On truth, let me stop here to say farewell, brother
I won't stop telling the truth, letting the world know
I won't stop speaking the truth, ever in all my life
And for my part I'll accept what truth I'm told

—September 1969

Kamliwaze

1 Tumishi inuka hima, utwae wangu waraka
Huko nitakokutuma, uwenende kwa haraka
Na haya mate natema, hima yasije kauka
      Inuka sasa inuka

2 Nenda kwa mwenzangu mja, kanisalimiye sana
Mwambe ni zetu pamoja, huzuni anazoona
Mambo hwenenda yakija, ni dasituri bayana
      'Kipeleleza 'taona

3 Nasivundikwe na moyo, kwa mambo yalotuswibu
Sisi kufikwa na hayo, si kitu kilo ajabu
Tushike tuliyonayo, tusiyawate swahibu
      Nyoyo zisife kwa tabu

4 Kama haya 'mewafika, walioanza azali
Walokuwa wakitaka, haki ishinde batwili
Walifikwa na mashaka, sampuli sampuli
      Nasi tusitahamili

—Oktoba 1969

Go and Console Him

1   Messenger, arise at once and take my letter
    There where I send you—you must go quickly
    Go fast, before the spittle dries
                Stand up now, stand up

2   Go to my fellow human being, bring him my warm greetings
    Tell him the sorrow he feels is shared by us both
    Things come and go, that's clearly the world's way
                If you investigate, you'll see

3   He should not be broken-hearted because of our affliction
    Our experiencing this is nothing strange, really
    Let's cling to what we have without giving in, my friend
                And not lose heart because of troubles

4   Such has happened from time immemorial
    People determined to see justice, to conquer what is unjust
    Have suffered trepidation of this kind and that
                So we too should endure

—October 1969

Tuza Moyo

Akhi tuliza mtima, uwate kusononeka
Hakuna lisilokoma, siku 'kifika 'tatoka
Kusubiri ni lazima, na kumuomba Rabuka
       Wasiya wako 'meshika

—*Novemba 1969*

Worry Not

Worry not, brother, you should stop grieving
Everything has an end; I'll be out when the day comes
It's necessary to wait and pray to the Almighty
          I've heeded your advice

—*November 1969*

Jipu

1   Towa taka masikiyo, upulikize uneni
Haya upulikizayo, uyatiye akilini
Kwani ni muhimu hayo, wendapo utabaini
Kwa hivyo fanya makini, upate kuyasikiya

2   Moyoni furaha sina, ningaitaka sinayo
Si usiku si mtana, ni mamoja kwangu hayo
Mateso n'nayoona, yaujuwa wangu moyo
Si mwako na wayowayo, uliyonifikiliya!

3   N'na jipu lin'tunza, linipalo tabu mno
Tangu liliponianza, kamwe sipati usono
Kwamba ni mara ya kwanza, kuuguwa ndwezi hino
Latoma kama sindano, utunguwe nakwambiya

4   Si jana wala si juzi, liliponianza tangu
Ni mingi mno miezi, n'nadhofu hali yangu
Nnakonda kama uzi, kwa kushitadi utungu
Kubwa tumaini langu, ni mwishowe nangojeya

5   Hitaka keti siwezi, kwamba li makaliyoni
Kutwa huwa yangu kazi, kusimama; n'tendeni?
Na usiku usingizi, siupati aswilani
Kucha nakesha mwendani, kwa utungu kuzidiya

6   Kili kipele mwilini, ndiyo mwanzo wake kuwa
Sikujuwa aswilani, kuwa jipu chaja kuwa
Ningekijuwa zamani, ningekitangiya dawa
Ni kwamba sikutambuwa, ndipo hakiwatiliya

The Boil

1   Listen up so you can hear me
    What you'll hear, your mind should absorb
    Because it's important, if you'll understand
    Pay attention and listen

2   I have a heavy heart; I'm not happy, much as I want to be
    It's all the same to me whether daytime or nighttime
    My heart well knows the suffering I'm undergoing
    The worries and trepidation that torment me

3   I have a boil that has formed, giving me endless grief
    Since it afflicted me, I've had no solace
    It's my first time experiencing such an ailment
    Its pain stabs like a needle, I tell you

4   It began not yesterday or the day before, but a long time ago
    For several months now my condition has worsened
    I'm thin as a thread because of the pain's intensity
    I'm awaiting its end; there lies my great hope

5   I can't sit, much as I'd like to, because it's on my behind
    I stand all day long; what else can I do?
    And during the night I can't catch a wink of sleep
    The whole night I'm awake, for pain overrides me

6   It was just a pimple on the body, that's how it all began
    I had no clue it would turn into a boil
    I'd have sought a remedy if only I'd known sooner
    But because I didn't know, that's why I didn't act

18 • *Jipu*

7   Jambo nilingojeyalo, ni kutimu yake siku
        Ningojeyalo ni hilo, tena kwa kubwa shauku
        Itimupo ndimi nalo, ja mwewe na mwana kuku
        Ni furaha hiyo siku, kwangu na wenzangu piya

8   Siku ya kuiva kwake, hiyo ndiyo siku kweli
        Huo ndiwo mwisho wake, na mwisho wa idhilali
        Idhilali in'ondoke, mimi nayo tuwe mbali
        Siku hiyo ni mawili, kuteka au kuliya

9   'Taliminya litumbuke, lisinisumbuwe tena
        Usaha wote utoke, utoke nikiuona
        Midamu itiririke, kama ng'ombe alonona
        Jipu hili mwana lana, M'ngu mbwalipa hizaya

10   Jasho jembamba litoke, ndiya mbili likitona
        Na hapo nitetemeke, si kwa baridi kuona
        Bali kwa utungu wake, utakaozidi sana
        Hapo ndipo nitasona, na moyo kufurahiya

11   Baada ya yote haya, jaraha niliuguze
        Kwa madawa kulitiya, ili kwamba yalipoze
        Irudi yangu afiya, na zaidi niongeze
        Nirukeruke niteze, kwa furaha kuningiya

12   Kalamu sasa natuwa, kaditamati lisani
        Nadhani nalotongowa, 'mekungiya akilini
        Jipu nitalitumbuwa, libaki kovu mwilini
        Suala kuu ni: lini? Ni siku ikitimiya

—*Januari 1970*

The Boil • 19

7   I'm waiting for its day to come
That's what I await, and with great anticipation
When the day comes, I'll pounce like a hawk on a chick
It will be a joyous day for me and my companions

8   The day when it ripens, that truly is the day
That will be the end of it, the end of humiliation
Humiliation will depart, I'll be far removed from it
It will be a day for one of two things: laughing or weeping

9   I'll squeeze it until it bursts, so it troubles me no more
So all the pus will ooze out, while I witness its oozing
Then blood will flow, as from a fat cow
This accursed boil, may God curse it more

10   A thin sweat will form, trickling in two streams
Then I'll quake, not from cold
But because of pain that will powerfully increase
And then I'll win solace and in my heart rejoice

11   After all this, I'll nurse the wound
By applying medicine so it heals
So that my health returns, and much more than that
I'll leap and dance in delight

12   I put down my pen, as I've reached the end
I think what I've divulged you've fully understood
I'll break the boil, leaving a scar on my body
The big question is—when? When the day comes

—January 1970

Siwati

1   Siwati n'shishiyelo, siwati; kwani niwate?
     Siwati ni lilo hilo, 'talishika kwa vyovyote
     Siwati ni mimi nalo, hapano au popote
     Hadi kaburini sote, mimi nalo tufukiwe

2   Siwati 'ngaadhibiwa, adhabu kila mifano
     Siwati ningaambiwa, 'tapawa kila kinono
     Siwati lililo sawa, silibanduwi mkono
     Hata ningaumwa meno, mkono siubanduwi

3   Siwati si ushindani, mukasema nashindana
     Siwati ifahamuni, sababuye waungwana
     Siwati ndangu imani, niithaminiyo sana
     Na kuiwata naona, itakuwa ni muhali

4   Siwati nimeradhiwa, kufikiwa na kila mawi
     Siwati ningaambiwa, niaminiyo hayawi
     Siwati kisha nikawa, kama nzi; hivyo siwi
     Thamma nakariri siwi, na M'ngu nisaidiya

     —*15 Machi 1970*

I'll Never Let Go

1   I'll never let go of what I've clung to, never; why should I?
I'll never let go but will cling to it come what may
I'll never let go; I'm with it here or anywhere
Until we're both in the grave, interred together

2   I'll never let go, despite being punished with punishment of every kind
I'll never let go, even if I'm promised a rich reward
I'll never let go of what's right, never release it from my hand
Even if I'm bitten, my hand won't let go

3   I'll never let go; don't say I'm being stubborn
I'll never let go; you respected ones should understand the reason
I'll never let go, for it is my conviction that I cherish
And letting it go is simply impossible for me

4   I'll never let go: I'd rather face the worst
I'll never let go, even when told what I believe is unachievable
I'll never let go and become like a fly; that I won't be
Let me repeat, I'll never let go, and God help me

—15 March 1970

Mamba

1 Nami nambe, niwe kama waambao
   Niupambe, upendeze wasomao
   Niufumbe, wafumbuwe wawezao

2 Kuna mamba, mtoni metakabari
   Ajigamba, na kujiona hodari
   Yuwaamba, kwamba 'taishi dahari

3 Memughuri, ghururi za kipumbavu
   Afikiri, hataishiwa na nguvu
   Takaburi, hakika ni ma'ngamivu

4 Akumbuke, siku yake ikifika
   Roho yake, ajuwe itamtoka
   Nguvu zake, kikomoche zitafika

5 Afahamu, mtu hajuwi la kesho
   Hatadumu, angatumiya vitisho
   Maadamu, lenye mwanzo lina mwisho

—*23 Machi 1970*

Crocodile

1   Now I would speak and be like those who speak
Let me adorn my poem so it appeals to readers
Let me compose a riddle so those who can may unravel it

2   There's a crocodile in the river, highly conceited
He brags and thinks himself invincible
He claims he'll live forever

3   Foolish arrogance has deceived him
He thinks his power will never fail
Certainly pride goes before a fall

4   He should remember: when his day comes
His spirit, he should know, will leave him then
His power will reach its end

5   He should understand: no one knows about tomorrow
He won't last, threaten though he can
Whatever has beginnings has an end

—23 March 1970

Nakukumbuka

1 Mi nawe mbali tungawa, nakukumbuka
Lau ngekuwa na mbawa, ningeliruka
Ni muhali hili kuwa, nasikitika

2 Mi nawe mbali tungawa, muhibu wangu
Kamwe hayatapunguwa, mapenzi yangu
Hili kaa ukijuwa, wewe u wangu

3 Mi nawe mbali tungawa, sitahamili
Pamoja 'takuja kuwa, sote wawili
Mwombe uhai Moliwa, na njema hali

—*1 Mei 1970*

I Remember You

1. Although we're far apart, I remember you
   If only I had wings, I'd fly
   But to my sorrow it's impossible

2. Although we're far apart, my beloved one
   My love for you will never diminish
   I want you to know you're mine

3. Although we're far apart, persevere
   We'll be together again, the both of us
   Pray to God for life and health

   —*1 May 1970*

Ukamilifu wa Mja

1 Twaa nakupa pokeya, pokeya usidharau
Yaliyomo ni ya ndiya, katika waadhi huu
Twaa kwa kuzingatiya, mazingatiyo makuu
Mtu kuwa na maguu, si kwamba mekamilika

2 Ameumbwa mwanadamu, kwa lililo zuri umbo
Bali si wote fahamu, waliyo na sawa mambo
Wako walio timamu, na wengineo wa kombo
Na mtu kuwa na tumbo, si kwamba mekamilika

3 Kuna walio werevu, ambao ni waelewa
Na kuna na wapumbavu, moja jambo wasojuwa
Piya kuna wenye nguvu, na dhaifu huonewa
Mtu kuwa na kifuwa, si kwamba mekamilika

4 Kuna wasemao kweli, na wasemaji urongo
Kuna walio na mali, zilizopita kiwango
Na wengine zao hali, nda kuinamisha shingo
Mtu kuwa na maungo, si kwamba mekamilika

5 Kuna walio wembamba, na walo wanene mno
Na wako ambao kwamba, wako kati ya hawano
Mwenyezi ametuumba, kwa mbali mbali mifano
Mtu kuwa na mikono, si kwamba mekamilika

6 Kuna walo mafidhuli, lugha yao ni matango
Na kuna wenye kauli, zisokuwa na ushingo
Kuna wake kwa wavuli, vipofu na wenye tongo
Na mtu kuwa na shingo, si kwamba mekamilika

Human Perfection

1 Here, take this I give you—take, don't despise it
It contains meaningful advice
Take it seriously, with greatest seriousness
Just having feet doesn't make one perfect

2 Humans are created with a charming physique
But not everyone, understand, has matters in order
There are those who have things right and others who don't
Just having a stomach doesn't make one perfect

3 Some are clever and fully grasp things
But there are also simpletons, knowing nothing at all
Also there are strong ones, and the weak get mistreated
Just having a chest doesn't make one perfect

4 Some speak the truth, while others lie
There are those with wealth, wealth without compare
And others in pitiful circumstances
Just having a back doesn't make one perfect

5 There are the slim ones and the very bulky ones
Also there are those in between
God has created us in many and varied ways
Just having hands doesn't make one perfect

6 There are rude people, always uttering obscenities
And there are those whose remarks lack sting
·There are women and men, blind people and one-eyed people
Just having a neck doesn't make one perfect

28 • *Ukamilifu wa Mja*

7 Kuna waja walo wema, kadhalika na waovu
   Wako wenye na hishima, na wenye adabu mbovu
   Na wako wenye huruma, piya na watenza nguvu
   Mtu kuwa na kidevu, si kwamba mekamilika

8 Kuna waliyo warefu, na wenye vifupi vimo
   Wako walo wahalifu, wa kupitisha kipimo
   Piya kuna watiifu, kwa vitendo na misemo
   Mtu kuwa na mdomo, si kwamba mekamilika

9 Kuna walo kimya sana, na wenye mengi maneno
   Kuna watu wa maana, wahishimiwao mno
   Wengine hilo hawana, ni wapuuzi hawano
   Na mtu kuwa na meno, si kwamba mekamilika

10 Kuna watu wakorofi, abadani hawatumi
   Na wako wataswarufi, moja huzalisha kumi
   Kuna wenye roho swafi, wengine zao sisemi
   Mtu kuwa na ulimi, si kwamba, mekamilika

11 Kuna walo makarimu, na mabakhili elewa
   Na wakubwa kwa hirimu, wazazi na wazaliwa
   Kadhalika madhalimu, na wanaodhulumiwa
   Na mtu kuwa na puwa, si kwamba mekamilika

12 Kuna walo makhawafu, 'kitishwa hwenenda mbiyo
   Na kuna wasiyokhofu, ni shujaa zao nyoyo
   Kuna walo wapotofu, na waongofu waliyo
   Na kuwa na masikiyo, huko si kukamilika

13 Kuna walio na haya, zilowajaa na mato
   Kuna watenda mabaya, wazi pasi na ufito
   Kuna wenye swafi niya, na kuna wenye vijito
   Na mtu kuwa na mato, si kwamba mekamilika

Human Perfection • 29

7 There are good people and wicked ones, too
 There are respectable ones and those without manners
 And there are compassionate ones and heartless ones, too
 Just having a chin doesn't make one perfect

8 There are tall ones and short ones
 And criminals whose criminality is limitless
 Also there are obedient ones, obeying in word and deed
 Just having a mouth doesn't make one perfect

9 There are introverts and extroverts, too
 There are honorable people who earn great esteem
 Others get none of that; they are nonsensical, these ones
 Just having teeth doesn't make one perfect

10 There are spendthrifts; they never see profit
 There are the shrewd people who from one produce ten
 There are the good-hearted; as for others, let me not say
 Just having a tongue doesn't make one perfect

11 Understand, there are generous ones and misers
 Adults and young ones, parents and offspring
 Also there are oppressors and the oppressed
 Just having a nose doesn't make one perfect

12 There are cowardly ones who when threatened run away
 And there are fearless ones with courageous hearts
 There are the crooked and the upright
 Just having ears doesn't make one perfect

13 There are those with shyness written all over their faces
 There are those who do evil openly, without hiding anything
 There are the well-intentioned and those full of envy
 Just having eyes doesn't make one perfect

30 • *Ukamilifu wa Mja*

14 Kuna walo na fikira, na wenye vibovu vitwa
Kuna walo na subira, husubiri kucha kutwa
Wengine tabiya bora, hino hawanayo katwa
Na mtu kuwa na kitwa, si kwamba mekamilika

15 Nilivyotaja si vyote, viungo vya muilini
Vinginevyo tuviwate, tuifupishe lisani
Ili kwamba tutafute, haya 'mesema kwa nini
Nikupe yangu maani, ya mja kukamilika

16 Hakuna mja kamili, ndivyo twalivyoambiwa
Kadhalika mimi hili, nasema li sawa sawa
Mkamilifu wa kweli, nakubali ni Moliwa
Maana yangu 'tatowa, ya mja kukamilika

17 Kukamilika kwa mja, ni mbali na kwa Moliwa
Kwa mja nitakutaja, ili upate kwelewa
Ni kufikiya daraja, ile aliyoumbiwa
Hapo ndipo huambiwa, mja amekamilika

18 Aiyelewe duniya, kwa marefu na mapana
Azipite zile ndiya, za miba mitungu sana
Avuke bahari piya, zilo na virefu vina
Hiyo ni yangu maana, ya mja kukamilika

19 Akishafikwa na hayo, si kwamba ndiyo akhiri
Lazima awe na moyo, wa kuweza kusubiri
Kuyasubiri ambayo, yote yatayomjiri
Kama huyo 'tamkiri, ni mja mekamilika

—*13 Mei 1970*

Human Perfection · 31

14   There are the thoughtful and the demented ones
There are the patient ones, persevering day and night
Others completely lack this good character
Just having a head doesn't make one perfect

15   These I've mentioned aren't all the body parts
Let's leave out others to cut the story short
So we can seek the reason for my mentioning them
So I can tell you what I mean by human perfection

16   There's no perfect person, so we have been told
I also believe it; this is quite true
The really perfect one, I admit, is God alone
I'll divulge my meaning concerning human perfection

17   Human perfection differs from God's
Human perfection—I'll clarify, so you understand—
Means attaining the status for which a human was created
That's when it can be said a human being is perfect

18   A person should comprehend what life is all about
Tread paths full of bitter thorns
Cross seas of unfathomable depths
That's my idea of human perfection

19   After going through all this, that's not the end
One must have a courageous and patient heart
To endure whatever befalls him or her
Such is the person I'll acknowledge to be perfect

—*13 May 1970*

Lilokuudhi ni Lipi?

1 Muhibu wangu muhibu, nakwita niitikiya
Nakwita ndoo karibu, upate kunisikiya
Nakuuliza nijibu, sinifite hata moya
Usinifite nambiya, lilokuudhi ni lipi?

2 Lililo langu ni lako, na lako ni langu piya
Liloudhi moyo wako, si vibaya kunambiya
Sifundike maudhiko, mwenzangu utaumiya
Usinifite nambiya, lilokuudhi ni lipi?

3 Jambo lisokupendeza, iwapo mekufanyiya
Ni vyema kuniongoza, hajuwa ya sawa ndiya
Kuliko kulinyamaza, na kunikasirikiya
Usinifite nambiya, lilokuudhi ni lipi?

4 Ufanyavyo si vizuri, mwendo kuninyamaziya
Sitojuwa takisiri, ilosababisha haya
Hakuna nimefikiri, baya nilokutendeya
Usinifite nambiya, lilokuudhi ni lipi?

5 Nieleza hicho kisa, ambacho 'mekutendeya
Kama ndiye nilokosa, nitakiri mara moya
N'ombe mswamaha sasa, kwa nililokukoseya
Usinifite nambiya, lilokuudhi ni lipi?

6 Nambiya nipate juwa, nambiya sasa nambiya
Wasiwasi umekuwa, ni mwingi uloningiya
Juwa utanitunguwa, ndilo ulokusudiya?
Usinifite nambiya, lilokuudhi ni lipi?

What Has Offended You?

1 My love, my love, please respond: I'm calling you
   I'm calling; come closer so you can hear me
   I'm asking you to answer; don't hide anything
   Don't hide, tell me: what has offended you?

2 What's mine is yours, and what's yours is mine
   What has hurt your heart? It's proper to inform me
   Don't harbor grievances—it's harmful, my dear
   Don't hide, tell me: what has offended you?

3 If I've done anything that offended you
   It's better to correct me so I know the right course
   Instead of going quiet and being angry with me
   Don't hide, tell me: what has offended you?

4 Your silent treatment isn't nice
   I won't know what problem has caused all of this
   I can't think of any wrong I've done you
   Don't hide, tell me: what has offended you?

5 Explain my fault: how I have wronged you?
   If I'm guilty, I'll readily admit it
   I'll beg for forgiveness for failing you
   Don't hide, tell me: what has offended you?

6 Tell me so I know; tell me now, tell me
   I've been worried, full of anxiety
   Know that you're breaking my heart—is that what you want?
   Don't hide, tell me: what has offended you?

34 • *Lilokuudhi ni Lipi?*

7   Iliyo sababu yangu, hata hauliza haya
Ni kwamba baruwa zangu, mbili nilokuleteya
Hujazijibu mwenzangu, mno umelimatiya
Usinifite nambiya, lilokuudhi ni lipi?

8   Kila siku ikipita, huwa nikitarajiya
Baruwa yako kupata, nijuwe yako afiya
Lakini sishi kudata, huwa karibu kuliya
Usinifite nambiya, lilokuudhi ni lipi?

9   Kuchelewa kunijibu, hiyo si yako tabiya
Ndipo haona ajabu, mara kunigeukiya
N'eleza yake sababu, nami ipate n'eleya
Usinifite nambiya, lilokuudhi ni lipi?

10   Mawazo kila namna, moyoni yanipitiya
Hata sasa nna dhana, juu ya yako afiya
Labda waumwa sana, kunijuza wacheleya
Usinifite nambiya, lilokuudhi ni lipi?

11   Ituze yangu nafusi, kwa baruwa kuneteya
Nileteya kwa upesi, 'sizidi kulimatiya
Unitowe wasiwasi, moyoni uloningiya
Usinifite nambiya, lilokuudhi ni lipi?

12   Usiniche niko radhi, nilokukosa nambiya
Lolote lilokuudhi, 'siwate kun'elezeya
Au kama ni maradhi, wauguwa nena piya
Usinifite nambiya, lilokuudhi ni lipi?

7   The reason I'm asking this
     Is that the two letters I've sent you
     You haven't answered; you've delayed much too long
     Don't hide, tell me: what has offended you?

8   With each passing day, I keep expecting
     To receive your letter, to know about your health
     But I keep being disappointed, nearing tears
     Don't hide, tell me: what has offended you?

9   Tardiness in replying isn't your nature
     That's why I'm wondering—why this sudden change
     Tell me your reason so I can understand
     Don't hide; tell me, what has offended you?

10   Thoughts of many kinds are flooding my mind
     And now I'm worried about your health
     Perhaps you're unwell and afraid to inform me
     Don't hide, tell me: what has offended you?

11   Comfort my heart by sending me a letter
     Send it fast, don't delay any longer
     So you can allay the fear that has overwhelmed me
     Don't hide, tell me: what has offended you?

12   Don't fear offending me; let me know my mistake
     Anything I've done wrong, don't hesitate to inform me
     Or if you are ailing, struggling with illness, say that too
     Don't hide, tell me: what has offended you?

36 • *Lilokuudhi ni Lipi?*

13   Tamma huku hitumai, baruwa utaneteya
Ilete upesi bui, sichelewe ni vibaya
Kwani mwenziyo ni hoi, sijifai pesa moya
Usiwate kunambiya, lolote lilokuudhi

—20 Mei 1970

What Has Offended You? • 37

13   I end here, hoping you'll write me a letter
Send it fast, dear one; it's not good to delay
For I am enfeebled, my state is pitiable
Don't hesitate to tell me: what has offended you?

—*20 May 1970*

Mnazi: Vuta N'kuvute

Alii: Ndugu ulo mnazini, wanitafuta balaa
Nakwambiya shuka tini, katakata wakataa
Wafanya ni masikani, mustarehe 'mekaa
Utashuka au la?

Badi: Ndugu tini ya mnazi, nilo juu nakujibu
Haya ni ya upuuzi, unambiyayo swahibu
Kushuka tini siwezi, pasi kujuwa sababu
Hiyo ni yangu jawabu

Alii: Sababu ya kukwambiya, ya kwamba ushuke tini
Ni kuwa nataka kweya, huko juu mnazini
Kwa ajili nami piya, nitunde nazi mwendani
N'shakweleza kwa nini

Badi: Hayo ni ya kutekesha, unambiyayo ndu yangu
Wataka niteremsha, juu ya mnazi wangu?
Wanistaajabisha, kuniamuru kwa changu
Una kishaa mwenzangu

Alii: Sina kishaa sinani, akili yangu kamili
Ni wewe usobaini, pale ulipo ukweli
Mnazi ni tangu lini, ukawa ni yako mali?
Sinitendee feeli

Coconut Palm: A Tug-of-War

Alii: My brother up in the coconut palm, you are causing me vexation
When I tell you climb down, you completely refuse
You've made it your abode and recline in utter comfort
      Are you coming down or not?

Badi: My brother beneath the coconut palm, this is my response
It's utter rubbish, what you are telling me, friend
I can't climb down without knowing the reason
      That is my response

Alii: The reason for telling you to climb down
Is that I want to climb up there as well
So that I too, my friend, can pick coconuts
      I've told you why

Badi: It's funny, what you're telling me, brother
Do you want to force me down my own coconut palm?
You surprise me, ordering me around my own property
      You must be mad, my friend

Alii: I'm not at all mad, my mind is quite sound
It's you who can't understand where the truth lies
When did the coconut palm become your property?
      Don't play tricks on me

Badi: Wabobojekwa maneno, yasokuwa na maana
Ni ya kipumbavu mno, hayo uliyoyanena
Iwapo mnazi huno, si wangu; mbwa nani bwana?
Sema nijuwe bayana

Alii: Mnazi ni wa shirika, mimi na wewe mwendani
Un'shakuwa wataka, kunitowa shirikani?
Hilo halitatendeka, wala haliwezekani
Sikubali abadani

'Takupa habari yake, kama wewe hufahamu
Kutokeya mwanzo wake, hata leo ikatimu
'Takweleza utosheke, kwa maelezo timamu
Ujuwe sina wazimu

Mnazi yake asili, uli mbwa wazazi wetu
Mbwa baba zetu wawili, pasi kungiya wa tatu
Mali yao ya halali, hawakunyang'anya mtu
Sasa wafile ni wetu

Badi: 'Takukatiza kauli, niwiya radhi mwenzangu
Hapa ninayo suali, ikerayo moyo wangu
Katika hawa wawili, ili babako na wangu
Yupi mwenye kubwa fungu?

Badi: You spout meaningless words
It's all foolishness, what you are uttering
If this coconut palm isn't mine, whose is it?
Speak up so I may know

Alii: The tree is collectively owned by both of us, friend
Are you therefore hell-bent on depriving me of my share?
That won't happen; it's impossible
I'll never agree

I'll tell you about it, in case you are clueless
From the very outset, until today
I'll tell you the full story, with detailed explanations
So you know I'm not crazy

Originally the coconut palm belonged to our parents
It belonged to our two fathers, with no third party
It was their rightful possession, not stolen from anyone
Now that they are dead, it's ours

Badi: I'll interrupt your speech; excuse me, my friend
I have a question for you that troubles my heart
Between these two, your father and mine
Who had more shares?

Alii: Siwe na pupa tuliya, tuwa ndugu yangu tuwa
Tamaa nyingi ni mbaya, mlimwengu humuuwa
Nisikiza nakwambiya, kusudi upate juwa
Wali na mafungu sawa

Walipoaga duniya, kwenenda zao kuzimu
Mnazi walit'watiya, baba zetu waadhamu
Tuurithi sote piya, ili tusiwalaumu
Je, un'shafahamu?

Badi: Tuseme ndivyo yalivyo, hivyo unenavyo wewe
Na hata kama ni hivyo, bado 'tavutana nawe
Sijaridhika vilivyo, na maelezo yakowe
N'eleza hili nijuwe

Nataka kukuuliza, suala nyengine kaka
Hivi punde 'men'eleza, mnazi ni wa shirika
Kwa nini kunihimiza, upesi nipate shuka
Na hali ni wa shirika?

Alii: Sababu ya kukwambiya, ushuke tini haraka
Mke na wanangu piya, wana ndaa 'mewashika
Nami nataka kukweya, nitunde nazi hakika
'Kauze wapate pika

Coconut Palm: A Tug-of-War • 43

Alii: Stop being greedy; be calm, my brother, be calm
Too much greediness is evil; it can kill you
Listen to what I say, so you'll be in the know
     They had equal shares

When they both died, joining the ancestors
They left us the coconut palm, our esteemed fathers
To inherit collectively, so we'd find no fault with them
     Do you get it now?

Badi: The way you put it, let's assume it's so
Even if it is, I'll still contend with you
I'm not satisfied with your explanations
     Say more so I can understand

I want to ask you another question, brother
You just told me now, the coconut palm is collectively owned
Then why do you urge me to climb down fast
     And yet we collectively own it ?

Alii: My reason for telling you to climb down fast
Is that my wife and also my children are hungry
I want to climb up, so I can pick coconuts
     To sell so my family can have a meal

Badi: Jambo hilo ndugu yangu, kitambo nilikwambiya
Ya kwamba chako na changu, tutanganye kwa umoya
Kisha tupige mafungu, atwae kila mmoya
Wake kuwapelekeya

Uliyakubali haya, kuwa tushirikiyane
Muda mfupi kusiya, ukayazuwa mengine
Ukashika yako ndiya, nami hashika nyengine
Ikabidi tutengane

Ndipo kunipiga vita, nisivyojuwa mwanzowe
Ulotafuta 'mepata, hasara ni kwako wewe
Mpiga ngumi ukuta, huumiza mkonowe
Wapigiyani mayowe?

Alii: Bure wajipambaniza, na kwingi kujimamasa
Maneno wayageuza, kusudi si kwa kukosa
Hivyo ulivyoy'eleza, ukweli hukuugusa
Wafita yako makosa

Kushirikiyana nawe, ni kweli nilikubali
Bali ulianza wewe, ya kwenenda ndiya mbali
Kutengana mimi nawe, haona ni afadhali
Kuliko kuwa wawili

Coconut Palm: A Tug-of-War • 45

Badi: On this issue, my brother, I told you long ago
That what is yours and mine, we should combine
Then we share out equally, each one taking his portion
To give to his household

You acceded to that, that we would share
But after a short while, you rocked the boat
You took your own path, and I took a different one
We had to go separate ways

I don't know why you're now quarrelling with me
You've gotten what you wanted, you're the one suffering loss
A person who hits the wall hurts his own hand
Why, then, are you screaming?

Alii: You're just obfuscating, and hiding the truth
You're twisting words—deliberately, not by mistake
In what you've spoken, you've never touched on truth
You hide your mistakes

It's true I agreed to cooperate with you
But you started it all by choosing a different path
I thought it better for us to separate
Instead of being partners

Pamoja tulipokuwa, vyetu tukivitanganya
Jambo moja hagunduwa, ulokuwa ukifanya
Hukuwa kinipa sawa, wakati wa kugawanya
    Changu ukinipokonya

Mwerevu ulijidai, fungu kubwa ukitwaa
Wanayo wala miyai, na vyakula vya kufaa
Wala hata hukinai, kwa mitumbo kuwajaa
    Na nguo njema wavaa

Hali kuwa wangu wana, wadhii mno kwa ndaa
Ndiyani ukiwaona, ni mitambara 'mevaa
Ni kwa kuwa kitu sina, kuwapa nilowazaa
    Kwa wewe changu kutwaa

Badi: Wanambiya nilikuwa, kilo kichache hikupa
Nami kingi hitukuwa, wanangu henda 'kiwapa
Ndiyo sababu wakawa, wanangu wamenenepa
    Na nguo njema kuwapa

Makosa haya si yangu, ya wanayo kudhikika
Lau hilo dogo fungu, kwalo ungeliridhika[1]
Watoto wako ndu yangu, wasingelitaabika
    Bali hili hukutaka

---

1. Correction of "ungaliridhika" in the original Swahili text.

Coconut Palm: A Tug-of-War • 47

When we were together, sharing our belongings
I discovered one thing that you were always doing
In dividing between us, you never shared equally
    You always shortchanged me

You deemed yourself smarter, often taking the bigger share
Your children eat eggs and sumptuous meals
They eat to satisfaction, filling their tummies
    And they have decent clothes

Whereas my children suffer pangs of hunger
If you see them out and about, rags are what they wear
It's because I'm too poor to provide for them
    Because you have dispossessed me

Badi: You claim I used to shortchange you
While I took the bigger share to give to my children
That is why my children are well nourished
    And I give them nice clothes

It isn't my fault that your children are suffering
If you'd contented yourself with your small portion
Then your children, brother, wouldn't be suffering
    But you refused this

48 • *Mnazi: Vuta N'kuvute*

Uliona ni vizuri, kichache kutokubali
Ukafanya nyingi ari, ya kukiwata kalili
Ni heri nusu ya shari, kuliko shari kamili
Au hufahamu hili?

Alii: Fungu ulo ukinipa, wakati unapogawa
Sababu iliyonipa, hakataa kutukuwa
Ulikuwa kinikopa, ukinipa kama dawa
Hali tuna haki sawa

Lau kama ningekuwa, 'meliridhi jambo hili
Ingeonesha ya kuwa, hiyo ni moja dalili
Ya kwamba kudhulumiwa, mwenyewe nimekubali
Na hali hili si kweli

Pili ni kuwa nyumbani, mke na wana hakika
Wangekuwa wakidhani, pesa nusu nafundika
Wao wasingeamini, kwamba wewe wanipoka
Dhalimu usotosheka

Tatu ningelaumiwa, na watu kila mahali
Wao wangeona kuwa, watu wangu nawadhili
Jina baya ningepawa, kwamba mimi ni bakhili
Na hali hili si kweli

Coconut Palm: A Tug-of-War • 49

You considered it better to decline your small share
You made a great effort to abandon that meager portion
Better the lesser of two evils
    Or don't you understand?

Alii: The portion you gave me in sharing out
The reason that caused me not to accept it
Was that you were dispensing it to me like medicine
    Yet we have equal shares

If I had given in to this unfairness
That would have shown that evidently
Being exploited is fine with me
    Yet this is untrue

Secondly, at home, surely my wife and children
Would have suspected I'd hidden part of my income
They'd hardly believe that you defraud me
    You insatiable exploiter

Thirdly, I'd have been blamed by people all around
They'd have thought I ill-treat my household
I'd have earned a bad name, that of a miser
    And this would be untrue

Kwani ningelidhaniwa, napata kilo adhimu
Kwamba hilo litakuwa, ni pato litalodumu
Wasingejuwa ya kuwa, dhalimu wanidhulumu
    Na kunyonya yangu damu

Ndipo haona ni vyema, nijitowe shirikani
Wajuwe wanaadama, na watu wangu nyumbani
Chombo kitakapozama, na kuzama walo ndani
    Nisiwemo lawamani

Badi: Ghadhabu zalokushika, na ghera za kijuhula
Zilikupa kun'epuka, kwamba waucha muhula
Ulokwisha kitapika, warudiani kukila?
    Hebu sema lahaula!

Alii: Kwa kuwa ni haki yangu, sitahayari kudai
'Tatumiya nguvu zangu, madhali ningali hai
Nilipate fungu langu, japo kwa ya ghali bei
    Nawe hapo uwe hoi

Badi: Wewe ni mbobokwaji, maneno mangi kanwani
Ambaye ni mtendaji, alilonalo haneni
Hutuliya kama maji, yaliyomo mtungini
    'Kangoja siku ya zani

People would have supposed I was earning something big
That I was enjoying a reliable income
They'd little know that you exploit me
  And suck my blood

That's why I felt I should quit our partnership
So people could know, and my household as well
That when the ship sinks with all its occupants
  I'm not to blame

Badi: The anger you felt and your foolish pride
Made you keep aloof from me, fearing how absurd you'd look
That which you have vomited, why then eat it again?
  Be careful: take heed!

Alii: Because I don't fear demanding my right
I'll use my power, so long as I'm alive
To get my share, even if it costs me a lot
  And you will suffer the consequences

Badi: You're a chatterbox, you talk too much
A serious doer doesn't reveal his intentions
He remains calm, like water in a pot
  And awaits the day of action

52 • *Mnazi: Vuta N'kuvute*

Alii: Ni ya waoga tabiya, hiyo usemayo wewe
Shujaa humuambiya, mvita wake ajuwe
Henendi kumuoteya, ja kifaranga na mwewe
Kama usemavyo wewe

Badi: Kama kweli una niya, ya kutenda usemalo
Kipi kilokuzuwiya, kunitimiziya hilo?
Au haujawadiya, wakati wa kutendalo?
Lipi ulingojeyalo?

Alii: Wanangu tangu kitambo, wangekuwa washafanya
Kila mtu yake fimbo, wali washajikusanya
Kuja kukuonya mambo, kwa changu kuninyang'anya
Lakini nikawakanya

Na sasa nalirudiya, nilokwambiya mwanzoni
Jambo nalilokwambiya, ni kwamba ushuke tini
Iwapo hutasikiya, shauri yako mwendani
Ukijafikwa ni zani

Badi: Mjinga usinifanye, wala usinishituwe
Wala usijidanganye, na urongo 'siambiwe
Alobwiya ndiye mwenye, alowata uzuzuwe
Hili kaa ulijuwe

Alii:	That is a sign of cowardice, what you've just said
	A valiant person speaks up, so his opponent understands
	He doesn't waylay him like a hawk does a chick
	In the manner you say

Badi:	If indeed you intend to do what you said
	What stops you from doing just that?
	Or is it not yet time for you to do so?
	What are you waiting for?

Alii:	My children would have already taken action against you
	Each one with his stick, they had already gathered
	To come and teach you a lesson for grabbing what is mine
	But I restrained them

	Let me repeat what I told you at the start
	I told you that you should climb down
	If you won't heed me, blame yourself for the outcome
	When disaster befalls you

Badi:	Don't suppose I'm a simpleton, and don't threaten me
	Don't fool yourself, and don't be deceived
	Whoever holds a thing owns it; whoever lets go is a fool
	This you must know

Mnazi: Vuta N'kuvute

Alii:

Kabla sijenda zangu, machache nataka sema
Umeninyang'anya changu, kwa kutumiya dhuluma
Pasi na shaka utungu, nitauwona lazima
      Sitasahau daima

'Tazidi kuvumiliya, ingawa wanidhulumu
Si mjinga wa duniya, kila jambo nafahamu
Si uwongo kuningiya, na wala sina wazimu
      Akili yangu timamu

Nilitakalo ni kuwa, waja wapate yaona
Wajuwe 'medhulumiwa, kwa muda mrefu sana
Siku 'kitwaa hatuwa, pamoja na wangu wana
      Pasiwepo wa kunena

Ijapokuwa nataka, kukustahamiliya
Iko siku nitachoka, zaidi kuvumiliya
Hapo litalokufika, litakudhuru vibaya
      Hilino nakuapiya

Ningenda zangu kumbuka, yote niliyoyanena
Siyatwae kidhihaka, 'kiketi yawaze sana
Iko siku itafika, haitakawiya tena
      Kujulikane bayana

—5 Juni 1970

Alii: Before I go off, I'll say a word or two
          You wrested from me what is mine, inflicting injustice on me
          As for pain, no doubt I'll feel it
                  I will never, ever forget

          I'll endure despite your injustice
          I'm not ignorant of the world; I understand its every aspect
          I'm not scared, nor have I lost my mind
                  I'm sound of mind

          What I want is for people to see
          To know who defrauded me for a very long time
          The day I take action alongside my children
                  Let no one object

          As much as I want to endure your injustice
          One day I'll get tired, I'll run out of patience
          And what befalls you then will devastate you
                  I swear this to you

          Remember, as I leave, all that I've told you
          Don't imagine it's a joke; ponder this when you sit quietly
          The day will arrive, and it will not take long
                  When the truth will be known

—*5 June 1970*

Kuno Kunena

Kuno kunena kwa nini, kukanikomeya kuno?
Kwani kunena kunani, kukashikwa kani vino?
Kani iso na kiini, na kuninuniya mno
Kanama nako kunena, kwaonekana ni kuwi

Kana na kuku kunena, kunenwa kakutakiwi
Kuna wanakokuona, kunena kwamba si kuwi
Kunena wakikuona, kukuita kawakawi
Kunena kana kwanuka, nikukome kukunena?

—*19 Julai 1970*

This Speaking Out

Why does speaking out cause me to be locked up?
What is in speaking out for it to be so forcefully resisted?
So much needless aggression unleashed and such frowns turned on me —
So! To others speaking out is apparently a vice

Yet if this speaking out seems to be unwanted
There are those with the view that speaking out isn't bad
When they encounter speaking out, they welcome it at once
So—if speaking out offends, should I stop speaking out?

—*19 July 1970*

Telezi

1 Mvuwa iliyonyesha, ya maradi na ngurumo
Kutwa na kucha kukesha, kunyesha pasi kipimo
Haikuwanufaisha, wenye kazi za vilimo
Wenye kazi za vilimo, walifikwa na hasara

2 Mimeya waloipanda, ilitekukatekuka
Kazi ngumu walotenda, yote ikaharibika
Hawakuvuna matunda, waliyo wakiyataka
Waliyo wakiyataka, yakawa ya mbali nao

3 Wenye kuicha mvuwa, isiwatose mwilini
Baadhi yao wakawa, wakimbiliya penuni
Wengine hawakutuwa, hadi mwao majumbani
Hadi mwao majumbani, na kukomeya milango

4 Wenzangu dhihaka kando, nisemayo ni yakini
Ilibwaga kubwa shindo, mvuwa hiyo jamani
Na mijaji kwa mikondo, yakawa barabarani
Yakawa barabarani, mvuwa kwisha kunyesha

5 Kunyesha iliposiya, kukatapakaa tope
Zilijaa kila ndiya, isibakiye nyeupe
Ukawa mwingi udhiya, pa kupita zisitupe
Pa kupita zisitupe, kwa ndiya kukosekana

Slipperiness

1   The rain that fell amid thunder and lightning
Day and night pouring, falling without end
Didn't benefit those whose occupation is farming
The farming community suffered great loss

2   The crops they'd sown were totally uprooted
All their hard work ended up a big waste
They didn't harvest the fruits they'd wanted
What they'd wanted remained out of reach

3   Among those who feared rain soaking their bodies
Some scampered for cover under shelters
While others raced up to their homes
Up to their homes and locked the doors

4   Friends, I'm not joking, I mean what I say
It caused quite a commotion, that downpour, my friends
And water was gushing, flooding the roads
Flooding the roads when the rain stopped falling

5   After the downpour there was mud everywhere
Not a single path remained clear
It caused a lot of trouble, leaving us nowhere to pass
Leaving us nowhere to pass, for no path remained

60 • *Telezi*

6   Japo hivyo zilikuwa, ndiya hazipitiki
    Bali mimi haamuwa, kwenenda japo kwa dhiki
    Kumbe vile nitakuwa, ni mfano wa samaki
    Ni mfano wa samaki, kuiendeya ndowana

7   Zikanibwaga telezi, sikujuwa kuzendeya
    Ningekwenda kwa henezi, yasingenifika haya
    Lakini tena siwezi, mwendo huo kutumiya
    Sitawata kutembeya, ila tabadili mwendo

    —*3 Agosti 1970*

6   Though the paths were that impassable
     Yet I decided to proceed, despite the hardships
     Little did I know I'd be like a fish
     Like a fish taking itself to the hook

7   The slipperiness brought me down; I didn't know how to walk on it
     I should have been more cautious to avoid what befell me
     But I won't ever again walk in that fashion
     Although I won't stop walking, I'll change my approach

—3 August 1970

Semani Wenye Kusema

1   Muko wapi wenye ndimi, zenye makali ya wembe?
Mbona leo hamusemi, mu kimya kama mapumbe?
Mwangoja yatimu kumi, halafu ndipo mulumbe?
Musijifanye migombe, semani wenye kusema

2   Ni mawi yaliyotuka, "ni ya ki-utu" musambe
Ni yupi mwenye kutaka, kama hayo yamkumbe?
Hao yaliowafika, ni kama 'mefumwa chembe
Musijifanye migombe, semani wenye kusema

3   Uwovu 'kiwa kwa watu, ijapokuwa u tembe
Utaona kila mtu, yu mbiyoni akaimbe
Mbona leo u kwetu, twaambizana tusambe?
Musijifanye migombe, semani wenye kusema

4   La damu kutanganyana, za tafauti viumbe
Ni hatuwa njema sana, watakayo wenye pembe
Pasi kukubaliyana, haifuzu hata tembe
Musijifanye migombe, semani wenye kusema

5   Engani yatendekayo, mato yenu musifumbe
Kisikizeni kiliyo, waliyao ni viumbe
Yapimeni yasemwayo, musimili moja pembe
Musijifanye migombe, semani wenye kusema

6   Lavuja paa la nyumba, wavimbaji nawavimbe
Na kila mlima shamba, natiye mpini jembe
Na wale waliyo simba, leo wangurume jumbe
Musijifanye migombe, semani wenye kusema

—*19 Oktoba 1970*

Speak Out, You Who Dare

1 Where are you whose tongues have the sharpness of razors?
Why aren't you talking today? You are mute like fools
Are you waiting for the count of ten before you speak up?
Don't be like sheep; speak out, you who dare[2]

2 It's evil what occurred, don't say "it's only human"
Who wishes for oneself that kind of misfortune?
The victims are as if an arrow had pierced them
Don't be like sheep; speak out, you who dare

3 When evil befalls other people, however small
You'll hear everyone speaking out
Why now that it's in our midst are we telling one another to be quiet?
Don't be like sheep; speak out, you who dare

4 Marriage between different peoples
Is a very good move that leaders desire
But it's unworkable without mutual consent
Don't be like sheep; speak out, you who dare

5 Behold what is happening, don't close your eyes
Listen to the cry—those crying are human
Consider what they say, don't be partial
Don't be like sheep; speak out, you who dare

6 The roof is leaking; repair it, thatchers
And every farmer should fix a handle to the hoe
And those who are lions should roar and make their voices heard
Don't be like sheep; speak out, you who dare

—19 October 1970

---

2. Literally, "don't be like cows," but the cow in the Swahili context has an association resembling that of the sheep in the English, with foolish docility. *—Ed.*

Muwerevu Hajinyowi

1 Mwenye nacho wajishasha, wajiona kama ndovu
   Kitu kimekulewesha, huutambuwi uwovu
   Ngoma yako itakesha, au ni nguvu za povu?
   Tangu lini muwerevu, akajinyowa mwenyewe?

2 Tangu ukipate kitu, 'megeuka mpumbavu
   Kattu huthamini mtu, ambaye kwamba mtovu
   Wafikiri kisu gutu, hakikati nyama pevu?
   Tangu lini muwerevu, akajinyowa mwenyewe?

3 Wangapi 'meonekana, mibakhili mishupavu
   Waliyo wakijitona, na mwingi usuluhivu
   Leo hawanasi tena, wageukile maivu
   Tangu lini muwerevu, akajinyowa mwenyewe?

4 Kupata kusikughuri, ukajidhani mwerevu
   Na hicho chako kiburi, ujuwe ni maangavu
   Iko siku itajiri, ujikute kwenye wavu
   Tangu lini muwerevu, akajinyowa mwenyewe?

5 Kila mwenye kukuonya, uiwate ndiya mbovu
   Huchelewi kumminya, kumvunda zake mbavu
   Fanya ambayo wafanya, baada mbiti ni mbivu
   Ungajidai mwerevu, hutajinyowa mwenyewe

   —27 Oktoba 1970

Even a Clever Guy Can't Shave His Own Head

1 You brag, oh! wealthy one, you think you're an elephant
Wealth has intoxicated you—you can't recognize evil
Will your drum thrum till morning, or does it have the power of foam?
Since when did a clever guy shave his own head?

2 Since becoming rich you have turned into a fool
You despise people who are deprived
You think a blunt knife can't cut tough meat?
Since when did a clever guy shave his own head?

3 How many people have emerged, notorious for their miserliness
Bragging about themselves, thinking they were smart
Today they're no longer with us; they've turned into ash
Since when did a clever guy shave his own head?

4 Don't let wealth trick you into supposing you're shrewd
That pride of yours will be your undoing
A day will come when you'll be trapped in the net
Since when did a clever guy shave his own head?

5 Everyone warning you against wicked ways —
You don't hesitate to pound them, breaking their ribs
Do as you like, but things change from unripe to ripe
However shrewd you pretend to be, you won't shave your own head

—*27 October 1970*

Yatakoma

1   Sitokuwanayo, dawamu daima
      Dhiki nilonayo, iliyon'egema
      Ta'wa mbali nayo, utuwe mtima

2   Utuwe mtima, na kutabaradi
      'Papatuwe kama, uwa la waridi
      Zitakapokoma, zakwe tashididi

3   Zakwe tashididi, zinganilemeya
      Nitajitahidi, kuzivumiliya
      Nipate muradi, ninaongojeya

4   Ninaongojeya, pasi ati ati
      Kwa moyo mmoya, tamaa sikati
      Ungalimatiya, si kwamba sipati

5   Si kwamba sipati, kwa kukawa kuja
      Hatuwa sivuti, mudawe nangoja
      Saa haipiti, 'talivaa koja

6   'Talivaa koja, la yangu subira
      Nipate natija, ilo barabara
      Subira kwa mja, ndilo jambo bora

7   Ndilo jambo bora, litakikanalo
      Hili kila mara, mtu awe nalo
      Makubwa madhara, kutokuwa nalo

—3 Novemba 1970

It Will End

1 It won't bedevil me forever and ever
  This agony I now have weighing on me
  I'll get far from it so my heart may gain relief

2 So my heart may gain relief and calmness
  So it will bloom like a rose
  When there is an end to its distress

3 Although its distress overwhelms me
  I'll try hard to endure it
  So I can attain the aim I await

4 I await it without wavering
  Whole-heartedly and ceaselessly
  Delay doesn't mean I'll miss it altogether

5 I'll not miss it altogether if its coming is delayed
  I'm not moving a step; I keep waiting
  In no time I'll wear the garland of flowers

6 I'll garland myself through my perseverance
  So I achieve a rightful reward
  Perseverance, for humans, is the best virtue

7 It's the best virtue, much preferred
  The virtue one should always possess
  What a disaster for someone without it

  —3 November 1970

Ah! Mwenzangu

1. Pulika wangu rafiki, rafiki nipulikiza
   Kukunasihi sichoki, ingawa wanipuuza
   Ijapokuwa hutaki, nasaha kuisikiza
   Ufanyayo ni ya pweza, kujipaliya makaa

2. Maadamu u mwenzangu, nilokuswafiya niya
   Wewe kama ndugu yangu, tulotoka tumbo moya
   Huwa wanipa matungu, utendapo jambo baya
   Sina budi kukwambiya, wajipaliya makaa

3. Ninenayo zingatiya, ung'aze yako maozi
   Najuwa ningakwambiya, waniona mpuuzi
   Mwisho utakuja liya, tena ya damu matozi
   Hili nakwambiya wazi, wajipaliya makaa

4. Wajivundiya hishima, kwa kitendo utendacho
   Kitendo hicho si chema, ungafurahi kwa hicho
   Ungenda enga na nyuma, ujuwe kikufwatacho
   Ingawa hunacho kicho, wajipaliya makaa

5. Mekufurahisha ngoma, mshipani mekungiya
   Mdundo ushakuvama, wauteza pasi haya
   Hata kimefika kima, cha njuga kuuvaliya
   Nakwambiya nisikiya, wajipaliya makaa

6. Najuwa tamu waona, kwa hilo ulitendalo
   Fahamu 'mekuwa huna, imekupoteya kwalo
   Hata watu wanganena, wewe hulijali hilo
   Si jema ulifanyalo, wajipaliya makaa

Alas, My Friend!

1   Listen to me friend, friend hear me out
    I won't tire of counseling you, although you ignore me
    Listen to advice, even if you don't want to
    You're acting like an octopus, heaping coals on yourself[3]

2   Since you're my friend to whom I wish good
    You're like my blood brother, born from the same womb
    You hurt me whenever you do wrong
    I have to tell you: you're heaping coals on yourself

3   Pay attention to my words, and open your eyes to see
    I know even as I talk to you—you think this is foolishness
    But in the end you'll weep, shedding tears of blood
    I tell you openly: you're heaping coals on yourself

4   You're bringing dishonor upon yourself by what you're doing
    Your actions are despicable, even if you delight in them
    As you move ahead, look back to know what is behind you
    Although you're fearless, you're heaping coals on yourself

5   The dance has elated you—it has entered your veins
    The drumbeat is rumbling, and you dance shamelessly
    You've reached the point even of dancing with bells on
    I tell you, listen to me: you're heaping coals on yourself

6   I know it feels sweet to do what you're doing
    You've lost your common sense because of it
    Whatever people say, you don't seem to care
    What you're doing isn't good: you're heaping coals on yourself

---

3. While being roasted, an octopus may in its spasmodic movements fling coals on its own body. —*Ed.*

70 • *Ah! Mwenzangu*

7 Donge la sukari tamu, ambalo 'melibugiya
Kati yake muna sumu, kama hujuwi sikiya
Utakuja jilaumu, wakati ukiwadiya
'Siseme sikukwambiya, wajipaliya makaa

8 Kipofu umegeuka, umepofuka maoni
Mtu japo angataka, kukuonesha huoni
Mkono angakushika, huukukuta yakini
Rafiki yangu fulani, wajipaliya makaa

9 Masikini wangu mwenza, nnakusikitikiya
Kitambo nililianza, jambo hili kukwambiya
Iwapo hutajitunza, ukawata mbovu ndiya
Madharani utangiya, wajipaliya makaa

10 Uliyo wajibu wangu, ndiyo huu naufanya
Nafanya hili mwenzangu, kusudi ni kukumbonya
Sina la zaidi kwangu, isipo ni kukukanya
Ndugu yangu nakuonya, wajipaliya makaa

11 Wewe hu mwana mtoto, hanena 'takukemeya
Wala kutwaa ufito, hasema 'takuchapiya
Haya kwangu ni mazito, siwezi kukutendeya
Langu ni kukuambiya, wajipaliya makaa

12 Wafahamu kila jambo, jema na lililo baya
Ya sawa na yalo kombo, yote hayo yakweleya
Wajifanyaje sombombo, kufanya yaso na ndiya?
Mwenzangu nakuapiya, wajipaliya makaa

13 Nakwambiya hichi changu, utakuja nikumbuka
Wambe nali na mwenzangu, kitako aloniweka
Akanamba mwendo wangu, niubadili haraka
Lakini sikuyashika, "wajipaliya makaa"

Alas, My Friend! • 71

7   The lump of sugar that you're eating
    There's poison in it—listen if you don't know
    You'll blame yourself when the moment comes
    Don't say I didn't tell you: you're heaping coals on yourself

8   You've become blind, your eyes are blinded
    Even if someone tries to show you, you can't see at all
    Even if he takes your hand, you shake it off
    My friend, you're heaping coals on yourself

9   Oh! poor friend of mine, I pity you
    I began much earlier, telling you this:
    If you won't take care of yourself and leave the wicked way
    Harm will befall you; you're heaping coals on yourself

10 This is my obligation I'm carrying out
    I'm doing this, my friend, to make you see
    I have no agenda other than to warn you
    I warn you, brother, you're heaping coals on yourself

11 You're not a small child for me to scold
    Or to grab a rod and threaten to smack
    That to me is impossible; I can't do that to you
    I can only tell you: you're heaping coals on yourself

12 You understand what's good and what's bad
    The straight and the crooked you fully differentiate
    Why are you then being so heedless and acting ruinously?
    I swear to you, my friend—you're heaping coals on yourself

13 I tell you what!—you'll come to remember
    You'll say—I had a friend who sat me down
    And told me I needed to change my conduct fast
    Yet I didn't heed "you're heaping coals on yourself"

72 • *Ah! Mwenzangu*

14   Aliponambiya haya, muwovu nikamuona
      Haanza kumtukiya, mimi naye hatengana
      Kumbe alokinambiya, yote yali nda maana
      Alinamba akinena, "wajipaliya makaa"

15   Kanama yali ni kweli, ni kheri 'ngemsikiza
      Lakini sikuyajali, alo akinieleza
      Nali fahali fidhuli, kila uchao hifuza
      Leo ndiyo naliwaza, wajipaliya makaa

16   Kaditama ukiketi, hili liwaze sikome
      Moyoni ulidhibiti, akilini ulipime
      Kiumbe mwanzo hajuti, majuto huja kinyume
      Mara ya mwisho niseme, wajipaliya makaa

      —17 Novemba 1970

Alas, My Friend! • 73

14 When he told me this (you'll say), I saw him as wicked
  I started to hate him and parted ways with him
  Little did I know what he said made sense
  He told me, saying, "you're heaping coals on yourself"

15 And so it was true—it would have been better to heed him
  But I didn't care then, whatever he told me
  I was like a rogue bull, day in and day out
  It's only today I realize: you're heaping coals on yourself

16 In conclusion: while you sit, ponder this ceaselessly
  Keep it in your heart, and weigh it in your mind
  One doesn't regret at first; regrets come later
  Let me say for the last time: you're heaping coals on yourself

—17 November 1970

Wasiwasi Enda Zako

1 Wasiwasi n'ondokeya, ondoka enenda zako
Ondoka andama ndiya, n'ondosheya uso wako
Ondoka! Wanisikiya? Ziwate jeuri zako
Jishughulishe na yako, yangu wayatakiyani?

2 Wasiwasi siitaki, suhuba yako si nzuri
Haisitahamiliki, uwovu umekithiri
Inganyoshwa hainyoki, ikukutene kikiri
Siitaki yako shari, enda zako wasiwasi

3 Huna kazi ufanyayo, ela kuwafitinisha
Viumbe na zao nyoyo, vitwa kuwagotanisha
Hiino ndiyo kaziyo, yenye kukufurahisha
Ni kazi isokuchosha, mno umeizoweya

4 Tukaapo wanambiya, hayawi niyatakayo
Kwamba tamaa ngatiya, nasumbuwa wangu moyo
Kwamba hata hingojeya, hayo niyangojeyayo
Ng'o! Siyapati hayo, ni bure najisumbuwa

5 Mara waja na habari, mambo yalivyo nyumbani
Ati mambo si mazuri, mambo yote tafashani
Wanitaka nifikiri, usemayo ni yakini
Nisononeke moyoni, upate kufurahika

Be Gone, Anxiety

1   Anxiety, go away from me, get out of here
    Go, get going, get out of my face
    I said go! Don't you hear me? Stop your stubbornness
    Mind your own business; what do you want with mine?

2   Anxiety, I don't need your friendship—it isn't good
    It's unbearable, there's too much evil in it
    It's impossible to straighten it, it's too hardened in its crookedness
    I don't want your wickedness: be gone, anxiety

3   You do nothing here but cause discord
    Driving a wedge between human beings and their hearts
    That's what you do, and you find joy in doing it
    This work never tires you, you're so comfortable with it

4   When I'm with you, you say what I want will never materialize
    That however much I hope, it's only hoping against hope
    That even if I await what I'm awaiting —
    Never! I'll never get it; it's a futile exercise

5   Sometimes you come with updates from home
    Saying things aren't good, everything is shambolic
    You want me to believe what you say is true
    You aim to break my heart so you can rejoice

76 • *Wasiwasi Enda Zako*

6 Au mara hunijiya, na kingine kisahani
   Kukhusu zao afiya, hao waliyo nyumbani
   Huwa hwishi kunambiya, hali zao taabani
   Zingawa; watakiyani? Ni zako au ni zao?

7 Na mara huja nambiya, nitakapotoka humu
   Ya kwamba yaningojeya, nde maisha magumu
   Ulilonikusudiya, ni kunitiya wazimu?
   Kama ndiyo yako hamu, basi unshatahayari

8 Huo urafiki wako, wa kuja niungulisha
   Kunipa masikitiko, na mateso yasokwisha
   Kutoka leo ni mwiko, sitautaka maisha
   Kamwe hutanikondesha, tokomeya mwana kwenda

   —*23 Novemba 1970*

6   Or you come to me with other tall tales
About the health of those at home
You never tire of telling me they're in bad shape
If so, what's it to you? Is it your health or theirs?

7   Sometimes you tell me that when I get out of here
A hard life awaits me outside
Is it your intent to drive me mad?
If that's what you want, you should be ashamed

8   This friendship of yours that comes to sear me
Giving me sorrow and endless suffering
Is from today forbidden—I don't want it ever again
You'll never make me waste away: get away from me

—*23 November 1970*

Mja si Mwema

1. Mkono inuka | inuka hima | twaa kalamu
   Upate ya'ndika | kwa khati njema | hino nudhumu
   Ipate someka | wenye kusoma | waifahamu
   Wapate yashika | na kuyapima | yaliyo humu

2. Kuandika anza | anza 'sikawe | mkono wangu
   Na mimi naanza | kisa chenyewe | cha mlimwengu
   Alivyonifanza | nao wajuwe | waja wenzangu
   Wapate jitunza | salama wawe | hawa ndu zangu

3. Mja sikudhani | sikudhaniya | 'tanizunguka
   Nikamuamini | hafikiriya | hatageuka
   Kumbe mwafulani | hakuzoweya | kuaminika
   N'shambaini | ingawa baya | lishanifika

4. Menitenda kisa | kisa adhimu | mja mcheni
   'Mezinduka sasa | n'shafahamu | najuwa kwani
   Ni yangu makosa | najilaumu | kumuamini
   Sikuwa napasa | hata sehemu | kumthamini

What a Bad Fellow!

1   Hand, rise   arise quickly   take the pen
       That you may write   in good handwriting   this verse
       That it may be read   that those who read   may apprehend it
       That they may grasp   and weigh   the contents

2   Start writing   start, don't delay   my hand
       And I begin   to tell the story   of this person
       What he did to me   that they may know   my fellow beings
       May protect themselves   and be safe   these my fellows

3   I didn't know this man   I didn't imagine   he'd plot against me
       I trusted him   I never thought   he would change
       Little did I know   he was unused   to being trusted
       I know him now   though calamity   has already befallen me

4   He's done me wrong   a great wrong   beware of him
       I've awoken   I've understood   I now know why
       It's my fault   I blame myself   for trusting him
       I wasn't meant   even a bit   to esteem him

80 • *Mja si Mwema*

5 'Meniuwa mja   mja ni nduli   tahadharini
   Mjaye daraja   nda kikatili   hana imani
   Muonapo mja   kaani mbali   mujitengeni
   Asije akaja   (kwani habali)   kuhasirini

6 Mja hana haya   haya hazimo   mwake usoni
   Mja ni mbaya   hutimba shimo   ungiye ndani
   Na ukishangiya   azome zomo   furaha gani!
   Mmoja kwa miya   ndiye hayumo   baya kundini

—*10 Januari 1971*

What a Bad Fellow! • 81

5 This man has done me in   he is lethal   be warned
   It's in his nature   to be cruel   he has no mercy
   When you see him   distance yourselves   stay away
   Lest he come   (for he cares not)   to cause you havoc

6 He has no shame   none at all   upon his face
   He is bad news   he digs a hole   so you can enter
   And once you're in   he taunts you then   oh! how nice!
   Only one in a hundred   happens not to be   among the evil ones

—*10 January 1971*

Lipi Litakalokuwa?

1   Lipi mojapo la kuwa? Naliwe lijulikane
    Liwe tupate lijuwa, tujuwe na tulione
    Naliwe tupate tuwa, liwapo ndilo tunene
    Halitakuwa jengine, ima ndilo au silo

2   Naliwe lijitokeze, bure lisifitamane
    Kama ni nuru ing'aze, ing'arishe pembe nne
    Ni giza? Lifunikize, kilo mbele tusione
    Halitakuwa jengine, ima ndilo au silo

3   Lisitudundishe nyoyo, naliwe nazo zisone
    Tangu hapo wayowayo, na nyoyo liembetene
    Yatosha ziliyonayo, lisizitweke mengine
    Halitakuwa jengine, ima ndilo au silo

4   Kama lataka naliwe, hakika ijulikane
    Bure lisitusumbuwe, kwa nini tusumbuwane?
    Lisipotaka lisiwe, wala tusiraiyane
    Halitakuwa jengine, ima ndilo au silo

    —14 Januari 1971

What Will Happen?

1   What will happen? Let it happen so it may be known
    Let it be, so we can know it, so we can know it and see it
    Let it be, so we can feel settled; if it's the one, we will say so
    It won't be something else: either it is or it isn't

2   Let it be and be apparent; it's pointless for it to be hidden
    If it's light, let it shine, illuminating the four corners
    If it's darkness? Let it spread, so we can't see in front of us
    It won't be something else: either it is or it isn't

3   Don't let it trouble our hearts; let it happen so they rest
    All along our hearts have been worried
    Our hearts have had enough; they don't deserve more anguish
    It won't be something else: either it is or it isn't

4   If it wants to be, let it be, so the truth may be known
    Don't let it trouble us: why trouble one another?
    If it doesn't want to be, let it not be, nor should we cajole it
    It won't be something else: either it is or it isn't

—14 January 1971

Mamaetu Afrika

1. Mamaetu Afrika, wanayo tu msibani
   Msiba umetufika, ndugu hatusikizani
   Kila mmoja ataka, awe mshika sukani
   Litawezekana lini? Hebu tuamuwe Mama

2. Wale maadui zetu, haweshi kutufitini
   Si watu hawa si watu, ni wanyama wa mwituni
   Hawapendi Mamaetu, kukwona u furahani
   Bali uwe simanzini, ndivyo watakavyo Mama

3. Hawa ndiwo wale wale, madhalimu wa zamani
   Usidhaniye wafile, wakalimo duniyani
   Na fikira zile zile, zikali mwao vitwani
   Wangali wakitamani, kukudhulumu we Mama

4. Mama madhalimu hawa, walikujiya zamani
   Wakakushika shokowa, nyayo hadi utosini
   Vyako vikatukuliwa, hata vilivyo mwilini
   Mali nyingi ya thamani, wakakupokonya Mama

5. Mali ulokuwanayo, ndiyo waloyatamani
   Wakajaza mali hayo, shehena mwao vyomboni
   Wakenenda nayo mbiyo, hadi mwao majumbani
   Ni wevi waso kifani, walokuibiya Mama

Our Mother Africa

1   Mother Africa, calamity has befallen us your children
Calamity has befallen us, siblings don't agree
Each one wants to grip the steering wheel
How can this be possible? Please resolve our dispute

2   Those foes of ours never stop nursing discord among us
These are not humans; they are wild animals
They don't want to see you elated, Mama
Sorrow, Mama, is what they desire for you

3   They are the very ones, the selfsame oppressors of the past
Don't think they died; they are still in the world
And the selfsame thinking is still in their heads
They still desire to exploit you, Mama

4   Mother, these oppressors came to you in the past
They tied you up from head to foot
They took all you had, even parts of your body
Plenty of precious wealth they grabbed from you, Mama

5   The wealth that you had, that is what they desired
They loaded your riches as cargo on their vessels
They rushed away with them to their homes
These are thieves like no others, those who stole from you, Mama

86 • *Mamaetu Afrika*

6   Mno waliyapapiya, pasi kuona imani
    Ilikuwa yao niya, kukuwata masikini
    Hawakukufikiriya, kisha'ye utafanyani
    Au utakula nini, na sisi wanayo Mama

7   Si mali tu Mamaetu, hawakutosheka kwani
    Vile vile ndugu zetu, wakatiwa utumwani
    Hawakuthamini utu, wa walo na ngozi hini
    Wakituona manyani, kwamba tu weusi Mama

8   Wakenda nao makwao, huko Bara Ulayani
    Ndugu zetu nguvu zao, zikatiwa makazini
    Pasi na kulipwa nao, ingawa malipo duni
    Walinali wakoloni, kwa bwerere hiyo Mama

9   Mama lau si wanayo, kupelekwa ugenini
    Lau kwamba si maliyo, kubwakurwa mikononi
    Hivi leo Bara hilo, liitwayo Ulayani
    Lingekuwa halifani, na kupawa sifa Mama

10 Ndiyo yaliyowalisha, na kutengezeya huko
    Miji wakasimamisha, kwa nguvu za mali yako
    Lililowatajirisha, ni jasho la mwili wako
    Na damu ya wana wako, ndiyo kuwa hayo Mama

Our Mother Africa • 87

6   They greedily grabbed your riches, showing no mercy
    They meant to leave you impoverished
    They didn't think about what you would do afterwards
    Or what you would eat with us, your children, Mama

7   It isn't just wealth, Mama; they couldn't be satisfied
    They enslaved our own brothers
    They had no regard for people with skin like ours
    They saw us as monkeys just because we're black, Mama

8   They took our brothers to their land, the continent of Europe
    They put our brothers' energy to use
    Without paying them wages, even negligible ones
    The colonists took all that for free, Mama

9   Had it not been for your children taken overseas
    Had it not been for your riches wrested from your hands
    Today that continent called Europe
    Wouldn't prosper or be praised, Mama

10 This is what fed them and built things over there
    Cities were erected on the strength of your wealth
    What made them rich is the sweat of your body, Mama
    And the blood of your children—so it was, Mama

88 • *Mamaetu Afrika*

11 Juu ya zao akili, zisifikazo kabisa
Walipungukiwa mali, mali ndicho walokosa
Wakaona afadhali, waje kwako kupukusa
Maliyo pasi ruhusa, wakakutwaliya Mama

12 Wakakunyang'anya vyako, hivi mtana mtana
Mmoja hakukuwako, wa kusubutu kunena
Mama uli peke yako, hata muombezi huna
Ila sisi wako wana, tukakuliliya Mama

13 Kwani siku hizo Mama, twali dhaifu yakini
Mtu akitusukuma, twali kianguka tini
Sisi nao kusimama, na kuwatiya mbaroni
Ikawa haimkini, sisi kuwashinda Mama

14 Tulipopata fahamu, kuweza kukuteteya
Wakaona madhalimu, yataw'endeya vibaya
Ndipo walipoazimu, kutumiya mpya ndiya
Kuzivunda zetu niya, wazidi kukula Mama

15 Hapo wakakatikiwa, kwamba watutenganishe
Kwani wamoja tukiwa, tutawakanyaga weshe
Wakaona kubwa dawa, wano watufarikishe
Ili wakukorofishe, na kukunyonya we Mama

Our Mother Africa • 89

11   Though they had brains, for which they are much acclaimed
They lacked wealth—wealth is what they lacked
They thought it better to come and harvest
Your wealth without consent; they stole from you, Mama

12   They stole your possessions in broad daylight
There wasn't a single one who dared to speak up
You stood alone, Mother, with no one on your side
Except for us, your children, who wept for you, Mama

13   Indeed in those days, Mother, we were weak for sure
If someone pushed us, we would fall down
For us to stand up and arrest them —
That was impossible, to defeat them, Mama

14   When we found our voices to speak up for you
The oppressors saw that things were looking bad
So they decided to use a new strategy
To break our will so they could keep profiting, Mama

15   They determined that they should divide us
Because if we remained one, we would annihilate them
They realized the best fix was to divide us
To cause discord and to exploit you, Mama

90 • *Mamaetu Afrika*

16   Tukawekewa mipaka, kila ukoo na pao
Walifanya kwa kutaka, umoja tusiwe nao
Walijuwa pasi shaka, u karibu mwisho wao
Wa kushungiwa makwao, wakuhame wetu Mama

17   Wakawa waendeleya, kutukuwa yako mali
Na sisi wanayo piya, wakitupa idhilali
Tukawa twalingojeya, mwisho wake jambo hili
Sikuye ikiwasili, tutende kitendo Mama

18   Tulipoona ya mno, yashatukoma kooni
Tukasema tabu hino, sasa natu'yondosheni
Tukakunduwa mikono, tukaingiya vitani
Kuwapiga wakoloni, wakwambae wetu Mama

19   Japo twali mbali mbali, kila ukoo pekee
Tukaona afadhali, kila tapo lisongee
Kila pembe na mahali, adui tumlemee
Wana na walo wazee, tukawa vitani Mama

20   Mama tukaanza vita, kukupiganiya wewe
Maguu tukayakita, tukasema tufe nawe
Minyoo tukaikata, ili kwamba huru uwe
Twalolitaka mwishowe, tukawa tunalo Mama

Our Mother Africa • 91

16   They imposed boundaries, each clan in its own domain
        Their intention in doing so was to break our unity
        They well knew their end was fast approaching
        They would soon be chased home, leaving our place, Mama

17   They continued taking your riches
        And humiliating us, your children
        We awaited the end of it all
        Awaited the day for acting, Mama

18   When we'd had more than enough, had it up to here
        We said—let's rid ourselves of this suffering!
        We rolled up our sleeves and entered the battle
        Fighting the colonists so they'd leave you alone, Mama

19   Although we were separated, every clan on its own
        We felt it would be better for each group to forge ahead
        From every nook and cranny to overwhelm the enemy
        Young and old, we fought the battle, Mama

20   We started the war, fighting for you
        We stood our ground, ready to die for you
        We cut the chains so we might be free
        In the end we obtained our objective, Mama

92 • *Mamaetu Afrika*

21   Nyingi mno damu yetu, ikabidi kumwaika
Baadhi ya ndugu zetu, roho zao zikatoka
Na kila kilicho chetu, kwa wingi kikatumika
Kwa kutaka kuiweka, hadhi yetu nawe Mama

22   Adui tukamshinda, ikawa sasa atoke
Tukamwamba toka nenda, na kumpiga mateke
Alikuwa yuwadinda, hakutaka kwenda zake
Kwa nyingi tamaa yake, ya kukudhulumu Mama

23   Baadhi ya wana wako, bado wangali tabuni
Wangali na masumbuko, kwa wateswavyo wendani
Wakoloni wangaliko, kwa wanayo wa Kusini
Bado wangali na kani, kutesa wanayo Mama

24   Msumbiji vile vile, bado hawajakwondoka
Nako Zimbabwe wa tele, hawajataka kutoka
Na Angola wabakile, wangali wakikushika
Guinea-Bissau kadha'ka, wamekugandama Mama

25   Watoto wako hawano, ni midume sawa sawa
Wamo kwenye mapigano, kutaka kukukombowa
Na kwa lao ungamano, na moyo wa kujitowa
Adui watamtowa, hilo litakuwa Mama

Our Mother Africa • 93

21 We had to shed a great deal of our own blood
    Some of our brothers lost their lives
    And we spent many of our resources
    Wanting to uphold our esteem and yours, Mama

22 We defeated the enemy, who now had to leave
    We told him—go—and kicked him out
    He was demurring, he didn't want to depart
    Because of his greed, his wish to exploit you, Mama

23 Some of your children are still in trouble
    They still suffer, experiencing torture
    The colonists still exist for your children in the South
    They still have the zeal to oppress your children, Mama

24 In Mozambique as well, they still haven't gone
    In Zimbabwe they are numerous; they don't want to leave
    And in Angola they remain, determined to cling to you
    Also in Guinea-Bissau, they've stuck to you, Mama

25 These your children, they are real men
    They are in the trenches, they want to liberate you
    And by their unity, and through their sacrifice
    They will smoke out the foe—that's a certainty, Mama

94 • *Mamaetu Afrika*

26 Adui hivyo kuona, kishamtoka kanwani
Chakula kitamu sana, tena hakipatikani
Akawa amedangana, hajuwi afanye nini
Ili kwamba mkononi, akirudishecho Mama

27 Ikawa anapokaa, huwa roho yampapa
Hurudiwa na tamaa, ya kuja tena kujepa
Bali aogopa baa, lau atarudi hapa
Ni mbwa kuona fupa, akacha guguna Mama

28 Kurudi yeye mwenyewe, kuja kuyatwaa mali
Au kutuma mwanawe, aitimize shughuli
Haya Mama utambuwe, yote kwake ni muhali
Ajuwa kwamba si kweli, hawezi faulu Mama

29 Kwani wingi wa wanayo, mato yao yako wazi
Kutokeya siku hiyo, hawanao usingizi
Hata yao masikiyo, daima ni masikizi
Angaja kwa unyenyezi, watamsikiya Mama

30 Tamaa hakuikata, ya kupata atakalo
Kufikiri hakusita, *lipi liwezekanalo?*
Litalonipa kupata, lile nilihitajilo
Kwani sina budi nalo, ndivyo kiwaza'ye Mama

Our Mother Africa • 95

26   When the enemy realized the food had dropped from his mouth
Very sumptuous food, and rare
He felt perplexed; he didn't know what to do
Whether he could get back what he'd held in his hand, Mama

27   Whenever he sat down he was troubled
His greed would return, urging him to come back and steal
But he feared calamity if he returned —
Like a dog that sees a bone and is scared to gnaw it, Mama

28   For him to return himself and carry off the wealth
Or to send his child to accomplish such a mission
Know this, Mama, it is impossible for him
He knows quite clearly he can't succeed, Mama

29   For a huge number of your children have their eyes wide open
Since that day, they never sleep a wink
Even their ears are ever alert
Even if he comes tiptoeing, they will hear him, Mama

30   But he didn't give up hope of achieving his goal
He didn't stop thinking—*What can I do*
That will enable me to get what I want?
I must devise a way; that's what he thought, Mama

96 • *Mamaetu Afrika*

31 Tahamaki akazuwa, jambo atakalofanya
    Akaona kubwa dawa, ambayo itamponya
    Ni wanayo hawa hawa, aanze kuwatawanya
    Mapande kuwagawanya, wamtumikiye Mama

32 Baadhi awatumiye, wawe vibaraka vyake
    Baadaye wakujiye, watimize kazi yake
    Wanayo wakuibiye, chako kipelekwe kwake
    Hiyo ndiyo haja yake, aliyoitaka Mama

33 Wanayo hao ni hawa, waletao machafuko
    Adui 'mewanunuwa, wamo ndani mwa mfuko
    Ndu zetu wameradhiwa, kuikosa radhi yako
    Watapata masumbuko, kwa wayatendayo Mama

34 Badala ya kuungana, tuwe ni kitu kimoja
    Tupate shirikiyana, sisi na wao pamoja
    Tukulinde sana sana, kwa kila litalokuja
    Bali wao yao haja, si sawa na yetu Mama

35 Ndiyo mwanzo ndugu zetu, wenda kinyume na sisi!
    Wakishika kila chetu, na kukiuza rahisi
    Waivunda hadhi yetu, sote tuliyo weusi
    Wapenda zao nafusi, na maaduizo Mama

Our Mother Africa • 97

31 Before long he devised a thing to do
He decided the medicine essential for his healing
Were these your very children: he should start scattering them
Dividing them into groups so they might serve him, Mama

32 He wants to use some as his puppets
Eventually they'll come to you to fulfill his bidding
That your children should steal from you and bring your things to him —
That is his wish; it's what he wants, Mama

33 Your children are the ones causing mayhem
The enemy has bought them—they are in his pocket
Our brothers have chosen to dispense with your blessings
They'll suffer ruin for their actions, Mama

34 Instead of a wish to unite as one
In cooperation, us and them together
To guard you without fail against whatever comes
Their desire, instead, differs from ours, Mama

35 But now our brothers have turned against us
They grab every one of our possessions and sell them cheaply
They soil the reputation of all of us who are black
They love themselves—and your enemies, Mama

98 • *Mamaetu Afrika*

36   Sisi hatutakubali, kurudishwa utumwani
Kurudiya idhilali, tuliyopawa zamani
Mama wala yako mali, kupelekwa Ulayani
Hatarudi mkoloni, tuamini wetu Mama

37   Tutakulinda vilivyo, pasipo kurudi nyuma
Na vyote ulivyonavyo, vitabakiya salama
Vitabaki vivyo hivyo, kimoja hakitahama
Tutamtafuna nyama, atayekugusa Mama

38   Tu tayari damu yetu, kwa mikondo imwaike
Tu tayari roho zetu, kwa maelfu zitoke
Tukuhami Mamaetu, kila baya likwepuke
Hishimayo tuiweke, Afrika wetu Mama

—*29 Januari 1971*

36   We won't accept being enslaved again
        Going back to the humiliation to which we were subjected before
        Nor will your wealth be ferried to Europe
        The colonist won't return—believe us, Mama

37   We will protect you ceaselessly
        And everything you possess will remain safe
        It will remain intact, not one thing will move
        We will destroy whoever touches you, Mama

38   We are ready for our blood to flow like streams
        We are ready to lose our lives, even by the thousands
        To protect you, our mother, from each and every evil
        So we uphold your honor, Africa our mother

—29 January 1971

Jana na Leo na Kesho

1 Jana ibakile jina, haipo tena haipo
  Hairudishiki tena, tungaitaka iwepo
  Yaliyokwenda na jana, yamepazwa na upepo
    Hunenwa: yalikuwapo

2 Tamani kuirudisha, jana irudi vivile
  Tamani kujiondosha, jana uifuwatile
  Hata 'kijibidiisha, jibidiishe milele
    Ni bure kwani haile

3 Asemaye 'tajaribu, yu mrongo hataweza
  Birri ajaribu hebu, tuone akitimiza
  Naapa hawezi swibu, angafanya miujiza
    Hataweza hataweza

4 Jana dasituri yake, ikipita inshapita
  Na kila kilicho chake, haiwati kuch'angata
  Hutwaa na kwenda zake, na wala hutaipata
    Haiji ungaiita

5 Ipaze yako sauti, isilikane mbinguni
  Tanuwa koo kwa dhati, liya gaagaa tini
  Jiapiziye mauti, uwondoke duniyani
    Haitaitika sini!

Yesterday and Today and Tomorrow

1 Yesterday remains in name, it's not here anymore, not here
It can't be brought back, however much we hunger for it
What went with yesterday has been swept away by the wind
   It can only be said: it used to be here

2 If you want to bring yesterday back just as it was
If you want to send yourself off in search of yesterday
However much you try, trying even forever
   It's futile because yesterday is not

3 Whoever says he'll try is lying; he surely can't
Or let him try, we'll see whether he can do it
I swear he can't succeed, even if he uses magic
   He won't be able to, he won't

4 The nature of yesterday—once it passes, it's past
And all its possessions, it clings to them
It takes its things and goes its way, and you can't find it again
   It won't come even if you call

5 Raise your voice high so it may be heard in the heavens
Shout as loudly as you can, wail as you roll on the ground
Swear upon death, on departing the world
   It won't respond at all

102 • *Jana na Leo na Kesho*

6   Jana ikishakuwata, kurudi 'situmaini
Ungenda kuitafuta, kattu haionekani
Huwapa watu kujuta, na *laiti* midomoni
        Laiti zitafaani?

7   Ya jana hufa na jana, yakawa ni marehemu
Kabisa hutayaona, hata maisha 'kidumu
Labda yalofanana, ndiyo yajayo kwa zamu
        Yenyewe haswa, haramu

8   Jana ni ya kukumbuka, vitendo vilivyopita
Watu hayo huy'andika, wajao wakayakuta
Wakajuwa yalotuka, faida wakaipata
        Baadhi wakafuwata

9   Wali na msemo wao, waliyokuwa zamani
Ulisemwa na ambao, jana wasoithamini
Mwisho wa msemo huo, huulizana wandani:
        Mla jana alileni?

10   Leo amka silale, silale leo amka
Kushakucha kulichele, asubuhi ishafika
Lete yako tuyaole, tujuwe yake hakika
        Nda kuliya nda kuteka?

Yesterday and Today and Tomorrow • 103

6   Once yesterday has left you, don't expect its return
Though you may search, you'll never see it
It makes people regretful, puts *if only* on their lips
        What will *if only* achieve?

7   What belongs to yesterday dies with it and becomes departed
You won't see it again, even if you live forever
Perhaps things that resemble it may come in turns
        But the real thing—never

8   Yesterday is for remembering, for actions that are past
People write about it so future generations can learn
And know what took place and benefit from it
        Some people take notice

9   They had a saying, people of long ago
It was spoken by those who didn't value yesterday
At the end of the saying, people ask one another
        What did he eat who ate yesterday?

10   Wake up today: don't sleep today, wake up
It has certainly dawned, the morning has come
Bring what you have, so we can understand its reality
        Is it for weeping or laughing?

104 • *Jana na Leo na Kesho*

11   Leo nawe ufunzike, kwa yaliyotuka jana
       Makosaye sijitweke, ukayarudiya tena
       Sandame hatuwa zake, iwa na hadhari sana
           Ya jana ushayaona

12   Leo ikisha kujiya, ikunduliye mikono
       Siwate kuipokeya, uipe mema maneno
       Hwenda ikakukidhiya, yalo manono manono
           Nisikiza langu neno

13   Itikiya ikwitapo, leo siinyamaziye
       Popote ikukutapo, shida zako iyambiye
       Iyambiye papo hapo, yako ikutimiziye
           Hima isikukimbiye

14   Siifanyiye usiri, ikawa ni ngoja ngoja
       Mujarabu ikijiri, zitimize zako haja
       Kwani haitasubiri, hwenda zake mara moja
           Nyengine ipate kuja

15   Iandike jito vyema, leo isikuponyoke
       Kisha ukaja lalama, ikisha kwenenda zake
       Ukabakiya kusema: kwa nini nisiishike?
           Ishike sasa ishike

Yesterday and Today and Tomorrow • 105

11   Learn today from the events of yesterday
    Don't carry its load by repeating those mistakes
    Don't follow in its steps—be very cautious
        You saw what happened yesterday

12   When today comes to you, open your hands to it
    Don't refuse to welcome it; speak to it choicest words
    It may fulfill all your dearest wishes
        Listen to what I say

13   Respond when today calls you; don't remain silent
    Wherever it finds you, tell it your problems
    Tell it there and then so it can sort them out
        Hurry, lest it fly away

14   Don't procrastinate, saying wait a moment, wait a moment
    The moment it arrives, carry out your intention
    For it won't stay long, it heads off at once
        So another day may come

15   Focus your eyes well so today won't escape you
    Leading you to complain after it's disappeared
    Leaving you saying, why didn't I grab it?
        Grab it now, grab it

106 • *Jana na Leo na Kesho*

16   Siku yako ndiyo leo, ipo uli duniyani
      Wewe na uwapendao, leo musiiwateni
      Musiiwatiye tao, isije kuponyokani
            Hivi sasa ibwiyeni

17   Ijayo mwisho ni kesho, ni ya mpatempate
      Kesho nda matayarisho, jitayarishe sisite
      Usubiri wake mwisho, tamaa usiikate
            Upatwe au upate

18   Ngojeya ungojeyalo, kwa moyo uliyotuwa
      Tumai ulilonalo, kwamba kesho litakuwa
      Siwe na hakika nalo, sema: huwenda likawa
            Liwapo ndipo pumuwa

19   Hujuwi yatakuwaje, hiyo kesho ikifika
      Hujuwi yatakwendaje, kesho ina shaka shaka
      Hujuwi mpaka ije, uiyone kwa hakika
            Ndipo ujuwe 'mefika

20   Kesho mithili ya mwana, aliyemo matumboni
      Hujuwi ni mvulana, msichana au nini
      Au kama atapona, ajapo ulimwenguni
            Huwa hunayo yakini

Yesterday and Today and Tomorrow • 107

16   Today is your day; it's there with you in the world
       You and your beloved ones, don't let it go
       Don't give it even an inch, enabling it to slip away
               Seize it right now

17   Last comes tomorrow, always just ahead
       Tomorrow is preparation: prepare yourself, don't delay
       Wait until its end; don't give up hope
               Whether you're gotten or you get

18   Wait for whatever you await with a calm heart
       The hope you have, that tomorrow it will happen
       Don't be too sure about that; say perhaps it may be
               If it happens, breathe your sigh of relief

19   You don't know how things will be when tomorrow comes
       Or what course things will take; tomorrow means doubts
       You don't know until it comes, when you see it for sure
               Then you'll know it's arrived

20   Tomorrow is like a baby in the womb
       You don't know if it's a boy, a girl, or how it may be
       Or whether it will survive when it arrives in this world
               You have no certainty

108 • *Jana na Leo na Kesho*

21   Kesho waweza kusema: 'tatenda jambo fulani
Nayo kesho ikikoma, ikawa haimkini
Ukawa unshautema, hu tena ulimwenguni
        Wenda tini mtangani

22   Kesho vyema uirai, kabla haijafika
Useme: nikiwa hai, na mzima hiamka
Hapo haja yangu hii, kuitimiza nataka
        Uingojee kufika

23   Vivyo isikugutushe, hayano ningakwambiya
Na wala isikuchoshe, ukachoka kungojeya
Ingoje hadi ibishe, upate ifunguliya
        Uiambiye: ingiya

24   Na siwe na pupa nayo, ngoja kwa moyo mtuvu
Wakati wa kufikayo, itakuja pasi nguvu
Usitake ije mbiyo, subiri uile mbivu
        Haitakuwa ni mbovu

25   Kuutiya kikomoni, huno utondoti wetu
Nataka taja thamani, ya hizino siku tatu
Ingawa hazifanani, hicho si kikubwa kitu
        Zote nda faida kwetu

Yesterday and Today and Tomorrow • 109

21 You could say: tomorrow I'll do such and such a thing
Then at the end of tomorrow, it turns out you didn't
Your life ended, you're no longer in the world
   But destined for the ground

22 You have to persuade tomorrow before it arrives
Say: If I'm alive, and when I wake up in good health
This my intention, I want to carry it out
   Then wait for tomorrow to come

23 Yet don't be perturbed by what I'm telling you
Neither let it tire you, so you tire of waiting
Wait till tomorrow knocks at the door so you can welcome it
   Tell it: Come in

24 Don't be greedy for tomorrow; wait with a calm heart
At its appointed time it will come effortlessly
Don't wish for it to come fast, wait so you can get what is ripe
   It won't have gone bad

25 To conclude this long explanation
I want to mention the value of these three days
It little matters that they don't resemble one another
   Each has its value

110 • *Jana na Leo na Kesho*

26   Jana japo inshapita, yafaa kuzingatiwa
      Jana ndoto huiota, leo ikaiyotowa
      Iswibupo ukapata, ulilolitaka kuwa
                'Kikosa siliye ngowa

27   Leo ina tafauti, si sawa sawa na jana
      Leo ndiyo ithibati, ya kuijuwa bayana
      Ndiyo roho ya hayati, mfano wake haina
                Leo itungeni sana

28   Kesho ndiyo darubini, huangaliliya mbele
      Kadhalika ndetu mboni, enga kwa kesho uole
      Kesho nda matumaini, tumai haya na yale
                Kesho daima i mbele

—*12 Februari 1971*

Yesterday and Today and Tomorrow • 111

26   Although yesterday is past, it deserves consideration
        Yesterday dreams and today fulfills the dream
        It may happen that you get what you desired
               If you miss out, don't be bitter

27   Today is different: it's not like yesterday
        Today is verification, for knowing clearly
        Today is the spirit of life, unparalleled
               Pay close attention to today

28   Tomorrow is a telescope that peers far ahead
        And it is the apple of our eye; look there so you may see
        Tomorrow is full of promise, that you may hope for this and that
               Tomorrow is forever ahead

—12 February 1971

Chema Hakidumu

1   Chema hakidumu, kingapendekeza
    Saa ikitimu, kitakuteleza
    Ungawa na hamu, kukingojeleza
    Huwa ni vigumu, kamwe hutaweza

2   Chema sikiimbi, kwamba nakitweza
    Japo mara tumbi, kinshaniliza
    Na japo siombi, kipate n'ongeza
    Mtu haniambi, pa kujikimbiza

3   Chema mara ngapi, kinniondoka!
    Mwanangu yu wapi? Hakukaa mwaka
    Kwa muda mfupi, aliwatilika
    Ningefanya lipi, ela kumzika?

4   Chema wangu babu, Kibwana Bashee
    Alojipa tabu, kwamba anilee
    Na yakwe sababu, ni nitengenee
    Ilahi Wahabu, mara amtwee

5   Chema wangu Poni, kipenzi nyanyangu
    Hadi siku hini, yu moyoni mwangu
    Yu moyoni ndani, hadi kufa kwangu
    Ningamtamani, hatarudi kwangu

    —*15 Machi 1971*

A Precious Thing Can't Last

1   A precious thing can't last, wonderful though it may be
     When time comes, it will slip away
     Although you may want it to remain
     Hard as it may be, that just won't happen

2   A precious thing—I don't demean it with my song
     Although many a time it has made me cry
     And though I don't pray to have my sorrow increased
     No one can tell me where to run

3   How many times has a precious thing gone!
     Where is my child? He didn't live beyond a year
     For just a brief moment—before he died, it wasn't long
     What could I do but bury him?

4   A good person, my great-uncle Kibwana Bashee
     The one committed to raising me
     For the sole purpose of seeing me prosper
     Then the Good Lord took him away

5   A good person, my beloved grandmother, my Poni
     Until today she remains in my heart
     She is in my heart until the day I die
     Though I long for her, she won't return to me

     —15 March 1971

Moyo Iwa na Subira

1   Usiliye moyo wangu, siliye moyo nyamaza
Usijitiye matungu, siliye 'tajiumiza
Huno ndiwo ulimwengu, muna yasiyopendeza
Kwa hivyo moyo nyamaza, zidi kuwa na subira

2   Yafute matozi yako, moyo sijiungulishe
Usijipe sikitiko, moyo usijikondeshe
Ituze nafusi yako, teka ujifurahishe
Hilino lisikuwashe, zidi kuwa na subira

3   Moyo nyamaa kuliya, matozi yako yaweke
Usizidi kuyamwaya, yaweke yatundizike
Matoziyo niwekeya, nifapo yatiririke
Huu si wakati wake, zidi kuwa na subira

4   Usiwe kama mkiwa, moyo wangu tangamka
Kwani mnyonge ukawa, na matama kujishika?
Ng'ara mfano wa juwa, uwate kuhuzunika
Sijiuwe kwa mashaka, zidi kuwa na subira

5   Mbona wazidi kuliya, na k'wanza kuomboleza?
Ni ya nini yote haya? Hebu moyo nieleza
Huruma nakuoneya, uliyapo waniliza
Moyo nakusisitiza, zidi kuwa na subira

Be Patient, My Heart

1   Don't cry, my heart: stop crying, quiet now
Don't embitter yourself, don't hurt yourself with crying
This is how the world is; there's unpleasantness
So heart, don't cry, but persist in being patient

2   Wipe your tears, don't sear yourself, heart
Don't bring sorrow on yourself, don't make yourself thin
Calm yourself down, laugh and be elated
Don't let this sting you; persist in being patient

3   Don't cry, my heart: store your tears away
Don't continue shedding them; let them accumulate
Keep them for me, and when I die let them flow
This is not the time: persist in being patient

4   Don't be like an orphan; cheer up, my heart
Why are you so despondent, chin in your hands?
Shine like the sun and stop being sorrowful
Don't kill yourself because of hardship; persist in being patient

5   Why do you keep crying, and why begin mourning?
What is the point of all this? Explain to me, my heart
I feel pity for you; when you weep, you make me weep
Heart, I stress to you: persist in being patient

Moyo Iwa na Subira

6   Utajiumiza mbavu, kuliya usiposita
Utashikwa na chechevu, na homa utaipata
Upate na maumivu, langu usipofuwata
Nyamaa matozi futa, zidi kuwa na subira

7   Duniya ni mdawari, hili moyo lifahamu
Na kuyapata mazuri, pasi mabaya vigumu
Kwa hivyo moyo subiri, tungu igeuze tamu
Usijiuwe kwa hamu, zidi kuwa na subira

8   Moyo kwamba halikuwa, ulilolitarajiya
Lisikupe kuingiwa, na simanzi na kuliya
Hivyo ndivyo mambo huwa, ni kama lumbwi duniya
Shika n'nalokwambiya, zidi kuwa na subira

9   Hebu tupa jito lako, ukuangaliye nyuma
Kutizame utokako, moyo kwangaliye vyema
Utokako na wendako, kupi kwenye nyingi pima?
Usianguke simama, zidi kuwa na subira

10   Subira ni kitu chema, nawe kwa hiyo jitande
Punguza na kulalama, 'sitatarike jipinde
Memla ng'ombe mzima, mkiya usikushinde
Umalize ndipo wende, zidi kuwa na subira

6 You'll hurt your ribs if you don't stop crying
You'll start hiccupping and get a fever
You'll feel pain if you don't follow my advice
Don't cry, wipe your tears, persist in being patient

7 The world is round, you must know that, heart
You can't have good fortune without misfortune too
So, heart, be patient, turn bitterness to sweetness
Don't kill yourself with longing, persist in being patient

8 That what you anticipated, heart, was never to be
Shouldn't cause despondency and weeping
That is how things often are; the world's like a chameleon
Listen to what I tell you: persist in being patient

9 Turn your eyes to look at the past
Look at where you come from, heart, do look well at it
From there or to your destination, where lies the greater distance?
Don't fall, stand up; persist in being patient

10 Patience is a virtue; clothe yourself in it
Quiet your complaining; don't fret, be tough
You've eaten the whole cow, don't let the tail defeat you
Finish it before you go; persist in being patient

118 • *Moyo Iwa na Subira*

11   Huu kwako mtihani, moyo wangu jitahidi
Yatuze yako makini, uwe mtuvu baridi
Faulu nikuthamini, nikutuze na zawadi
Hii nakupa ahadi, zidi kuwa na subira

12   Haya ni mafunzo kwako, funzika moyo funzika
Tabu na misukosuko, si mwishowe kukufika
Katika uhai wako, hutaweza kuy'epuka
Muda yakikudirika, zidi kuwa na subira

13   Huwezi kuligeuza, lililolekeya kuwa
Kwa hivyo moyo nyamaza, uwate kujisumbuwa
Ufaalo kufanyiza, omba uwe na afuwa
Hakuna nyingine dawa, zidi kuwa na subira

14   Halikuwa ni la kuwa, si kama yale yawayo
Na yale ambayo huwa, huwa ni ya kuwa hayo
Na hili kwa kutokuwa, pengine ni heri hiyo
Basi tuwa ewe moyo, zidi kuwa na subira

—20 Machi 1971

Be Patient, My Heart • 119

11   This is a test for you, my heart: exert yourself
       Be fully alert and keep your cool
       If you emerge victorious, I'll reward you
       This is my promise to you; persist in being patient

12   This is a lesson for you—learn from it, heart, learn
       For trouble and trepidation, it's not the last of these for you
       Throughout your life you'll be unable to avoid them
       When they come upon you, persist in being patient

13   You can't change what's destined to be
       So, heart, don't cry; stop troubling yourself
       What you must do is pray for good health
       There is no other antidote: persist in being patient

14   It wasn't meant to be, it wasn't like what becomes
       And whatever becomes is usually what is meant to
       And this not becoming might well be good fortune
       So be calm, you heart, persist in being patient

—*20 March 1971*

Usiniuwe!

1. Mama nimekukosani? Nambiya nami nijuwe
   Nimetenda jambo gani, ovu liso mfanowe?
   Lazima hiyo nda nini, ushikayo uniuwe?
   Hebu iwa na imani, mamangu nihurumiya

2. Lazima hiyo nda nini, uliyoishikiliya?
   Yangu ni makosa gani, lipi nilokutendeya?
   Nieleza nibaini, yapate kunieleya
   Hela iwa na imani, mamangu nihurumiya

3. Simi niliyekwambiya, utende ulilotenda
   Wala sikukupangiya, wenende ulikokwenda
   Ni mwenyewe yako niya, na hawaa kukushinda
   Ni bure wanioneya, mamangu nihurumiya

4. Ulipokwenda kutana, na huyo wako fulani
   Kabisa sikuwaona, wala sijuwi ni lini
   Ni usiku ni mtana, sinayo yake yakini
   Wala ni mahali gani, mamangu nihurumiya

5. Mato yalipokutana, yako na huyo mwendani
   Ndipo mukasemezana, maneno yalo laini
   Kwishapo kusikizana, mukangiya faraghani
   Zenu hamu mukeshana, mamangu nihurumiya

Don't Kill Me!

1   Mama, what wrong have I done? Tell me so I may know
    What have I done that is so evil beyond compare?
    What is this compulsion that drives you to kill me?
    Mama, be compassionate; feel pity for me, mama

2   What compulsion is this to which you've clung?
    What are my mistakes, what did I do to you?
    Tell me so I may know and fully comprehend
    But be compassionate; feel pity for me, mama

3   I'm not the one who told you to do what you did
    Nor did I arrange for you to go where you went
    It was out of your own volition and lust overtaking you
    You do me injustice for nothing; feel pity for me, mama

4   When you went to meet with a certain individual
    I didn't see you at all, and I don't know when it was
    Whether it was nighttime or daytime, I have absolutely no clue
    Or where it all took place; feel pity for me, mama

5   When your eyes met, yours and your lover's
    Then you spoke to one another, sweet soft nothings
    After consensus, you went off to privacy
    You satisfied your desire; feel pity for me, mama

122 • *Usiniuwe!*

6   Hukutenda kwa hiyari, hukutenda ukijuwa?
     Hukufahamu athari, mwishowe itavyokuwa?
     Piya ukaona kheri, upawe ulilopawa
     Mwenyewe ulikhitari, mamangu nihurumiya

7   Uliridhika mwenyewe, hukulazimishwa sini
     Ulikubali upawe, na kwa furaha moyoni
     Hukwambiwa utukuwe, alokwambiya n'nani?
     Basi kwani niuwawe? Mamangu nihurumiya

8   Ni manii tone moja, la maji madhalilifu
     Tone lililojituja, kutoka maji machafu
     Ndicho chanzo changu kuja, na bado ndiya ni ndefu
     S'anze sasa kunifuja, mamangu nihurumiya

9   Tone lilipoanguka, mahalipe maalumu
     Hapo likahifadhika, kungoja muda utimu
     Kisha likabadilika, nikawa pande la damu
     Wata roho kunipoka, mamangu nihurumiya

10   Na hilo pande la damu, likakaa kwa salama
     Likingoja yake zamu, aloiweka Karima
     Zamuye ilipotimu, nikawa nofu la nyama
     Basi usinihukumu, mamangu nihurumiya

Don't Kill Me! • 123

6   Wasn't it your own choice? You didn't do it knowingly?
    You didn't know the outcome, what it would be like?
    Also, you deemed it good to receive what you received
    It was your own choice; feel pity for me, mama

7   You were contented; no one forced you
    You were glad to receive, with joy in your heart
    No one told you to take it, who told you to do so?
    So why I should be killed? Feel pity for me, mama

8   One drop of semen, of feeble water
    That distilled itself from impure water
    That is my beginning, and the journey is still long
    Don't start destroying me now; feel pity for me, mama

9   When the drop fell in its special place
    There it was preserved, waiting for its time to come
    Then it changed, becoming me, a lump of blood
    Don't rob me of my soul; feel pity for me, mama

10 That lump of blood was well secured
    Awaiting its turn, appointed by the Almighty
    When the time came, I became a piece of flesh
    So don't condemn me; feel pity for me, mama

124 • *Usiniuwe!*

11   Bado sijamalizika, halijesha umbo langu
      Sitakwisha kwa haraka, zitapita siku tungu
      Huna haki kunipoka, uhai ni haki yangu
      Niwata 'takamilika, mamangu nihurumiya

12   Huna haki kuniuwa, japo sijakamilika
      Huna haki kunitowa, kabla siku kufika
      Niwata nipate kuwa, mimi mwenyewe 'tatoka
      Mama wata kuniuwa, mamangu nihurumiya

13   Kunipa ulikubali, uhai tangu kitambo
      Kabla sijawaswili, humuno ndani mwa tumbo
      Sasa niya 'mebadili, wataka geuza mambo
      Usiwe sawa na nduli, mamangu nihurumiya

14   Kama kweli hukutaka, tokeya hapo mwanzoni
      Hukutaka kuniweka, humu mwako matumboni
      Hadi siku ya kutoka, nende zangu duniyani
      Kwani tweka kujitweka? Mamangu nihurumiya

15   Ngoja! Usinisongowe, niweka mama niweka
      Niweka hadi nikuwe, halafu ndipo 'tatoka
      Kama hunitaki wewe, ulimwengu wanitaka
      Mwanayo usiniuwe, mamangu nihurumiya

Don't Kill Me! • 125

11   I am not yet finished—my body is still taking shape
        I won't be done that quickly—many days must pass
        You have no right to deprive me; life is my right
        Just let me develop fully; feel pity for me, mama

12   You have no right to kill me, though I'm not fully developed
        You have no right to force me out before the day arrives
        Just let me grow until I can come out by myself
        Mama, don't kill me; feel pity for me, mama

13   You agreed from the start to give me life
        Before I arrived inside this very womb
        Now you've changed your mind, you intend something else
        Don't be like a murderer; feel pity for me, mama

14   If you didn't want from the very beginning
        To keep me in this, your womb
        Until the day of my emergence to wander in the world
        Why did you take up this load? Feel pity for me, mama

15   Wait! Don't strangle me; keep me alive, mama, keep me alive
        Keep me until I grow, then I will come out
        If you don't desire me, the world desires me
        I am your child—don't kill me; feel pity for me, mama

126 • *Usiniuwe!*

16   Kama hunitaki mama, piya waniuliyani?
Nakuomba nikisema: usiniuwe tumboni
Mama nizaa salama, kisha nitupa ndiyani
Mja alo na huruma, an'okote kunileya

17   Ngojeya upige kite, matumboni unitowe
Kisha nibwaga popote, bora pa salama pawe
Aniokote yoyote, ili niwe mbali nawe
Lakini sasa niwate, mamangu nihurumiya

18   Sitakosa mlimwengu, ambaye atanileya
Anionee utungu, kama tulo damu moya
Si kama wewe mamangu, usonisikitikiya
Nisikiza ombi langu, mamangu nihurumiya

19   Sikosi wa kunitwaa, aniswafishe ujusi
Niliyapo ng'aa! ng'aa! Aniongowe upesi
Hataniwata na ndaa, atanipa na libasi
Bora salama nizaa, mamangu nihurumiya

20   Sikosi wa kunifaa, hili sina wasiwasi
Sitakosa pa kukaa, sikosi kamwe sikosi
Duniya haijajaa, ingali tele nafasi
Bora salama nizaa, mamangu nihurumiya

16   If you don't want me, mama, why are you killing me?
     I plead to you, saying: don't kill me in your womb
     Mama, just give birth to me, then abandon me on the path
     Someone with sympathy will pick me up and raise me

17   Wait until you wail as you give birth to me
     Then throw me anywhere, so long as it is safe
     That anyone may pick me up, so I can be far from you
     But for now leave me alone; feel pity for me, mama

18   I won't lack someone to take care of me
     Someone who will feel for me as a blood relative would
     Unlike you, mother, who feel no compassion for me
     Listen to my plea; be merciful to me, mama.

19   I won't lack someone to clean me after birth
     Whenever I wail ng'aa! ng'aa! she will comfort me quickly
     She won't leave me hungry; she'll clothe me
     You only have to give birth to me safely; be merciful to me, mama

20   I won't lack someone to care for me, I have no doubt about this
     I won't lack a place to stay; I won't lack it, surely
     The world isn't full, there's still plenty of space
     You only have to give birth to me safely; be merciful to me, mama

128 • *Usiniuwe!*

21 Duniya menipangiya, mipango japo ni ndani
    Yaliko yaningojeya, mamangu usinikhini
    Wajibu na yangu niya, ni kuitimiza hini
    Wata kunipanguliya, mamangu nihurumiya

22 Niwata nipate kwenda, nishuhudiye mwenyewe
    Sitawata kujipinda, kwamba sawasawa yawe
    Na hata yakinishinda, hutalaumiwa wewe
    'Tavuna nitachopanda, mamangu nihurumiya

23 Hapo ukisha nitowa, henda zangu duniyani
    Naniwe nitavyokuwa, niwe hata kitu gani!
    Kama 'takuwa mtawa, au 'takuwa shetwani
    Ni yangu majaaliwa, mamangu nihurumiya

24 Kwamba waicha aibu, na makanwani kutiwa
    Hizino ndizo sababu, za kutaka kuniuwa?
    Haya yasingekuswibu, ungelitunga muruwa
    Mwenyewe uliharibu, mamangu nihurumiya

25 Kutaka ustahiki, na kuitaka hishima
    Hakuwezi kupa haki, kuniuwa wangu mama
    Na ovu lako kubaki, litabakiya lazima
    Hilo halizamishiki, mamangu nihurumiya

Don't Kill Me! • 129

21 The world has plans for me, even though I'm enclosed
Things await me, mama, don't deprive me
My role and intention are to fulfill these plans
Don't undo them; be merciful to me, mama

22 Let me go my way, so I can see for myself
I'll do my utmost to make things right
And even if I fail, no one will blame you
I'll reap what I sow; be merciful to me, mama

23 Once you put me out there, I'll go my way in the world
I'll be whatever I'll be, it doesn't matter what I become
If I become a saint or if I become a devil
That will be my fate; be merciful to me, mama

24 That you fear shame and being the subject of gossip —
Is that cause for wanting to kill me?
This wouldn't have happened had you kept your honor
You messed things up; be merciful to me, mama

25 Wanting esteem and wanting respect
Don't grant you the right to kill me, my mama
And your vice will remain, it certainly will remain
It can't be wished away; be merciful to me, mama

130 • *Usiniuwe!*

26   Japo menipaka dowa, lililo rangi nyeusi
      Japo ningalikwanguwa, kufutika si rahisi
      Lakini kuhukumiwa, kwa kosa lako sipasi
      Mama wata kuniuwa, mamangu nihurumiya

27   Uhai! Nakuliliya, wewe ndiye upendwaye
      Uhai! Huna ubaya, yupi akutukiyaye?
      A! Uhai niombeya, mama yangu sema naye
      Pengine atasikiya, asiniuwe mamangu

28   Nawe Haki nisemeya, kwa ya dhati matamshi
      Sema na kuniombeya, nihurumiwe niishi
      Mamangu anioneya, anioneya bilashi
      A! Haki nihukumiya, asiniuwe mamangu

29   Mauti! Nihurumiya, Mauti! 'Sinitukuwe
      Lipi nilokukoseya? Hatuna vita mi nawe
      Toba! Nisikitikiya, nisalimisha na wewe
      Magoti nakupigiya, simsikize mamangu

      —*18 Aprili 1971*

26 Although you besmirched me, giving me a black spot
    Although however I scrub, it is hard to erase
    Yet I shouldn't be condemned for your mistakes
    Mama, don't kill me; be merciful to me, mama

27 Life! I cry out to you, you the beloved one
    Life! You are blameless—who is it that would loathe you?
    Aa! Life, intercede for me, speak to my mother
    Perhaps she'll listen and not kill me, my mother

28 Justice, speak up for me, with sincere proclamations
    Speak up and plead for me to be pitied that I may live
    My mother treats me unjustly, unjustly for nothing
    Aa! Justice, judge for me, that my mother may not kill me

29 Death! Feel pity for me, Death! Don't take me away
    What wrong did I do you? There's no quarrel between us
    Have mercy! Feel sorrow for me, save me from you
    I kneel before you; don't listen to my mother

    —18 April 1971

Mambo Yana Mambo Yake

1. Mambo yataka buswara, kinguvunguvu hayendi
   Yataka tuvu fikira, nyofu ziso na mapindi
   Fikira za kitwa bora, kitwa bupu hakiundi
   Msonayo hayatendi, akanyokewa na mambo

2. Kutenda pasi kuwaza, mambo hayawezi nyoka
   Yataka bongo kutuza, lituzike kwa hakika
   Kwani mambo ya kusoza, yasozwapo husozeka
   Yote yakavurujika, yasifaidiwe mambo

3. Mambo yataka kupima, na kujuwa ndiya zake
   Yataka na kutizama, yaliyoko mbele yake
   Ndipo yapate simama, vizuri yaimarike
   Mtu haya nayashike, afanikiwe na mambo

4. Mambo yataka wekevu, na bongo lilo razini
   Bongo la akili pevu, litambuwalo maani
   Mambo si ya mpumbavu, aso na kitu kitwani
   Mwenye vidoto matoni, asoweza ona mambo

5. Hutwaliwa kwa hikima, mambo hutwaliwa hivyo
   Hayashikiwi lazima, hivyo sivyo yatakavyo
   Hayatatendeka vyema, kama yatakikanavyo
   Yataka tendwa vilivyo, yapate kufana mambo

Things Have Their Own Ways

1   Things require wisdom; using force doesn't work
    They need deep thoughts, correct and not crooked
    Thoughts of a good head—an empty head can't handle them
    One lacking these fails; things never go right for him

2   Things never go well when one acts without thinking
    One must calm the mind, calm it completely
    For things once squandered, when squandered remain so
    They become ruined, proving profitless

3   Things need weighing and ascertaining
    They require scrutiny of whatever may lie ahead
    So that they may stand upright, may be quite stable
    One must heed this advice to succeed in things

4   Things need understanding, a truly sound mind
    Maturity in one's mind, and ability to decipher meaning
    Things are not for the simpleton with an empty head
    One with blinders on his eyes so he can't see things

5   Things are grasped through wisdom, that's how they're grasped
    Not held by force—that's not how it's done
    Things won't happen properly then, the way they're supposed to
    Things want to be done just so, so all will go well

134 • *Mambo Yana Mambo Yake*

6   Mambo yataka subira, hino ni moja sharuti
Na hiyo si maskhara, yataka mtu thabiti
Kwani nayo kila mara, haishi kutuswaliti
Mambo kuwa madhubuti, nayasubiriwe mambo

7   Mambo hayapatikani, bila ya misukosuko
Yana tabu kama nini, na tumbi ya masumbuko
Mtu kamwe nasidhani, mambo ni mteremko
Yanayo vingi vituko, mambo si matezo mambo

8   Yataka moyo mgumu, moyo wa sitahamala
Uliyokwisha hitimu, kuvumiliya madhila
Moyo unaofahamu, kwamba mambo si kulala
Na wala si kama kula, si kazi rahisi mambo

9   Mambo kamwe hayataki, mtu wa moyo laini
Muda 'kifikwa ni dhiki, akawa yu taabani
Akiona hayanyoki, akayawata ndiyani
Kabisa hasikizani, mtu huyuno na mambo

10   Mambo yataka ujuzi, kijinga hayatakwenda
Yataka mtu maizi, mjuzi wa kuyatenda
Zitatanapo tatizi, kama matandu kutanda
Ziwe hazitamshinda, kuyatatuliya mambo

Things Have Their Own Ways • 135

6   Things want patience; this is one of the requirements
It's not a joke: one has to be firm
For every so often patience betrays us
And for things to go well, patience there must be

7   Nothing is attained without turmoil
So much trouble, in fact, and endless vexation
Let no one suppose things are easily attainable
Things have strange antics; they're no joke, things

8   Things require a strong heart, a persevering heart
A mature heart, able to withstand difficulties
A heart that understands: this isn't like sleeping
And it's not like eating: things are no easy task

9   Things don't go well for a faint-hearted person
When he meets with hardship, he's overwhelmed
He feels things have gone wrong and then gives up
A person like this can't manage well with things

10   Things require knowledge; they founder when done foolishly
They want an astute person who knows how to do things
So when things get twisted like tangled cobwebs
They won't defeat him; he'll find ways of untangling them

136 • *Mambo Yana Mambo Yake*

11   Mambo yataka kujuwa, ujuzi ulo kamili
       Yataka alo mwelewa, atumiyae akili
       Si yoyote kuambiwa, tenda lile au hili
       Pasi mambo kuyajuwa, hayatengenei mambo

12   Mjinga huvunda mambo, yakawa ni mvurugo
       Akumbwapo na vikumbo, ijapokuwa kidogo
       Huweza zamisha chombo, mambo yakenda upogo
       Ikawa ni kubwa pigo, kwa kuharibika mambo

13   Mambo asiyoyajuwa, mtu asiyajaribu
       Kwani yatamsumbuwa, na kumtiya aibu
       Sababu hayatakuwa, bure atajipa tabu
       Mambo si ya mtu dubu, 'sojuwa kwenda na mambo

14   Mambo yangawa ni male, hupelekwa kwa daraja
       Hupelekwa polepole, kwa hatuwa moja moja
       Ndiwo mwendo tangu kale, ufuwatwao na waja
       Asotaka kuyafuja, nende nayo hivyo mambo

15   Yeshapo kutendwa kwake, mambo yataka ngojewa
       Yangojewe yapikike, kuiva kwake hukawa
       Mambo si tabiya yake, saa hiyo hiyo kuwa
       Yataka muda kupawa, ndipo yawe rara mambo

Things Have Their Own Ways • 137

11   Things require thorough knowledge
     From a discerning person who uses the mind
     Not someone who has to be told—do this or do that
     Without knowledge of things, things won't go right

12   A foolish person wrecks things, making them haywire
     If he gets shoved around, even a little
     He'll sink the ship, ensuring things to go awry
     It becomes a great blow, with things falling apart

13   Things one doesn't know, one shouldn't try
     For they'll vex and disgrace him
     Because they won't happen, he'll trouble himself uselessly
     Things are not for the simpleton, unaware of how things work

14   Even if things are deep, they are taken in degrees
     They are taken gradually, step by step
     This is the ancient pace that humans tend to keep
     If you don't want to ruin them, take things at that pace

15   After it's all been done, things require some waiting
     Wait until they cook, until they are fully cooked
     It's not the nature of things to be done on the spot
     They need time before they're ready, things

138 • Mambo Yana Mambo Yake

16   Mambo hayataki moyo, ulo na pupa na mambo
     Kwani yake matokeyo, ni ya kupambuwa pambo
     Mambo ya kupekwa mbiyo, hayabali kwenda kombo
     Pupa ndilo mtaimbo, wa kuyavundiya mambo

17   Mambo yana wakatiwe, hutendwa ukiwadiya
     Kwa makini yawekewe, saa ya kuyafanyiya
     Hayataki yachelewe, wala kuutanguliya
     Mambo huleta udhiya, yakitopangiwa mambo

18   Yataka pimiwa hali, kabla kutendwa kwake
     Hali ya hapo mahali, vizuri ibainike
     Kama itayakubali, ili mambo yatendeke
     Zipimwe yatengezeke, yana hali zake mambo

19   Hali isipowafiki, haufai ushindani
     Kabisa hayafanyiki, hayanyoki asilani
     Kwani mambo hayataki, kushikiwa nyingi kani
     Iwatwe tabiya hini, mambo ndipo yawe mambo

20   Nguvu mwenye kutumiya, kwa kujiona fahali
     Akataka jifanyiya, mambo kinyume cha hali
     Hatawata kuumiya, sababu ya kutojali
     Mambo kuwa bulibuli, yategewe hali mambo

Things Have Their Own Ways • 139

16   Things reject a heart full of impatience
     For that will mess things up
     Things that are rushed must indeed fall apart
     Impatience is the crowbar that breaks things to pieces

17   Things have their time; they're accomplished when that time comes
     Carefully set the time of completion
     They shouldn't be delayed or done beforehand
     Things cause vexation when not well planned

18   Gauge conditions before doing things
     The conditions of a particular place must be known
     To see that they are conducive for things to be done
     Gauge them, rectify them; things have their conditions

19   If conditions are unsuitable, there's no need for stubbornness
     Things are unattainable; they can't be sorted out
     For things can't be grasped through force
     Leave off that habit so that things become themselves

20   Anyone who uses force, thinking himself like a bull
     Will be acting contrary to conditions
     His carelessness will harm him
     For things to be good, conditions must be right

140 • *Mambo Yana Mambo Yake*

21   Aliye mtu mwerevu, hali hashindani nayo
'Kiona hali ni mbovu, haatuwi wake moyo
Huingoja kwa utuvu, hali imruhusuyo
Ijapo akenda nayo, na kuyapeleka mambo

22   Yataka kusumbukiwa, yatafutwe kila ndiya
Yataka kulimbikiwa, na bidii jari moya
Yataka jasho kutowa, na moyo kujitoleya
Mambo yahitaji haya, kwamba yafaulu mambo

23   Mambo mtu hayaoni, bila kujitaabisha
Mambo hayapatikani, bila viungo kunyosha
Hayaokotwi jaani, wala mbingu kuy'angusha
Mambo kujihangaisha, 'sidhani ni bure mambo

24   Mambo ayangojeyaye, yamjiye kitandani
Naawe mtu awaye, naawe hata yu nani
Hayatamwendeya yeye, kwamba yeye ni fulani
Mvivu ni tangu lini, kuwa rafiki na mambo?

25   Asojuwa namwambiya, tena asikize sana
Tangu mwanzo wa duniya, mambo bwerere hakuna
Na haswa majira haya, ndiyo kabisa hayana
Bila ya jasho kutona, ni yapi yawayo mambo?

Things Have Their Own Ways • 141

21   A wise person doesn't contest conditions
If conditions aren't right, it doesn't trouble his heart
He waits patiently for favorable ones
When they come, he goes with them and moves things along

22   Things need to be worried over and pursued by every means
They require patient accumulation, effort and strength all at once
They require sweat and a devoted heart
They need these to succeed, things

23   One can't see things without troubling oneself
Things can't be attained without stretching the limbs
They're not plucked from the dustbin, nor do they drop from heaven
When one troubles oneself for things, it's not for nothing

24   Whoever waits in bed for things to come to him
Whatever person he may be, whoever he may be
They'll never go to him because he's so-and-so
When did the lazy person become a friend of things?

25   Whoever doesn't know, let him listen to me keenly
From the beginning of the world, free things never existed
And especially now, there are none at all
Without someone sweating, what things have come to be?

142 • *Mambo Yana Mambo Yake*

26 Ya "mtuzi nitiliya, ni pakavu hapa pangu"
    'Kiwata kujitekeya, ujitiliye mwenzangu
    Ukawa utangojeya, utiliwe ndugu yangu
    Naapa haki ya M'ngu, huwezi yapata mambo

27 Mambo yataka imani, mtenzi awe anayo
    Imani ya kuamini, kwamba atendayo ndiyo
    Asiwe nayo moyoni, ile itetelekayo
    Hii si hiyo ambayo, yatakikana na mambo

28 Yataka imani kweli, tena ilotimilika
    Thabiti kama jabali, isoweza kuondoka
    Ikumbwapo na kitali, 'siwe nda kutikisika
    Ili vyema kutendeka, yataka imani mambo

29 Mambo hayataki yule, aliyekosa imani
    Mamboye hayalekele, ha-ya-juu ha-ya-tini
    Huyo ni kama muwele, muwele aweza nini?
    Mkosefu wa imani, hatengenewi na mambo

30 Mambo yendapo popote, imani isiwe nyuma
    Yendapo yenende wote, ndipo mambo yawe mema
    Katika mambo yoyote, imani ni kama mama
    Mambo kuwa mwana mwema, yasitengwe nayo mambo

Things Have Their Own Ways • 143

26 By saying "give me some soup, my plate is dry"
And not getting it oneself, ladling the soup oneself
But waiting instead to be served, my brother —
I swear to God, you will never get things

27 Things require that their doer have strong conviction
Strong conviction that what he does is right
Not conviction that is easily shaken
That's not the sort needed for things to happen

28 It has to be conviction that's true and complete
Strong like a rock that can't be moved
That when bombarded won't be shaken
To go well, things take conviction

29 Things reject the person without conviction
His things don't go well, they're neither here nor there
He's like someone ailing: what can a sick person accomplish?
A person lacking conviction finds nothing going right

30 Wherever things go, conviction must be there
They should move together so things are good
In all things, conviction is like a mother
To be a good child, things can't be separated from it

Mambo Yana Mambo Yake

31 Nipumzishe mikono, pamwe na vidole vyake
Kwani n'shachoka mno, nataka nipumzike
Na haya yangu maneno, watenda mambo mushike
Mambo yana mambo yake, yatimizwe yawe mambo

32 Asoweza kutimiza, hizino sharuti zake
Ningependa kumweleza, kwamba asitaabike
Mambo asiyoyaweza, ni heri asiyashike
Mambo bila mambo yake, hayawezi kuwa mambo

—9 Mei 1971

Things Have Their Own Ways • 145

31   Let me rest my hands and their fingers too
For I'm so tired, I really must rest
And these my words—heed them, all you doers of things
Things have their own terms, if they're to be things

32   Whoever can't fulfill these requirements for things
I'd like to warn him not to waste his time
Things he can't manage are better left alone
Things without their conditions can't become things

—9 May 1971

Watiliye Pamba

1 Fitina za waja, usizisikize
  Kubwa yao haja, ni wakupoteze
  Kisha watakuja, shere wakuteze

2 Muda wakilumba, hao mafatani
  Watiliye pamba, za masikiyoni
  Uwe kama kwamba, u duko yakini

3 Waja hawapendi, tubaki wawili
  Hila hawatindi, na nyingi feeli
  Wa mbiyo mafundi, tuwe mbali mbali

4 Hao masabasi, kaa mbali nao
  Hauna kiyasi, uvundifu wao
  'Siwape nafasi, kutimiza lao

5 Ituze akili, vyema ituzane
  Fanya kila hali, tusifarikane
  Tuishi wawili, hadi tuzikane

—1 Juni 1971

Don't Listen to Them

1   Ignore people's intrigues
    Their great wish is to lead you astray
    Then at last they'll ridicule you

2   When they speak, those who cause discord
    Turn a deaf ear
    Be like someone who is completely deaf

3   They hate the two of us remaining together
    There's no end to their tricks, mischief all around
    They are bent on seeing us part ways

4   Those sowers of discord—give them wide berth
    There's no limit to their destructiveness
    Don't give them a chance to fulfill their aim

5   Keep your sanity, protect it well
    Do all you can so we may never be estranged
    Let's live together until we bury one another

—1 June 1971

Tendekezo

Tendekeza tendekezo, nazo zikutendekeze
Ziongezee mtwazo, nawo uziandamize
Yupi mwenye haja nazo? Nazitwae 'sizisaze
Upendaye tendekezo, twaa zikakupoteze

—*28 Juni 1971*

Pampering

Pampering, pampering, so you become thoroughly spoiled
Add to it pretension, making the one follow the other
Who wants these things? Let him take them, leaving nothing behind
You who love pampering, take it and be led astray

—*28 June 1971*

Leo N'singekuwako

1   Kama tabu ni mauti, leo n'singekuwako
Ningekuwa ni maiti, 'mebakiza sikitiko
Ningekuwako tiyati, mtanga ndilo funiko
Leo n'singekuwako, kama tabu ni mauti

2   Hivi leo n'ngekuwa, kana kwamba sikuwako
Kitambo n'shafukiwa, nimo kaburini huko
Kungebaki kuambiwa: "Atifu alikuwako"
Leo n'singekuwako, kama tabu ni mauti

3   Marehemu ningekuwa, n'shaoza ni mnuko
Hawata kusumbuliwa, ni tabu na masumbuko
Na tabu haondokewa, ingenijiya niliko?
Leo n'singekuwako, kama tabu ni mauti

4   Kwa siku ningeliliwa, na jamaa waliyoko
Na maduwa kuombewa, nende salama nendako
Kisha hasahauliwa, kwa moyo na matamko
Leo n'singekuwako, kama tabu ni mauti

5   Na kwamba hata yakawa, hadi leo hawa niko
Ni kuwa huu moyowa, wahimili masumbuko
Ngeliya kwa yalokuwa, hakika singekuwako
Leo n'singekuwako, kama tabu ni mauti

—*14 Juni 1971*

I Wouldn't Be Here Today

1   If hardship were death, I wouldn't be here today
I'd have become a corpse, leaving sorrow behind
I'd be under the ground, covered by soil
I wouldn't be here today if hardship were death

2   Today I'd be as if I'd never existed
I'd be interred already, be occupying the grave
People would be saying: "Atifu was once here"
I wouldn't be here today if hardship were death

3   I'd be the departed, rotten and reeking
I'd now be undisturbed by hardship and uneasiness
I'd be hardship-free; would hardship follow me there?
I wouldn't be here today if hardship were death

4   My relatives would have mourned me for a while
Praying for me so I could travel safely to my destination
Then I'd be forgotten in hearts and in words
I wouldn't be here today if hardship were death

5   And as things turned out, that I'm still alive today
It's because this heart of mine is able to bear so much hardship
Had I wept over what happened, for sure I wouldn't be here
I wouldn't be here today if hardship were death

—*14 June 1971*

Kokoiko!

Kokoiko! Kokoiko! Awika jimbi awika
Vitandani muliyoko, namuanze kurauka
Asoitika mwitiko, atachelewa kufika
Yule aliyekutweka, ndiye atayekutuwa

—3 Julai 1971

Cockadoodle-do!

Cockadoodle-do! Cockadoodle-do! The rooster is crowing
Those of you sleeping, time to get up
Whoever ignores the rooster will be late
The one who put the load on you will be the one to take it off

—3 July 1971

'Sikakawane na Kimya

1   Ndugu yangu Ahmadi, kwani kunitenda haya?
Kimya chako kinzidi, hata kishapindukiya
Leo hawa sina budi, ila kukiuliziya
Kimya kingi ni kibaya, usikakawane nacho

2   Nyaraka nikweteyazo, ambazo hukufikiya
Na salamu niwapazo, watu ili kukweteya
Hujishughulishi nazo, japokuwa mara moya
Kimya kingi ni kibaya, usikakawane nacho

3   Nieleza nami hebu, kwani kuninyamaziya?
Au kuna gani tabu, iliyo kukuzuwiya?
Nataka juwa sababu, inipunguze udhiya
Kimya kingi ni kibaya, usikakawane nacho

4   Watu ni kuambiyana, na kuswafiyana niya
Lau iwapo waona, liko nilokutendeya
Ngelifurahika sana, iwapo ungenambiya
Kimya kingi ni kibaya, usikakawane nacho

5   Nakusisitiza tena, kabla sijatuliya
Kimya hakina maana, kwani wakishikiliya?
Safari hii kazana, upate niandikiya
Kimya kingi ni kibaya, usikakawane nacho

Don't Cling to Silence

1 My brother Ahmadi, why are you doing this to me?
Your silence is too much, this indeed is too much
Today I can't help but inquire of you
Long silence is bad; don't cling to silence

2 The letters I sent you, the ones that reach you
And the messages I send people to bring
You don't bother with them, not even for a moment
Long silence is bad; don't cling to silence

3 Tell me, please: why are you silent towards me?
Or what trouble is there that has hindered you?
I want to know the reason, to lessen my agitation
Long silence is bad; don't cling to silence

4 People need to communicate and talk sincerely together
If in any way I've done you wrong
I'd be very glad if you told me about it
Long silence is bad; don't cling to silence

5 I stress to you again, before I keep quiet
Silence is meaningless: why do you cling to it?
This time exert yourself so you can write to me
Long silence is bad; don't cling to silence

156 • 'Sikakawane na Kimya

6   Salamu kwako nyumbani, kwa mama na Fursiya
     Na watu wote Uwani, wajuze yangu afiya
     Na jamaa mitaani, wa Kuze na Dundee piya
     Wambiye nawaambiya, 'takuwa nao mwakani

7   Ni Atifu ndugu yako, mulozawa tumbo moya
     Alo kwenye masumbuko, alokwisha yazoweya
     Tabu na misukosuko, ndiko kujuwa duniya
     Asiyefikwa na haya, hajawa yu mlimwengu

—*5 Septemba 1971*

Don't Cling to Silence • 157

6   Greetings to you at home, to Mama and Fursiya
     And to everyone in Uwani, update them on my health
     And the people in the neighborhoods, Kuze and also Dundee
     Tell them I say I'll be with them next year

7   It's I, your brother Atifu, from the same womb as you
     The one in bad straits but accustomed to that condition
     Trouble and anxiety are ways of knowing the world
     One not beset by these is not yet a worldling

     —5 September 1971

Wasafiri Tuamkeni

1   Bado safari ni ndefu, wasafiri tusichoke
    Natusiwe madhaifu, twendeni hadi tufike
    Tusafiri bila hofu, wenye nazo ziwatoke
    Huu ndiwo mwanzo wake, siwo mwisho wa safari

2   Twendeni tusonge mbele, twendeni tusianguke
    Mwaona mlima ule? Pale ndipo mwisho wake
    Tupande chake kilele, bendera tuitundike
    Huu ndiwo mwanzo wake, siwo mwisho wa safari

3   Twendeni tukifahamu, kila mtu akumbuke
    Safari yetu ni ngumu, si rahisi ndiya yake
    Kuna miba yenye sumu, tunzani tusidungike
    Huu ndiwo mwanzo wake, siwo mwisho wa safari

4   Ni ndiya yenye misitu, na mirefu miti yake
    Imejaa nyama mwitu, kila mmoja na pake
    Na wakionapo kitu, ni lazima wakishike
    Huu ndiwo mwanzo wake, siwo mwisho wa safari

5   Na kuna bahari pana, na kirefu kina chake
    Mawimbi makubwa sana, ni ajabu nguvu zake
    Hiyo hatuna namna, ni lazima tuivuke
    Huu ndiwo mwanzo wake, siwo mwisho wa safari

Travelers, Let's Wake Up

1   The journey is still long: let's not tire, travelers
Let's not become weaklings before we reach our destination
We should travel without fear; let the fearful discard it
This is but the beginning, it's not the end of the journey

2   Let's move ahead, let's go without falling
Do you see that mountain? That's the destination
Let's climb to the summit and hoist the flag
This is but the beginning, it's not the end of the journey

3   Let's go with understanding: everyone should remember
The journey is difficult, the way isn't easy
There are poisonous thorns; beware they don't prick us
This is but the beginning, it's not the end of the journey

4   It's a forested path with very tall trees
It's replete with wild animals, each one in its lair
And once they see something, they're determined to snatch it
This is but the beginning, it's not the end of the journey

5   And there's a vast sea of great depth
The waves are massive, of unimaginable force
We have no choice but to cross it
This is but the beginning, it's not the end of the journey

160 • *Wasafiri Tuamkeni*

6   Japo ni ngumu safari, wendaji tusigutuke
'Ingawa ina hatari, twendeni tusitishike
Ingawa ndefu safari, lazima imalizike
Huu ndiwo mwanzo wake, siwo mwisho wa safari

7   Tamaa tusiikate, niya zisiteteleke
Ndiya natuifuate, nyoyo zisituvundike
Haja yetu tuipate, bendera yetu tutweke
Huu ndiwo mwanzo wake, siwo mwisho wa safari

8   Vibobwe tujifungeni, tuvifunge vifungike
Tuvikaze viunoni, waume kwa wanawake
Tungiyapo safarini, twende tusibabaike
Huu ndiwo mwanzo wake, siwo mwisho wa safari

9   Wenzangu nawahimiza, haya! Shime muinuke
Tuwate kujilegeza, wala tusitetemeke
Haja ni kuimaliza, isiwatwe nusu yake
Huu ndiwo mwanzo wake, siwo mwisho wa safari

10   Tuenukeni twendeni, mwenye chake najitweke
Ngiyani misitarini, safu safu mupangike
Wana na wazee ndani, pamoja tutanganyike
Huu ndiwo mwanzo wake, siwo mwisho wa safari

6   Although the journey is long, let's not be shocked, travelers
Though it's rife with dangers, let's not be scared
Though it's a long journey, we must complete it
This is but the beginning, it's not the end of the journey

7   Let's not give up hope, let's not be irresolute
Let's pursue our aim, let's not be discouraged
So we attain our goal, hoisting our flag
This is but the beginning, it's not the end of the journey

8   Let's tie our loin cloths as tight as we can
All of us determined, both men and women
When we embark on the journey, let's go without faltering
This is but the beginning, it's not the end of the journey

9   I exhort you, my friends, now—please stand up
Let's not relax or be unduly shaken
The point is to finish, not leave off halfway
This is but the beginning, it's not the end of the journey

10   Let's arise and go and carry our belongings
Form a single line, stand one after the other
Young and old alike should join together
This is but the beginning, it's not the end of the journey

162 • *Wasafiri Tuamkeni*

11 Kusafiri ni lazima, tukitaka tusitake
Wale waliyo wazima, maguu nayanyosheke
Na aliye na kilema, naabebwe na mwenzake
Huu ndiwo mwanzo wake, siwo mwisho wa safari

12 Mwenye kutaka safari, ya kwamba isifanyike
Huyo aduwi dhahiri, kwetu pamoja na kwake
Na wala asifikiri, atafaulu kwa lake
Huu ndiwo mwanzo wake, siwo mwisho wa safari

13 Na mshikaji bendera, kwa vizuri naishike
Daima nawe imara, wala asilainike
Ay'ongoze barabara, huko twendako tufike
Huu ndiwo mwanzo wake, siwo mwisho wa safari

—*4 Septemba 1971*

Travelers, Let's Wake Up • 163

11   Journeying is imperative, whether we like it or not
      Those in good health should stretch their legs
      And the disabled person be carried by a friend
      This is but the beginning, it's not the end of the journey

12   Whoever wishes this journey would not commence
      Is clearly a foe, both to us and to himself
      He shouldn't suppose he will succeed
      This is but the beginning, it's not the end of the journey

13   And the flag-bearer should hold the flag firmly
      And be steadfast, unwavering
      He should lead the way so we reach our destination
      This is but the beginning, it's not the end of the journey

—*4 September 1971*

Zindukani

1 Sikuja weka baraza, au hadithi kutowa
 Sikuja kuzungumza, maneno yasiyokuwa
 Nnakuja kuw'eleza, ambayo yatusumbuwa
 Tuyatafutiye dawa, twongokewe maishani

2 Muzowele kubwagaza, na kungoja majaliwa
 Viungo mumviviza, hamutaki jisumbuwa
 Hamuna munaloweza, mwataka ya kufanyiwa
 Daima tutapwelewa, jamani amshanani

3 U-Badi mewapoteza, mukakosa kuelewa
 Ndiwo ulowamaliza, leo mu kama mabuwa
 Mno ukawalegeza, mapwetepwete mukawa
 Tutazidi kupwelewa, mbona hatuhimizani?

4 Lenu kubwa kujitwaza, na kupenda kusifiwa
 Na kupenda kujijuza, mtu alivyozaliwa
 Apite akitangaza, watu wapate mjuwa
 Ili apate ambiwa, yu Fulani wa Fulani

5 Na kwingi kujitukuza, na utukufu kupawa
 Na kupenda kujikuza, popote ambapo huwa
 Lau kama mungeweza, mungetaka sujudiwa
 Muwe mukiabudiwa, kama kina Mwafulani?

Come to Your Senses

1   I haven't come to chit-chat or tell stories
    I haven't come to talk about what doesn't exist
    I've come to tell you about what ails us
    So we can find a solution and enjoy a good life

2   You're used to sitting still and waiting for destiny
    You stunt your own limbs; you don't want to trouble yourselves
    You do nothing for yourselves; you want others to serve you
    We'll be stranded forever; let's awaken one another

3   Hubris has led you astray and blinded you
    That's what ruined you; now you're like stalks
    Enfeebled, you've turned spineless
    We'll remain stranded, so why not encourage one another?

4   All you do is brag and enjoy flattery
    And make yourselves known through your family name —
    Someone going around proclaiming, so people will know
    So people can tell him he's so-and-so

5   And glorifying oneself, and being glorified
    Making oneself big wherever one goes
    If only you could, you'd have people prostrate before you
    Do you want to be deified, like Certain Folks?

166 • *Zindukani*

6   Nyuso mlipogeuza, na mato kuyafumbuwa
     Kuona walivyojaza, wale walofanikiwa
     Haanzanyi kuuliza, waliyapataje hawa?
     Kama bure hutolewa, au kwokotwa jaani

7   Mato muka'nza konyeza, na midomo kupanuwa
     Hasira zikawakaza, na husuda kuingiwa
     Kwamba vipi waliweza, kukweya juu wakawa
     "Si nao twali tu sawa, na kwani leo tu tini?"

8   Juu walipojikweza, na kuwa wahishimiwa
     Nyinyi kwani mwaliiza, kwandama zao hatuwa?
     Kwani hamukujikaza, hali mu viumbe sawa?
     Ni hivi yalivyokuwa, musojuwa sikizani

9   Mulipo mun'jilaza, na huku mukipepewa
     Mukawa 'mejitandaza, vitandani maridhawa
     Wenzenu wakiangaza, kwa kazi wakijiuwa
     Ndipo nywi nao mukawa, leo hamulingamani

10   Hawakujitendekeza, wakangoja kufanyiwa
     Si usiku wenye giza, wala mtana wa juwa
     Bidii wakifanyiza, na jasho jingi kutowa
     Hawakuwa 'kipumuwa, saa zote wa mbiyoni

6   When you turned your faces and opened your eyes
     Seeing how they have prospered, the successful ones
     You began wondering: how did they get this?
     Through gifts, was it, or by scavenging in the trash?

7   You started blinking with mouths agape
     Anger seized you and jealousy crept in
     As you wondered how these people ascended so high
     "We were the same as they; why we are now below them?"

8   When they ascended, becoming venerated
     Why did you desist from following in their steps?
     Why didn't you exert yourselves, as you're the same creatures?
     That's how it was: listen, those of you unaware

9   When you were lying down and being fanned
     Stretching yourselves on lovely beds
     Your fellows were awake and hard at work
     That's how you've become, very unlike them

10   They didn't pamper themselves, awaiting things to be done for them
     In the dark night and in the sunny day
     They worked diligently and sweated copiously
     With no chance to catch their breath, always on the go

168 • *Zindukani*

11 Vyenu mulipovisoza, na kwa fujo kutumiwa
Wenzenu wakijikaza, matumbo kutopanuwa
Wakila na kubakiza, kwa ya kesho kutojuwa
Ndipo hi' leo wakawa, wako juu muko tini

12 Vyenu mukaangamiza, kwa kuupenda uluwa
Mato yakafunga giza, mukawa 'mumechachawa
Fakhari ziliwakaza, mno zikawapotowa
Na ndipo leo mukawa, mwambwa hamuna thamani

13 Si kwamba walikiiza, wenzenu kamanywi kuwa
Lakini wakijikaza, na kujinyima uluwa
Wao wakijihimiza, kupanda siku ya mvuwa
Kusudi siku ya juwa, waje kula kwa makini

14 Vyenu ngoma mukiteza, na wake wingi kuowa
Mijana mukasambaza, musoweza watukuwa
Raha mulitanguliza, nazo zikawapotowa
Mpaka mukaishiwa, ha mu nyinyi ha mu nani

15 Mukauza mukauza, na watu 'kivinunuwa
Mukawa mwavipunguza, kila juwa likituwa
Vyote mukavimaliza, mukawa 'mekaukiwa
Wenyewe mulijiuwa, mutamlaumu nani?

11   While you squandered your wealth and spent recklessly
Your peers tried hard not to stuff themselves
They would eat and save leftovers for an unpredictable tomorrow
That's why they're up there today, and you're down below

12   You wiped out your wealth in your desire for prestige
You were blinded and became confused
You were full of pride, and it let you astray
And that's why you're told you are valueless today

13   It isn't that your fellows didn't want to be like you
But they exerted themselves and denied themselves luxury
They exhorted themselves to sow on a rainy day
So on a sunny day they might surely eat

14   You spent your wealth on dances and polygamy
You fathered children you couldn't support
You put pleasure first and lost your way
Until you used it all up and made yourselves nothing

15   You sold and sold, and people bought things
You kept using things up, every single day
You depleted your stock and left yourselves with nothing
You ruined yourselves: who else would you blame?

170 • *Zindukani*

16 Baada ya kupoteza, vyenu na vya kurithiwa
Halafu mtu huweza, hi' leo kujiinuwa
Kidole akalekeza, na huku asema kuwa
"Pale pangu palikuwa", leo hajuwi pa nani!

17 Ndipo hapo hauliza, ili nipate jibiwa
Musimame kunijuza, nami nipate elewa
Vipi leo mutaweza, nyinyi nao kuwa sawa?
Hali mulipotolewa, na raha za duniyani?

18 Wenzenu lilowakweza, ni jasho walilotowa
Si raha si miujiza, wala si majaaliwa
Na si kwa kujitukuza, wala kwa kwao kuzawa
Hawakujiviza hawa, nasi natukazaneni

19 Kabla sijamaliza, shauri nataka towa
Nawaomba kusikiza, mushike 'talotongowa
Mukae na kuliwaza, tupate tengenekewa
Lipi la kutuinuwa, twondoke hapano tini?

20 Ni nyendo kuzigeuza, ambazo 'metupotowa
Na hatuwa kuz'ongeza, zaidi zipate kuwa
Petu tupate pakuza, kwa jasho letu kutowa
'Kingoja kusaidiwa, tutakufa masikini

16   After squandering your possessions and those you inherited
What can one do but arise today
Pointing his finger and uttering the words
"That place used to be mine," with no clue who owns it now

17   That's why I ask, so I can be answered
Stand and bring me up to speed, so I can comprehend
How can you today be equal to them
When you were led astray, lolling in the pleasure of this world?

18   What elevated your fellows was their sweat
Not pleasure or miracles, neither destiny
And not self-glorification or the accident of their birth
They didn't loiter around, so let's also exert ourselves

19   Before I stop, let me give you counsel
I urge you to listen and grasp what I say
Ponder it, so things might go well with us
What will lift us up, so we can leave this low place?

20   We have to change our ways, which have led us astray
And take steps to move ourselves ahead
So we can improve our home through our own sweat
If we wait for help, we'll die poor

172 • *Zindukani*

21 Ni lazima kufanyiza, kila la kutuinuwa
    Tuanze kujihimiza, tusingoje kuambiwa
    Petu tupate pakuza, kwa sote kujisumbuwa
    Hapo tutahishimiwa, tuhisabike tu nani

22 Iwapo tutaigiza, ya waliyofanikiwa
    Iwapo tutapunguza, kupenda vyetu vifuwa
    Kama tutajikataza, kupenda mwingi uluwa
    Hapo tutafanikiwa, basi shimeni jamani

23 Kiyoo cha wangu moyo, nilipokiangaliya
    Kikanionyesha hayo, tulivyopoteya ndiya
    Kikanamba nije mbiyo, hayano kuw'elezeya
    Kila mwenye kusikiya, ajuwa n'nasemani

24 Hii ni kweli ambayo, hata'mi meniumiza
    Kwamba mbwa sehemu hiyo, kweli hii yaniliza
    Yauliza wangu moyo, wala hautanyamaza
    Hakuna cha kuupoza, mpaka twondoke tini

    —*22 Septemba 1971*

21 We have to do what we can to elevate ourselves
Let's take initiative and not wait to be told
So we can improve our home through our own effort
Only then will we be respected and counted worthy

22 If we emulate those successful people
If we work ourselves harder
If we check our desire for prestige
Then we'll succeed, so let's work hard at it

23 When I looked into the mirror of my heart
It showed me how we went astray
It urged me to hurry here to tell you this
Everyone listening knows what I'm talking about

24 This is the truth that hurts even me
Because it concerns our home, this truth makes me weep
My heart weeps because of it and will not quiet
Nothing can comfort my heart till we leave this low place

—22 September 1971

Kwa Heri

1. Nakuaga ndugu yangu, kwa heri ya kuonana
   Naondoka nenda zangu, hiwa na simanzi sana
   Simanzi moyoni mwangu, kwa tulivyozoweyana
   La kutenda ndilo sina, ela kwenenda nendako

2. Nawe kaa kwa salama, salama wa salimini
   Nakutakiya uzima, na furaha ya moyoni
   Siku moja ni lazima, tutakutana wendani
   Kwa hili nina yakini, bora sote tuwe hai

3. Siwati kukukumbuka, popote nitapokuwa
   Na ingawa naondoka, mimi mbali nawe kuwa
   Daima hutanitoka, ndani ya changu kifuwa
   Hakuna cha kukutowa, nendapo 'takwenda nawe

4. Ndu yangu Israili, mambo huwenda yakija
   Kwamba tutakuwa mbali, si hoja hiyo si hoja
   Mbali ni yetu miili, bali nyoyo zi pamoja
   Moja na moja si moja, lakini kwetu ni yiyo

5. Beti tano namaliza, mbele hakusongeleki
   Ningetaka kuongeza, lakini mbele sifiki
   Mengine nayabakiza, yote hayaelezeki
   Kwa heri ndugu rafiki, kwa heri ya kuonana

—*9 Oktoba 1971*

Goodbye

1. I bid you farewell, my brother, goodbye till we meet again
   I'm departing, going my way in sorrow
   There's sorrow in my heart because of how close we've grown
   There's nothing I can do but go where I go

2. May you dwell in peace, peace and tranquility
   I wish you a good life and happiness in your heart
   One day we'll surely meet, my dear companion
   Of this I have no doubt, so long as we're both alive

3. I won't forget you, wherever I may be
   And although I depart, headed far from you
   You will never, ever leave my heart
   Nothing will remove you; where I go, I go with you

4. Israel, my brother, things come and go
   That we'll be far apart isn't the point, not the point
   We're apart in body, but our hearts are joined
   One plus one isn't one, yet for us it's so

5. I end here on the fifth verse; I can't go further
   I'd like to say more, but I just can't manage
   Some things I leave unsaid; they're inexplicable
   Goodbye brother, friend; goodbye till we meet again

—9 October 1971

La Mjini na la Shamba

Mwateni apige mbawa, na kwingi kutaratamba
Nakifutishe kifuwa, na aridhi kuitimba
Ni bure ajisumbuwa, haamshi moja nyumba
Tangu lini jimbi shamba, likawikiya mjini?

Jawabu:
Uliyelifumba fumbo, hukujuwa kulifumba
Usibaranganye mambo, simba awapo ni simba
Si leo tangu kitambo, kwajulikanwa ya kwamba
Lau si huyo wa shamba, wa mjini hangekuwa

—*2 Novemba 1971*

The Town Cockerel and the Country One

Let him flap his wings and strut all over
And let him puff his chest and scratch the ground
He's wasting time: he won't awaken any household
Since when did a country cockerel crow in town?

Response:
You who composed this riddle lacked the know-how
Don't confuse things: a lion's a lion anywhere
It's well known now and from times long gone
The town cockerel wouldn't be here were it not for the country one

—*2 November 1971*

Muosheni

1   Muosheni, mpaka atakasike
     Na sabuni, mwili wote mumpake
     Utosini, hadi kwenye nyayo zake

2   Mswafini, uchafu ndani utoke
     Mpakeni, mafuta anan'ganike
     Duniyani, leo ndiyo mwisho wake

3   Mtangani, ndipo kulala endapo
     Ni nyumbani, kwetu sote tuliyopo
     Muosheni, awe swafi azikwapo

4   Simwateni, ati sababu afile
     Ni kanuni, ya tangu zama za kale
     Muosheni, mabuu yende yamle

5   Muosheni, alele haamshiwe
     'Simukhini, ni haki yake napawe
     Muosheni, aozapo swafi awe

6   Uhaini, japo ali yu mchafu
     Na mwilini, 'kitowa mbaya harufu
     Muosheni, kwa vile leo yu mfu

Wash Him

1   Wash him until he is spotless
Smear his whole body with soap
From his head down to his feet

2   Make him clean, removing all dirt
Apply ointment until he shines
On Earth, today is his end

3   He's going to lie in the soil
It's a home for all of us here
Wash him, so he's clean when interred

4   Don't abandon him because he's now dead
It's the custom from time immemorial
Wash him, that he may be eaten by worms

5   Wash him; he sleeps and won't be awakened
Don't deprive him; it's his right, let it be granted
Wash him, that he may be clean when he rots

6   Although in life he may have been dirty
And smells may have spread from his body
Wash him, because today he is dead

180 • *Muosheni*

7 Muosheni, na huku twamliliya
  Kwa huzuni, mwenzetu kutwondokeya
  Masikini, twali tunamzoweya

8 Muosheni, leo zimfika zake
  Muosheni, mabegani tujitweke
  Muosheni, twenende tukamzike

  —19 Novemba 1971

7   Wash him as we bewail his death
    In sorrow: our companion has left us
    What a pity—we'd grown attached to him

8   Wash him; today his days have ended
    Wash him so we can hoist him on our shoulders
    Wash him so we can go and bury him

    —*19 November 1971*

Naja

1. Naja sasa ni ndiyani, naja kwetu mzalendo
   Naja nirudi nyumbani, nilowekwa nako kando
   Kwetu 'mi nakutamani, kulo na mwingi uhondo
   Nijaye ni ile nyundo, misumari hadharini

2. Naja ni ndiyani naja, taratibu ndiwo mwendo
   Siku ambayo nangoja, kunyakuliya mdundo
   Iko karibu na kuja, siifanyii kishindo
   Nijaye ni ile nyundo, misumari hadharini

3. Naja kwengine kuwapi, kulojaa langu pendo?
   Henda nende kwenginepi, sawa nako kwa muundo?
   Kaa kwengine anapi, ela kwenye lakwe gando?
   Nijaye ni ile nyundo, misumari hadharini

4. Naja nije rudi papo, panigendeme mgando
   Ningaambwa kwetu hapo, kwamba kwanuka uvundo
   Sitakwenda penginepo, 'tarudi kuko kwa mwando
   Nijaye ni ile nyundo, misumari hadharini

5. Naja sitapakimbiya, ningambwa kuna vimondo
   'Takuja kuvilekeya, vinganijiya kwa rundo
   Nilipozawa 'tafiya, sikimbii kwenda kando
   Nijaye ni ile nyundo, misumari hadharini

I'm Coming

1   I'm coming now: I the patriot am coming back
I'm returning home from where I was torn apart
I yearn for our home, where there are wonderful things
I the hammer am on the way: nails, beware

2   I'm coming, slowly coming but surely
I await the day when my journey will start
That day is approaching—I won't be impatient
I the hammer am on the way: nails, beware

3   I'm coming; where else lies my affection?
What place could I go that has the same shape?
What place does the crab have besides its own shell?
I the hammer am on the way: nails, beware

4   I'm coming right back there; we're joined to each other
Even if I'm told that home smells rotten
I won't go anywhere else, I'll return there to my beginning
I the hammer am on the way: nails, beware

5   I'm coming and won't flee, even if I'm told there's trouble
I'll come to confront it, even if it arrives in plenty
I'll die where I was born, I'm not running away
I the hammer am on the way: nails, beware

184 • *Naja*

6   Naja hiwa 'mekomaa, kuzidi nilivyo mwando
    Tena nnajiandaa, kwa fikira na vitendo
    Kwetu nije kuifaa, na kuitiliya pondo
    Nijaye ni ile nyundo, misumari hadharini

7   Naja munaoningoja, kwa vigele na misondo
    Ningojeyani 'takuja, nyuso z'ondoweni kundo
    Tuje pigana pambaja, wangu wenza wazalendo
    Nijaye ni ile nyundo, misumari hadharini

8   Naja na ambao kwamba, waningoja kwa vihendo
    Wazidi kukaza kamba, wasizibadili nyendo
    Wangajiita ni simba, sitazicha zao kondo
    Nijaye ni ile nyundo, misumari hadharini

9   Naja huu wangu moyo, hauningii mdundo
    Sitatishika kwa hayo, niyazowele maondo
    Mimi kutishika nayo, huo siwo wangu mwendo
    Nijaye ni ile nyundo, misumari hadharini

10 Naja na ingawa naja, siwaekei mifundo
    Moyo wangu ushatuja, mawi nalotendwa mwando
    Ela wataoningoja, na vyao viwi vitendo
    Nijaye ni ile nyundo, misumari hadharini

I'm Coming • 185

6   I return more mature than I was at the start
Also I'm prepared in thought and action
So I can benefit my home and help it prosper
I the hammer am on the way: nails, beware

7   I'm coming; you who await me with ululations and drums
Just wait, I'll come; wipe the frowns from your faces
So we can embrace one another, my fellow patriots
I the hammer am on the way: nails, beware

8   I'm coming, and those awaiting me with ill-will —
Let them redouble their efforts, let them not change their ways
Though they may call themselves lions, I won't fear war with them
I the hammer am on the way: nails, beware

9   As I come, this my heart has no iota of fear
I'm not scared at all—I'm inured to tribulation
To be frightened of that isn't my way
I the hammer am on the way: nails, beware

10   And even as I come, I bear no grudges
My heart has sieved away the evil done against me
Except for those who await me with their evil actions
I the hammer am on the way: nails, beware

186 • *Naja*

11 Naja wenye niya hizo, na watotezi vidondo
Naja sitaki matezo, matezo nayawe kando
Naja wakizituwa'zo, 'tawanwisha sichi kondo
Nijaye ni ile nyundo, misumari hadharini

—*19 Disemba 1971*

11   I'm coming: those with such intentions, fanning fires—
I'm coming, I'm not joking: set jokes aside
I'm coming and if they start, I'll finish them, for I fear no battle
I the hammer am on the way: nails, beware

—*19 December 1971*

Ndiya Panda

1 Safari naloiyanza, bado ningalimo kwenda
Sitawata kujikaza, isipate kunishinda
Nataka kuimaliza, ndivyo nipendavyo tenda
Sasa niko ndiya panda

2 Napo singepafikiya, falau singejipinda
Kwani hiiangaliya, ndiya nalimoenenda
Ningekuwa 'mewatiya, kwisha tu kuiyanda
Singefika ndiya panda

3 Maana ndiya yenyewe, si ndiya ya mtu kwenda
Sivyo ilivyo na mawe! Ya kuvikongowa vyanda!
Yataka isafiriwe, kwa farasi au punda
Kupafika ndiya panda

4 Haitaki mlegevu, na ambaye ajipenda
Kwa mtu mtepetevu, 'wapo ndiya hiyo enda
Atafurikwa na povu, na pumzi kumpanda
Hapafiki ndiya panda

5 Yataka mvumilivu, tabu alokwisha onda
Mwenye moyo wenye nguvu, mgumu usiyopinda
Na tena awe mwekevu, ndipo azipite nyanda
Kupafika ndiya panda

Crossroads

1   I'm still on the journey, the one I began
I won't relax, so as not to be vanquished
I want to stay the course, that's what I want to do
        Now I'm at the crossroads

2   I wouldn't have come here if I'd not taken a turn
For when I look at it, this path I've come along—
I should have abandoned it as soon as I started
        I wouldn't have reached the crossroads

3   Because the path itself isn't made for a person
Look! So many rocks that hurt the toes
It wants traveling by horseback or donkey
        To get to the crossroads

4   It doesn't suit the fickle person, or one who loves himself
A lazy person, if he goes this way
Will foam at the mouth and gasp for breath
        He won't reach the crossroads

5   It takes a patient person, one who has tasted trouble
One with a strong heart, an immovable heart
Someone who is stoical, so he can cross the plains
        To get to the crossroads

190 • *Ndiya Panda*

6   Pamoja na tabu kuu, hazipita hizo nyanda
     Kiyakokota maguu, tafu henda 'kinipinda
     Pamwe kuchoka hiyau, safari sikuivunda
         Haja hadi ndiya panda

7   Tabu nalizozikuta, zakondesha alowanda
     Nyayo'za zilinikata, zikawa pwi vidonda
     Vivyo hajivutavuta, hiteteya huku henda
         Na sasa ni ndiya panda

8   Nali 'kijuwa si sasa, kwamba ndiya hiyo chenda
     'Takumbana na mikasa, yatayonikundakunda
     Na vivyo sikujiwasa, ilinilazimu kwenda
         Ndipo kuja ndiya panda

9   Ilipofika safari, silijuwi la kutenda
     Nimekwisha kufikiri, lakini limenishinda
     Nawatakanyi shauri, nijuwe ndiya ya kwenda
         Mojapo ya ndiya panda

10   Shauri jema munipe, enyi binadamu wenda
     Nipani musinitupe, musiwe wa kunivunda
     Nipate juwa kweupe, ndiya ipi ya kwenenda
         Kwenye hii ndiya panda

Crossroads • 191

6   Despite great tribulation, I crossed the plains
    Dragging my feet along, muscles cramping me
    And despite tiring this way, I didn't abandon the journey
            I came to this crossroads

7   The trouble I experienced would make a fat person thin
    The soles of my feet cut me with many wounds
    Yet I kept on dragging myself, limping along
            And now I'm at the crossroads

8   It's not only now that I understand how taking this path
    Means encountering crushing hardships
    But I was determined, having no choice but to go on
            That's why I'm at the crossroads

9   Where I've now reached, I have no idea what to do
    I've mulled it over, but I find no answers
    I seek your guidance, so I can know which way to go—
            One of these at the crossroads

10   Give me good advice, my fellow humans
    Give it to me: don't abandon me, don't dissuade me
    So I know clearly which way to go
            At these crossroads

192 • *Ndiya Panda*

11   Nnapigwa na pumbao, akili inniganda
Kila usiku uchao, na mtana nikishinda
Bongo silipi kituo, linijuvye la kutenda
        Hukumu ya ndiya panda

12   Kila niitupiyao, jito ili kuitunda
Kila moja kati yao, hunipa ya kunitanda
Huniita: "huku ndoo, ni hii ndiya ya kwenda"
        Yanitanza ndiya panda

13   Na zote mbili hunena, hizi ndiya kwenye panda
Kwamba lau 'tashindana, nendee nnayopenda
Basi nijuwe bayana, maguu itanivunda
        Yanambiya ndiya panda

14   Ni kama niloangama, na kushuka kwanishinda
Na hata lau nasema, nijitupe kama bunda
Sitaanguka salama, kwenye mawe 'tajidunda
        Ni hayo ya ndiya panda

15   Enyi wenda nambizani, nambizani enyi wenda
Mwenzenu nimo tatani, moyo hawishi kudunda
Nitowani mashakani, munijuvye la kutenda
        Yanishe ya ndiya panda

Crossroads • 193

11 I'm confused, and my mind has stalled
  Every single night, and by day as well
  My brain finds no respite, struggling to unravel the choice
    Deciding at the crossroads

12 Whenever I glance towards them
  Each of the paths gives me a confounding message
  It calls to me: "come here, this is the way to go"
    The crossroads confound me

13 And both paths proclaim, these paths at the crossroads
  That if I insist, I should take whichever way I choose
  But I must understand clearly that my feet shall be broken
    The crossroads tell me

14 It's like I'm suspended and unable to climb down
  And even if I decide to toss myself like a bundle
  I won't land safely, I'll land on rocks
    This is the trouble with crossroads

15 Fellow humans, tell me; tell me, fellow humans
  I, your fellow, am entangled; my heart won't stop pounding
  Save me from this anxiety by letting me know what to do
    That I may finish with the crossroads

194 • *Ndiya Panda*

16   Nichalo ni kujisoza, kisha haja uma vyanda
Ndipo'nywi hawaambiza, munishauri ya kwenda
Nipani la muwangaza, safari 'sije ivunda
       Ajili ya ndiya panda

—*23 Januari 1972*

Crossroads • 195

16   I fear ruining myself and regretting things later
        That's why I call upon you to advise me where to go
        Enlighten me, that I may not abandon the journey
                    Because of the crossroads

—*23 January 1972*

Kichu Hakiwi ni Uchu

1   Ni nyani ambidhiweo, yu nchu kwa chake kichu?
Ni nyani nnena hao, ntaka hadaa vachu
Nadhengee vangineo, jura hatopacha kwechu
Nchu kwambiwa yu nchu, ni uchuwe kwa wendiwe

2   Na kana ni chwambiwavo, kichu na uchu ni chicho
Dhiko na dhingi dhilidho, dhenye dhichu kochokocho
Chwambe dhina uchu nadho, thibabu ni lavo pacho?
Nchu si kwa lake pacho, ni uchuwe kwa wendiwe

3   Hela ndovu chunchunde, awe ni mfano wechu
Chumuawanye dhipande, awe dhipande dhichachu
Ili kasidi chwenende, chufahamishane uchu
Chuyive nchu ni kichu, au uchu kwa wendiwe?

4   Kwanda ni muwili wake, uliyo nkuru nno
Kwa nama mwichu wendake, hauna wakwe mfano
Apeche umbo la pweke, kuru tena lilo nono
Si chanda si lakwe ino, si madodi ila mato

5   Ndhengee avoneo, mwene kuwavona vachu
Vachu ndovu wavoneo, awapo kachika mwichu
Umvudhe: vachu hao, wavonapo hicho kichu
Achi huwaye wendechu, sura wataajabuvo?

A Thing Can't Be Human

1   Who is considered human because of the things he has?
    Whoever says so intends to deceive people
    Let him look for others; he won't find fools among us
    What makes someone human is his humaneness towards others

2   If we are told objects and humane qualities are the same
    There are propertied people possessing things in plenty
    Can they be said to have humanity because of their riches?
    Humanity isn't in things, but in humaneness towards others

3   Let's take the elephant as our example
    Let's think about it in parts, in three aspects
    With the intent of learning what it is to be human
    So we can tell if humanity is a thing or is humaneness towards others

4   First, there's its body so humongous
    Among its wild peers there's no compare
    It has a distinctive figure, fat and enormous
    Everything is big, toe to teeth, save the eyes

5   Find a person who has seen, who has seen people
    People who saw an elephant in the wilderness
    Ask him: when they saw it
    How surprised were they?

198 • *Kichu Hakiwi ni Uchu*

6   Pili nguvu alonadho, dhiyani dhalomweneya
     Ni nguvu dhiwachishadho, dhiumbe na michi piya
     Dhidirikanao nadho, hadhina budi kuliya
     Au mbiyoni kungiya, kwa kucha kudhidirika

7   Vako ambao hunena, nguvudhe kudhisifiya
     Kwamba huwedha vuchana, na hata na vachu miya
     Na hata vangaungana, kumvucha kwa pamoya
     Hawawi kuwedha piya, kwa nguvu alidhonadho

8   Ata dhiumbe vanche, kwa nguvù alidhopowa
     'Kichumiya kifuwache, awapo andoudhiwa
     Michi isiyo michache, hungiliya kuang'owa
     Nyuteni yivani kuwa, hawi mbwa kudhivilika

9   Kando ni lakwe iteke, libikapo hwangamidha
     Pumudhidhe pweke yake, chwaambiwa huumidha
     Dhivudhiyapo chendake, mbali hukichokomedha
     Humbiriya dhikapadha, na tiyati kuchangusha

10   Chachu ni yakwe thamani, asoiyiva hakuna
     Ichengee duniyani, kupi kaiyulikana?
     Dhiungani na miyini, nno huchambulikana
     N'nyani m'wene kunena, haiyisi thamaniye?

6   Second, the power it has, how it fills its body
      It's the power that scares creatures and trees, too
      Encountering it, they suffer that force
      Or run away fast, in fear of facing it

7   There are those who speak out, praising its power
      How the elephant can pull even a hundred people
      And even if they unite, trying to pull it together
      They won't succeed because of its might

8   Creatures fear it because of its power
      It can use its force whenever it is aggrieved
      It will indeed uproot countless trees
      All of you must know: it can't be held back

9   Besides its kick—when it kicks it devastates —
      The elephant's breath alone is said to wound
      When it breathes on another animal, the animal vanishes
      Its breath throws that animal far and fells it with a thud

10   Third is the elephant's value: no one is unaware of it
      It is recognized worldwide; where is it unknown?
      In the outskirts and in the towns it's widely known
      Who would say he doesn't know the elephant's value?

200 • *Kichu Hakiwi ni Uchu*

11   Pacha kwenda utukuni, pembedhe dhidhanyiwapo
      Au nenda nnadani, kwahali dhinadiwapo
      Uyivwonee matoni, n-da dhinunuliwapo
      Ndipo utayiva hapo, thamani ya nama huu

12   Thamani yakwe si chocho, thamani ya nama huu
      Chakwe iye kidhanywacho, hoko kwene utukuu
      Mwene kukinunuwacho, hulipiya bei kuu
      Beiye kwamba i yuu, ndipo kudhanywa hiyau

13   Kiswahili cha Kigunya, kwacho 'kiwazungumza
      'Mejaribu kubambanya, kiyasi n'livyoweza
      Sasa n'takalofanya, nataka kukigeuza
      Kwamba n'pate maliza, n'lilolikusudiya

14   N'likijuwa zamani, tangu utotoni mwangu
      Wakati ni Magunyani, pamoja na babu yangu
      Na tangu huko nihuni, si leo miyaka tungu
      Kwa hivyo fahamu yangu, kwacho 'menipungukiya

15   Changu ni cha Kimvita, tangu mwa mama tumboni
      Sikwenda kukitafuta, n'likikuta nyumbani
      Mi nacho ni kama pata, twendapo hatuwatani
      Na tangu kwinukiyani, hicho ndicho hutumiya

11   Go to the market where its tusks are sold
Or go to the auction, see how they are auctioned
See with your own eyes how they are purchased
Then you'll understand the value of this animal

12   Its value isn't small, the value of this animal
When part of it is sold at the market
The one purchasing it does so at a high price
That price is high, that's how it's sold

13   The Kiswahili I've been speaking is the Kigunya dialect
I've only tried to fumble as far as I could
Now what I intend to do is change style a bit
So I can complete what I intended

14   I knew it long ago, from the time of my childhood
When I lived in Magunyani along with my great-uncle
And it's many years since I moved from there
Hence my knowledge of the dialect has long faded

15   Kimvita is my dialect, right from my mother's womb
I never went looking for it, I found it at home
Kimvita and I are like twins, together wherever we go
In all my growing up, this is what I've used

202 • *Kichu Hakiwi ni Uchu*

16 Kwangu ndicho mahashumu, mno nakipendeleya
Ndicho kinishacho hamu, mashairi hitungiya
Huwa siyaoni tamu, hiwata kuchandikiya
Huyaona ni mabaya, ha ya tamu ha ya nyamu

17 Hicho ndicho Kiswahili, ambacho chanipendeza
Kwake sioni badali, ndipo nikakitukuza
Kwangu ki kama asali, tamu isokinaiza
Ndicho hunitosheleza, wakati wa kutungiya

18 Kwanza nataka fasiri, maana ya neno "kitu"
Tuelezane vizuri, afahamu kila mtu
Maanaye idhihiri, kwa kila mmoja wetu
Mtu kiambiwa "kitu", lipate kumueleya

19 Ni mengi maana yake, nikianza yadondowa
Lau yote niandike, niwe kuyafafanuwa
Ndugu zangu mukumbuke, kazi kubwa itakuwa
Basi yote sitatowa, ingawa yanieleya

20 Katika lugha iweyo, hata iwe nda Kichina
Kuna maneno ambayo, kwa mato ukiyaona
Utayadhaniya hayo, hayana maana pana
Yaani yao maana, moja hayakuzidiya

A Thing Can't Be Human • 203

16 To me this is something special; I prefer it to anything else
  It satisfies me when I'm writing poems
  I find no pleasure when I cease writing in it
  The poems appear poor to me, neither sweet nor interesting

17 This is the Kiswahili dialect that appeals to me
  I see no substitute for it, that's why I celebrate it
  To me it's like honey, with endless sweetness
  It's what brings me contentment when I'm composing

18 First I want to define the word "thing"
  Let's explain well to one another, so that everyone knows
  So its meaning is evident to each one of us
  And when mention of "thing" is made, all may understand

19 It has multiple meanings, if I may begin enumerating
  If I were to write them all down and elucidate them
  Remember, my brothers, it would be hard work
  So I won't give all, although I know them

20 In any language, even Chinese
  There are some words which if you see with your eyes
  You will think they have no multiplicity of meaning
  That their meaning is only one

204 • *Kichu Hakiwi ni Uchu*

21 Lakini sivyo yalivyo, si hivyo ambavyo huwa
Vilivyo ambavyo ndivyo, ambavyo vilivyo sawa
Hutegemeya ambavyo, neno lilivyotumiwa
Ndipo utapambanuwa, maanaye mbalimbali

22 Na Kiswahili ni vivyo, vyenginewe usidhani
Neno ulitumiyavyo, liwapo li kifunguni
Nalo ndivyo likupavyo, tafauti ya maani
Ukaweza kubaini, maana yatakiwayo

23 Kwa maana ya jumla, ya neno "kitu" wenzangu
Ni ambacho au kila, kilo kwenye ulimwengu
Mfano nguo, chakula, neno, roho au rungu
Jiwe, mtu au tungu, kila kimoja ni kitu

24 Ndipo mfano hatowa, wa ndovu alivyonavyo
Ukubwa aliopawa, ni kama hivyo ulivyo
Na nguvuze twazijuwa, zistaajabishavyo
Na thamaniye ilivyo, si ndogo 'meelezeya

25 Vyote hivino ni vitu, tena si vitu vidogo
Ndivyo vitu kila mtu, huviwekeya mitego
Kimojapo mwenzi wetu, 'kipata hutupa shingo
Hufurahi hadi jego, likawa laonekana

A Thing Can't Be Human • 205

21 Yet that isn't the case, that's never how things are
    The way things are, how they really are
    Depends largely on the use of the word
    That's how one recognizes its various meanings

22 Even Kiswahili is that way—don't think otherwise
    The way you use a word in a given sentence
    That's how it conveys to you a connotation
    So you can determine the intended meaning

23 Generally speaking, the term "thing," my friends
    Is the *which* or *each* of all that's found in the world
    For example: clothes, food, a word, a spirit or a club
    A stone, a person, or an ant; each is a thing

24 That's why I furnished the example of an elephant
    Its massive size is the way it is
    Its might that we all know, that never ceases to amaze
    And the nature of its value; it's quite invaluable

25 All of these are things, and they aren't small
    These are things every person attempts to capture
    If any of us gets one, he's surely delighted
    His joy is so great as to expose his molars

206 • *Kichu Hakiwi ni Uchu*

26   Iwapo ni hicho kitu, mno kinachosifiwa
Ndicho kimpacho mtu, naye yu mtu kwambiwa
Basi huyu nyama mwitu, ambaye meelezewa
Kitu chamfanya kuwa, kwambiwa naye yu mtu?

27   Licha mtu na akili, ambayo iko razini
Hata mjinga wa kweli, mtopeya ujingani
Hataweza kukubali, kabisa hataamini
Ati nyama wa mwituni, awe yu sawa na mtu

28   Lau hayo watamka, na kumwambiya mwendani
Hakika atakuteka, akutiye uzuzuni
Maana kufikirika, hayangii akilini
Hilo haliwezekani, ni bure ungamwambiya

29   Basi na mtu ambaye, yuna vitu kwa milima
Maadamu vyake yeye, hafalii binadama
Bali huvikusanyaye, na kupenda vitizama
Huwa sawa na mnyama, tuliyemuelezeya

30   Mfano awe na mali, yalokiuka mipaka
Akatupiliya mbali, wenye shida na mashaka
Akawa hata hajali, tabu zinazowafika
Huyo si mtu hakika, kwani mtu mbwake utu

A Thing Can't Be Human • 207

26 If a particular thing that is much praised
    Is what gives a person the right to be called human
    So shall we say of the beast we've discussed
    That a thing earns him the right to be called human?

27 Not to mention a sane person, one with a sound mind
    Even a mere simpleton whose foolishness is great
    Won't accept, won't be able to believe
    That a wild beast should be considered the same as a person

28 If you said that, telling it to a friend
    He'd surely laugh at you and count you among fools
    Because it's unthinkable, utterly inconceivable
    It's not possible, and it would be futile telling him so

29 So someone who has mountains of things
    As long as they are his, yet he doesn't profit humanity
    But would instead gather them and enjoy looking at them —
    This person is the same as the animal we just discussed

30 Or take someone who has wealth without limit
    And forsakes those with problems and hardships
    Not caring what trouble befalls them
    He isn't human, really, because one becomes human through humaneness

208 • *Kichu Hakiwi ni Uchu*

31   Au awe yuna nguvu, kikubwa kifuwa chake
Ziwe nguvu za mabavu, na magumi na mateke
Iwe sasa utulivu, hawaupati wenzake
Iwe ni watetemeke, muda'ye akitokeya

32   Nguvu hizo sasa ziwe, hatumii ajikinge
Bali ndiyo mwanzo awe, kwenye mitaa arange
Akidhulumu wenziwe, ambao kwamba wanyonge
Yawe "mnyonge msonge", hana wa kumzuwiya

33   Au awe yuna cheo, juu ya wenziwe wote
Na kisha wenziwe hao, alonao saa zote
Wawapo na shida zao, hawafai kwa chochote
Iwe "poteleya pote", hataki kuwasikiya

34   Badili hiyo furusa, kuitumiya vizuri
Kwake sivyo; bali sasa, huanzisha takaburi
Wende awe kuwatesa, awatendee jeuri
Huyo ni nyama wa pori, hafai kuitwa mtu

35   Waliwo na sifa hizo, viumbe niwanenao
Mali wangakuwa nazo, ukubwa wangawa nao
Wangawa na nguvu hizo, wadhiliyazo wenzao
Siweki viumbe hao, kwenye daraja ya watu

A Thing Can't Be Human • 209

31   Or if a person is mighty, with a hefty chest
     And acts brutally with fists and kicks
     So that his peers find no peace
     So that they start quaking the moment he arrives

32   If he uses his might not to protect himself
     But as his basis for bragging in the neighborhoods
     Exploiting his fellows, who are essentially weak
     So it becomes "oppress the wretched one," and no one can stop him

33   Or if he has a position above all his fellows
     And eventually his fellows, who are with him all the time
     Have problems, and he doesn't help at all
     But says "I don't care" and won't listen to them

34   Instead of using well the chance given him
     Quite to the contrary, he now becomes arrogant
     So he mistreats them and deals with them insolently
     Then he is a wild beast, not deserving to be called human

35   Those with such attributes, the creatures I allude to
     Even if they have wealth, as well as high positions
     Even if they have might with which they oppress others
     I don't place such creatures in the category of human

36 Uliyo wangu muradi, wa kuyaneneya hayo
Viumbe hao idadi, pamoja na ndovu huyo
Sikioni cha zaidi, kati ya waliyonayo
Naona wa sawa kwayo, kipi walopitaniya?

37 Iwapo ni hayo mali, watu yasosaidiya
Sababu ya ubakhili, wakawa wayabaniya
Wasijali wasibali, dhiki za wapita ndiya
Na ndovu anayo piya, kama nalivyoeleza

38 Ndovu na bakhili sawa, hawambali kwa masafa
Ya bakhili hurithiwa, baada ya kwake kufa
Mara nyingi hutumiwa, ovyo pasi maarifa
Na ya ndovu ni kwa kufa, ndipo yake yatwaliwe

39 Kwa hivyo hapa twaona, viumbe hivi viwili
Ambavyo wamfanana, kwa hayano yao mali
Hayawi kupatikana, ela watwawe na nduli
Kuna gani afadhali, baina wawili hawa?

40 Na kwa wa nguvu upande, 'taweleza pasi shaka
Iwapo ni wa makonde, na mabavu kutumika
Watu iwe mbiyo wende, kwa kucha kuzidirika
Vifenene kadhalika, viumbe viwili hivi

A Thing Can't Be Human • 211

36   The whole point of my saying all this
About these many creatures, including the elephant
Is that I don't see the difference between them at all
I see them as the same: what differentiates them?

37   If the difference is that wealth which doesn't help people
Which, because of stinginess, they keep to themselves
Not caring about the trials of passersby
Even the elephant has those attributes, as I've explained

38   The elephant and the miser are the same in their ways
The miser's wealth is inherited upon his demise
Often it's misused quite recklessly
As for the elephant, upon death all that belongs to him is taken

39   Thus we see here two creatures
Who resemble one other in that their wealth
Is unobtainable except when they are snatched by the angel of death
Who is the better of the two?

40   And as to the use of force, I'll tell you without a doubt
If he uses fists, and whatever other force
People must flee in fear of his attacks
Then they look alike, these two creatures

212 • *Kichu Hakiwi ni Uchu*

41   Apandwapo na ghadhabu, huyu ndovu 'mewambiya
        Vilivyo naye karibu, na alivyovilekeya
        Huanza kuviharibu, vikawa kuangamiya
        Huulaza mwitu piya, manyasi na miti yake

42   Kwani muda hifikiri, hizo nguvu walonazo
        Ni nguvu za kuhasiri, na kudhili wasonazo
        Hazitumiwi kwa kheri, bali kwa maangamizo
        Basi wafenene kwazo, ipi tafauti yao?

43   Na iwapo ni ukuu, huyo mtu alonao
        Ukuu wa kudharau, wasiwo na hicho cheo
        Basi ndovu nao huu, na yeye pia anao
        Ipi tafauti yao, walotafautiyana?

44   Basi tusidanganyike, tusiwe mbwa kuhadawa
        Mtu si kwa kitu chake, japo kwacho asifiwa
        Utu wake kwa wenzake, ndiwo wa kuhisabiwa
        Vyengine sitaambiwa, nami nikaviamini

—4 Oktoba 1971

A Thing Can't Be Human • 213

41   When he is incensed, I tell you, this elephant
The things near him or those facing him
He begins to destroy, devastating them completely
He flattens the forest, also the grass and the trees

42   When I think about it, the power these two have
Is a damaging power of tormenting the powerless
It isn't used for good, but for devastation
Indeed they resemble one another this way: what is their difference?

43   And if it's position that a person has —
Position from which to despise those below
Then the elephant, too, has such position
What is their difference, what really distinguishes them?

44   Let's not be misled, not be like the deceived
One isn't human because of possessions, even if they bring adulation
Humanity towards fellow humans, that's what counts
I can't be told otherwise and believe it

—*4 October 1971*

Kutendana

1   Mwanamume:
Kama bure utanipa, nipa sinisimbuliye
Kama hutaki 'takopa, nikulipe baadaye
Hivi sasa cha kukupa, sina; kweli nikwambiye
Mtu huwa hakutupa, amfaapo mwenziye

2   Mwanamke:
"Sina" kila siku "sina", "sina" kwako i maisha
Huna siku utanena: ninacho 'kanirambisha?
Hiyo "sina" yako Bwana, sasa ishanichokesha
Nyege ni kunyegezana, kwangu huba zin'kwisha

3   Mwanamume:
Nnatoka nitokako, mwendo kiguu na ndiya
Sikujali masumbuko, ya mvuwa kuninyiya
Mwenzi wako nina mwako, tafadhali niridhiya
Nipa kwa hisani yako, wata kunisimbuliya

4   Mwanamke:
Rudi kuko utokako, siniletee udhiya
Tafutiya mwako wako, ndiya ya kuutoleya
Mimi ndiye jaa lako, takazo kunitupiya?
Mwanamume nenda zako, sina n'talosikiya

Tit for Tat

1   HE:
If you're going to give it to me, give it without mocking me
If you don't want to, I'll take it on credit and pay you later
As for now, I have nothing to give you, I'm telling you the truth
A person loses nothing by helping a friend

2   SHE
"I don't have," every day "I don't have"; "I don't have" has become life to you
There isn't a single day you say: I have something for you to enjoy
I'm now tired, sir, of your "I don't have"
Life is give and take, for me our love is dead

3   HE:
I've come from where I came, walking a long way on foot
I've endured discomfort from the rain falling on me
I, your companion, am on fire; please accept my request
Just give it to me out of kindness; stop mocking me

4   SHE:
Go back where you came from, don't trouble me
Seek other ways of dousing the fire burning inside you
Am I a dump for depositing your litter?
Go away, man, I won't listen to you

216 • *Kutendana*

5   Mwanamume:
Laiti kwamba wajuwa, uhisivyo wangu moyo
Laiti ungetambuwa, niumiyavyo mwenziyo
Kattu hungenisumbuwa, na kunifanyiya choyo
Ndiwe wa kuiyondowa, hii dhiki nilonayo

6   Mwenziyo n'nalemewa, si dhihaka n'semayo
Sina pa kwenda itowa, hii hamu nilonayo
Na hata wewe wajuwa, kwamba sina badaliyo
Ni mgonjwa nauguwa, na dawa yangu ni hiyo

7   Mwanamke:
Kila mambo naelewa, yaliyo ndiyo na siyo
Si mwana wa kuhadawa, khaswa kwa unambiyayo
Japo wasema ni dawa, sikupi ngakuwa nayo
Na kama yatakuuwa, kufa kwa maradhi hayo

8   N'lishakupeleleza, hata n'kakubaini
Muda pesa ukijaza, humo mwako mfukoni
Huanza kujikimbiza, na kunigura nyumbani
Ngapita kukuuliza, uliko hujulikani

9   Ukisha kuzimaliza, kutolibakisha peni
Ndipo ndiya huongoza, hadi kwangu mlangoni
Na kuanza kujiliza, n'kuonee imani
Leo sitakusikiza, hata unganambiyani

Tit for Tat • 217

5 HE:
If only you knew how my heart feels
If only you fathomed how I am suffering
You wouldn't vex me and deprive me
You are the one who can solve this problem for me

6 I'm overwhelmed, it's no joke at all
I have no other place where I can satisfy this urge
And even you are well aware that I have no substitute
I'm ailing now, and the antidote is this

7 SHE:
I understand everything, what is right and what isn't
I'm not a child to be hoodwinked, especially about your proposition
Though you say it's an antidote, I'm not giving it to you, though I have it
If this ailment will kill, may you die from it

8 I've examined you until I know you fully
The moment you fill your pocket with money
You start running around and abandoning me at home
However much I ask, your whereabouts are unknown

9 Once you've depleted the money, not leaving even a penny
That's when you follow the path back to my door
And then you begin weeping, asking for my sympathy
Today I won't listen to you, whatever you tell me

218 • *Kutendana*

10   Mwanamume:
Amma um'badilika, hu tena kama zamani
Waniona nadhikika, hutaki kuniauni
Mwenziyo nataabika, hunionei imani?
Hufanyi hafarijika, hatowa pepo kitwani?

11   Waniwata nateseka, hali ni wako mwendani
Huwati hafarijika, haondosha tabu hini?
Jambo la chache dakika, bure nyonda wanikhini
Nipa nipate ondoka, nikwondokee matoni

12   Mwanamke:
E mtu mume ondoka, sin'etee kisirani
Hilo ambalo wataka, kwangu halipatikani
Ni bure utasumbuka, sikupi ungasemani
Usidhani ni dhihaka, nisemayo ni yakini

13   Usemayo ni hakika, si urongo aswilani
Ni kwa kuwa nnachoka, kukufanya muhisani
Ndipo n'kabadilika, hakutowa maanani
Mjinga 'meerevuka, mwerevu u mashakani

14   Pepo aliyekushika, mimi anikhusiyani?
Kumtowa ukitaka, nenda naye kilingeni
Mimi sitashughulika, kumpunga pepo duni
Tafuta pa kumpeka, pepo wako masikini

Tit for Tat · 219

10   HE:
For sure you have changed: you aren't like before
You see me in anguish, and you won't help me
I, your friend, am in distress, won't you feel pity for me?
Won't you comfort me so I can purge my mind of the devil?

11   You leave me suffering, yet I'm your intimate companion
You won't allow me to be comforted and banish this distress?
You're denying me, darling, something that takes just few minutes
Just give it to me and I'll soon be out of your way

12   SHE:
You, man, get out of here, don't bring me trouble
Whatever you want, you won't get it from me
You're wasting your time; I won't give it no matter what you say
Don't imagine it's a joke—I'm serious about this

13   What you say is certain, it is without a doubt true
I'm tired of being your benefactor
That's why I've changed; to me you are inconsequential
When the fool wakes up, the clever one is in trouble

14   The evil spirit that plagues you, how does it concern me?
If you want to purge yourself, go to the healer's clinic
I won't bother myself with purging a useless spirit
Search for a place to take your poor demon

220 • *Kutendana*

15   Kwa huyo unakopeka, pesa zako mwafulani
Na leo kuko geuka, nenda akakuauni
Apate kukutunuka, akuondowe tabuni
Sikubali kusumbuka, na faida siioni

16   Mwanamume:
Zako sijaziafiki, jawabu za ukaidi
Ungazijibu sichoki, na wala nyuma sirudi
Kwa sababu n'na dhiki, nami kwako sina budi
Ni kweli kwamba hutaki, au ni yako inadi?

17   Mwanamke:
Hata usipoafiki, huo si wangu muradi
Lako halitimiziki, leo Bwana hufanidi
Mzito hutukuliki, mno n'najitahidi
Kikwelikweli sitaki, ni heri kuko urudi

18   Mwanamume:
Tushakaa wewe nami, kwa siku tumbi nzima
Sijainuwa ulimi, kukueneza lawama
Baya kwako silisemi, la kukuudhi mtima
Bali hayano hamami, ya leo yannitoma

19   Mwenziyo nili sikomi, sichoki kukuandama
Mahaba hawa sipimi, hikupenda pasi kima
Leo unani na mimi, haja yangu kuninyima?
Mwenzangu huyatizami, twalotoka nayo nyuma?

15 The one to whom you often take your money
Today, turn around and go right there for help
So she can bail you out and rescue you from hardship
I can't agree to suffer for nothing

16 HE:
I don't agree with your stubborn response
And despite your answer, I'm not giving up
I'm in dire straits, and I'm bound to you
Is it true that you don't want this, or are you pretending?

17 SHE:
Even if you disagree, it's no concern of mine
Your wish is unattainable; today you won't succeed
I can't stand you—I tried very hard
I refuse absolutely, you'd better go back

18 HE:
We've stayed together, you and I, for countless days
I've never raised my voice to lambast you
I never speak ill of you, causing you heartache
But these words today have surely seared me

19 I, your friend, never gave up following you
I didn't measure my love, I loved you boundlessly
What problem do you have with me today, that you deny me my wish?
My friend, aren't you considering how far we've come together?

222 • *Kutendana*

20   Nyuma ungeangaliya, toka twalipoanzana
        'Ngekumbuka mazoweya, na wema tulotendana
        Ungejuwa ni vibaya, kunifanyiya khiyana
        Mwenzako nihurumiya, si vizuri kutesana

21   Siku zote twalokuwa, pamoja tukiwekana
        Nili sijakutunguwa, kukwelewa ewe nana
        Leo n'nafunukiwa, mahaba na mimi huna
        Tamaa itakuuwa, iwa na hadhari sana

22   Mwanamke:
        Wajuwa yake maani, ya la wema kutendana?
        Naapa n'na yakini, huyajuwi; hungenena
        Lau ungeyabaini, vilivyo haya maana
        Wallahi hungetamani, uso wako kwonekana

23   Fadhila ungekumbuka, hayano usingenena
        Kwako mno 'mesumbuka, tena kwa kila namna
        Nikawa nakueleka, kana kwamba mbwangu mwana
        Hayo usingetamka, lau wajuwa maana

24   Mato unnifumbuwa, ya wazi sasa yaona
        Hili kaa ukijuwa, kwako huba sina tena
        Mizizi n'shaing'owa, hayawezi shikamana
        Uwate kujisumbuwa, mi nawe tushatokana

Tit for Tat • 223

20 If only you'd look back to consider how we began
   You'd remember affection and the good we did for each other
   You'd know that doing me mischief is evil
   Feel pity for me, your friend; it's not right to vex one another

21 In all our past days together
   I hadn't examined you to understand you, woman
   Today it's dawned on me that you have no love for me
   Greed will kill you; you should be very careful

22 SHE:
   Do you know the meaning of treating each other well?
   I swear I'm sure you're clueless; otherwise you wouldn't speak
   If you recognized the meaning of your words
   I swear you wouldn't want your face to be seen

23 If you'd remembered those favors, you wouldn't have said what you did
   I've suffered for your sake in every way
   I carried you on my back as if you were my own child
   You wouldn't have said that if you knew its meaning

24 You've opened my eyes; I can now see clearly
   I want you to know this: no longer do I love you
   I've pulled up the roots—love can't take hold again
   Don't waste your time; it's over for you and me

224 • *Kutendana*

25 N'likuwa sina niya, nawe kukashifiyana
Kwani si yangu tabiya, maneno kutupiyana
Ni jambo nalitukiya, silipendi kuliona
Hishima kumuwekeya, kiumbe napenda sana

26 Lau hungenianziya, singesubutu kunena
Kwa kuwa 'metanguliya, kunipaka baya jina
N'nakuwa sina ndiya, ela ni kujibizana
Siwezi kuvumiliya, kutukanwa nikiona

27 Na ambayo 'takwambiya, sidhani waweza kana
Kwani ni mambo sawiya, urongo ndani hamuna
Urongo sitatumiya, kweli tupu 'tainena
Mwanamume huna haya, hunayo; kabisa huna

28 Mwanamume:
Sikuja kukwandamiya, kwamba tuje kuzozana
Na wala sikukujiya, tuje kuhutubiyana
Nililolifuwatiya, kitambo n'shalinena
Au unkusudiya, mwenzangu kunitukana?

29 Mwanamke:
Ungapandwa na hamaki, sitakuwata kusema
Lile ambalo ni haki, kulisema ni lazima
Endaye tokoza nyuki, pana budi kumuuma?
Mwenzangu huswarifiki, si leo n'nakupima

Tit for Tat • 225

25   I had no intention of trading insults
    Since it isn't my nature to engage in verbal duels —
    It's something I abhor, I hate to see it happen —
    Respecting others is important to me

26   If you hadn't started it all, I wouldn't have spoken
    Because you've started it, soiling my name
    I have no choice but to engage in the match
    I can't stand being insulted

27   And the things I'll tell you, I don't think you can deny them
    Because they're indeed true; there are no lies in them
    I won't speak lies; I'll speak nothing but the truth
    You have no shame, man, none—none at all

28   HE:
    I didn't seek you out so we could quarrel
    Nor did I come so we could make speeches to one other
    What brought me here, I've already said to you
    Or is it your aim to hurl insults at me?

29   SHE:
    You may be angry, but I won't stop speaking
    Concerning what is right, speaking is a must
    Is it a wonder when bees sting the person who disturbs them?
    My friend, you're hard to deal with; I took your measure before today

226 • *Kutendana*

30   Si kutaka kujinaki, kulipiga langu goma
    Na wala sifurahiki, kukusimbuliya njema
    Na kunyamaa ni dhiki, bure 'tajipa nakama
    Unamtokoza nyuki, ndipo sasa akuuma

31   Un'nitafuta baa, pasi kukuanza shari
    Kwa kuwa n'nakataa, haja yako kuikiri
    Wasema n'na tamaa, na kwamba nitahadhari
    Wajuwa wajihadaa, hili wajuwa vizuri

32   Hakika lin'niwasha, tamshi ulotamka
    Sitaweza kuipisha, ila ulonibandika
    Ndipo nami najibisha, japo hili sikutaka
    Na un'nilazimisha, ya zamani kukumbuka

33   Naanza kukukumbusha, kama ushaghafilika
    Ni habari 'takupasha, ambazo zin'tendeka
    Nawe 'kiweza jibisha, uonalo lajibika
    Au iwa kukanusha, ambalo lakanushika

34   Nali hijikalifisha, kwamba nipate kuweka
    Hifunguwa langu kasha, kila likihitajika
    Nikawa nikikulisha, pamoja na kukuvika
    Vipi wanambiya kisha, tamaa in'nishika?·

Tit for Tat • 227

30   I didn't want to brag, blowing my own horn
     And I won't delight in naming the good I've done you
     And keeping silent is agonizing; I'd be torturing myself for nothing
     You've disturbed the bee, and that's why it's stinging you now

31   You wish me evil without my provoking you
     Because I decline to fulfill your desire
     You claim I'm greedy and conceited
     You're deceiving yourself, of this you're well aware

32   The things you've said have hurt me for sure
     I can't overlook the taint you cast on me
     So I respond, even though I was unwilling
     And now you've forced me to remember the past

33   Let me remind you, if you have forgotten
     These are facts I'll recount, of what really happened
     As for you, if you can, counter with how you see it
     Or go ahead and discount whatever can be discounted

34   I used to trouble myself so I could keep you
     I'd open my money box whenever it was needed
     I'd feed you, and clothe you as well
     Why, then, do you claim I'm seized by greed?

228 • *Kutendana*

35 Nikikusitarehesha, kwa kila unachotaka
  Hikupa mema maisha, upate kufurahika
  Hikupa cha kukutosha, cha kula na cha kuweka
  Vipi wanambiya kisha, tamaa in'nishika?

36 Ulikuja un'kwisha, muwili untujuka
  Ulikuwa un'tusha, uso un'sawidika
  Umbo likawa latisha, kwa kukobokakoboka
  Vipi wanambiya kisha, tamaa in'nishika?

37 Mno ukisikitisha, kwangu miye hakuweka
  Hawa hikutononesha, nawe ukatononeka
  Ndipo hakunenepesha, ukawa wanang'anika
  Vipi wanambiya kisha, tamaa in'nishika?

38 Hawa 'kijibidiisha, dakika kila dakika
  Kila la kutangamsha, na furaha kukuweka
  N'kawa hikusemesha, usipate ungulika
  Vipi wanambiya kisha, tamaa in'nishika?

39 Mtu wewe hutanisha, zingapita nyingi nyaka
  Un'jisahaulisha, ulivyonipa mashaka?
  Mno un'nikutisha, tabu zisoelezeka
  Vipi wanambiya kisha, tamaa in'nishika?

Tit for Tat • 229

35   I used to bring you pleasure by providing all you desired
       I gave you a good life to make you happy
       I gave you enough for spending and for saving
       Why, then, do you claim I'm seized by greed?

36   When you came you were emaciated; your body was faded
       You weren't a pleasant sight, the way your face was crooked
       Your physique was frightful, disfigured all around
       Why, then, do you claim I'm seized by greed?

37   You were quite pathetic when I took you in
       I made you prosper to considerable prosperity
       Then I fattened you up until you shone
       Why, then, do you claim I'm seized by greed?

38   I worked hard, every single minute
       I brought you everything that makes you happy
       I'd often talk with you so you wouldn't be despondent
       Why, then, do you claim I'm seized by greed?

39   I'll never forget, even after many years
       Do you pretend to forget how you brought me anguish?
       You made me undergo suffering, indescribable hardship
       Why, then, do you claim I'm seized by greed?

230 • *Kutendana*

40   Pesa 'kinitumilisha, idadi isosemeka
     Matumizi yasokwisha, ungiyapo na kutoka
     Nazo kila zikikwisha, hikupa huku nateka
     Vipi wanambiya kisha, tamaa in'nishika?

41   Raha nkikuonesha, 'kikupa unachotaka
     Japo kwa kujidhikisha, upate kusitirika
     N'lilo 'kiliepusha, usipate azirika
     Vipi wanambiya kisha, tamaa in'nishika?

42   Hilo halikunichosha, siku moja sikuchoka
     Wala sikukimwa; hasha! Na wala kunung'unika
     Bali 'kinifurahisha, hiona wafurahika
     Vipi wanambiya kisha, tamaa in'nishika?

43   Mwanamume:
     Ewe wangu mliwaza, yote hayo yajiyani?
     Badili ya kunituza, na kunitowa tabuni
     Wazidi kuniumiza, na kunitoma moyoni
     Yaliyokwisha jilaza, wayaamshiya nini?

44   Mwanamke:
     Ndiwe uloyaamsha, mimi siye niletaka
     Siku tumbi zin'kwisha, 'mepata kuyatamka?
     Kidonda 'menitonesha, ndipo nami n'karuka
     Kwamba 'menikokomosha, pana budi kutapika?

Tit for Tat • 231

40   You'd ask me for money, incalculable amounts
You had endless expenses as you entered and exited
And whenever you were broke again, I'd smile and give you more
Why, then, do you claim I'm seized by greed?

41   I used to give you leisure, granting all your wishes
Though it meant suffering for me, so that you'd be protected
I wanted only to ensure that you remained undisgraced
Why, then, do you claim I'm seized by greed?

42   That didn't tire me out, not even one day did I tire
And I wasn't fed up, not at all! Nor did I whine
Instead I'd be happy if you were delighted
Why, then, do you claim I'm seized by greed?

43   HE:
My dear comforter, what is the point of all this?
Instead of comforting me and rescuing me from distress
You exacerbate my pain and stab me in the heart
Why do you awaken what was sleeping?

44   SHE:
You're the one who's awakened things; it's not I who wanted that
Many days have passed, but did I mention these matters?
You've opened my wound—that's why I leaped up
When you've pressed me hard, how do you expect me not to vomit?

232 • *Kutendana*

45 Ilipoanza kunisha, akiba nilokiweka
Haanza kuviswafisha, vyangu vya kuthaminika
Mpaka mwisho langu kasha, likawa linkauka
Vipi wanambiya kisha, tamaa innishika?

46 Vyombo vya thamani tosha, rahani nikaviweka
Kimoja sikubakisha, dhahabu na kadhalika
Vyote n'kavisozesha, upate kusitirika
Vipi wanambiya kisha, tamaa in'nishika?

47 Rahani 'kiviwekesha, bila kuwa na hakika
Itakayoniwezesha, kuvikombowa hitaka
Piya nikajasirisha, haidhuru hitamka
Vipi wanambiya kisha, tamaa in'nishika?

48 Na hivyo vilipokwisha, vikawa vishasozeka
Hayo hayakunitosha, mengine n'kajitweka
Hangiliya kukopesha, kwa n'naoaminika
Vipi wanambiya kisha, tamaa in'nishika?

49 Hapo hajirafikisha, kwa walio na maduka
Kwao hajiaminisha, wasinitiliye shaka
Wakawa wanikopesha, kila n'nachokitaka
Vipi wanambiya kisha, tamaa in'nishika?

Tit for Tat • 233

45   When it began to be depleted, the savings I'd created
       I started cleaning out all my valuable things
       Eventually my treasure box emptied
       Why, then, do you claim I'm seized by greed?

46   I pawned all my valuable items
       I didn't leave any, not gold or anything
       I let them all be lost so you'd be protected
       Why, then, do you claim I'm seized by greed?

47   I mortgaged them, without being too sure
       What would enable me to redeem them when I wished
       I encouraged myself: it's no big deal, I said
       Why, then, do you claim I'm seized by greed?

48   And when those things were gone, having been squandered
       That wasn't all; I carried more burdens
       I began borrowing, as people trusted me
       Why, then, do you claim I'm seized by greed?

49   I befriended the shop owners
       I gained their trust so they wouldn't doubt me
       They sold me everything I wanted on credit
       Why, then, do you claim I'm seized by greed?

234 • *Kutendana*

50   Kwa kucha kuwajulisha, deni hazitolipika
Nikawa nabadilisha, duka baada ya duka
Kote n'kajizungusha, hadi yakamalizika
Vipi wanambiya kisha, tamaa in'nishika?

51   Deni zikanikondesha, kwa zilivyonizunguka
Afiya yangu ikesha, na muwili kunyauka
Zikawa zanikosesha, usingizi ngautaka
Vipi wanambiya kisha, tamaa in'nishika?

52   Wakawa wakinitisha, pesa zao wazitaka
Sizidi kuchelewesha, wazitaka kwa haraka
Au watanifikisha, mbele kwenye mashitaka
Vipi wanambiya kisha, tamaa in'nishika?

53   Kwa kutaka kuy'ondosha, japo nusu ya mashaka
Nguo zangu hafungasha, niuze za kuuzika
Nipate kujiepusha, na deni zilonifika
Vipi wanambiya kisha, tamaa in'nishika?

54   Nguo sikuzibakisha, ela zisotamanika
N'kawa n'kijivisha, nguo zilizotatuka
Haya zikinionyesha, nde hishindwa kutoka
Kisha baada ya kwisha, "tamaa in'kushika"!

Tit for Tat • 235

50 In fear of revealing to them that the debts wouldn't be paid
I'd change from one shop to another
I went from one to another till no shop was left
Why, then, do you claim I'm seized by greed?

51 The debts that engulfed me made me thin
My health deteriorated, and my body became emaciated
I lost my sleep, however much I sought it
Why, then, do you claim I'm seized by greed?

52 They began threatening me as they demanded their money
That I shouldn't delay any longer—they wanted it fast
Or else they would drag me before the courts
Why, then, do you claim I'm seized by greed?

53 In trying to reduce my distress at least by half
I packed my clothes and sold them off
To rescue myself from the crippling debts
Why, then, do you claim I'm seized by greed?

54 I didn't spare any clothes except the unattractive ones
I started wearing tattered garments
I felt so ashamed, I could no longer go out —
Then you claim, "You're seized by greed"!

236 • *Kutendana*

55   Amma yan'nitekesha, hayo uloyatamka
Kwisha kunikorofisha, n'kawa ndaa nanuka
Leo wajisimamisha, na kuanza kupayuka
Ati wanihadharisha, tamaa in'nishika

Maelezo

56   Tangu hapo mwanamke, akisema kwa ukali
Na rangi ya uso wake, ikawa im'badili
Mwili umtetemeke, mkali ja pilipili
Kwa sababu ya mwenzake, alivyo kumfidhuli

57   Ukali ulimzidi, palipotajwa tamaa
Na khaswa nyuma 'kirudi, kwa maisha walokaa
Hapo akaona hadi, mwanamume ajifaa
Ndipo akakosa budi, maudhiko kumjaa

58   Na kwa hakika laudhi, tamko la huyo Bwana
Lavundiya mtu hadhi, kwa ajuwaye maana
Ni yupi mwenye kuridhi, mtu aje mtukana?
Kisha hayo ayaridhi, bila ya kujibizana?

59   Mwanamume ali tuli, Bibi alipokinena
Ameituza akili, asikiza vyema sana
Huku nyuso zao mbili, zali zin'lekeyana
Bwana asikiza kweli, ambayo asema nana

Tit for Tat • 237

55 What you said really tickles me
    After messing things up for me so I became abject
    You stand here today and start spouting nonsense
    Why, then, do you claim I'm seized by greed?

Explanation

56 From the very outset, the woman spoke in bitterness
    And the color of her face was transformed
    Her body was shaking, she was burning like pepper
    Because of how her partner had mistreated her

57 She became more embittered when greed was mentioned
    And especially after looking back at the life they'd lived
    It dawned on her that the man was selfish
    That's why she had no choice but to be infuriated

58 The man's utterance was certainly hurtful
    It's degrading to the person who understands its meaning
    Who will consent to being taunted —
    And to withstand all that, without answering back?

59 The man was mum as the woman spoke
    His mind was calm as he listened quite attentively
    While they stood face to face
    The man was listening to what she said

238 • *Kutendana*

60   Mwanamume alidhani, ni maneno ya dhihaka
Mwanzo hakuyaamini, Bibi alokitamka
Hakujuwa Mwafulani, kwamba mambo 'megeuka
'Kiona kana zamani, 'tapata anachotaka

61   Hakuiona sababu, ya bibiye kumnyima
Itakwendaje muhibu, leo awe atagoma?
Hajapata kujaribu, maisha yetu mazima
Akawaza taratibu, na kwenye moyo kusema

62   Hakuweza kukumbuka, japokuwa siku moja
Ambayo 'mehangaika, kuipata yake haja
Muda alipokitaka, hakuwa 'kipawa hoja
'Kitimiziwa haraka, bila ya kwambiwa ngoja

63   Alipo kufunukiwa, dafule halifuliki
Katakata 'mekatawa, hataki Bibi hataki
'Kazidi mnyonge kuwa, maguu hayamshiki
Yu mgonjwa auguwa, na mwenye twiba hataki

64   Akija akiyapima, aloambiwa na Mwana
Vyema akayatizama, kwa marefu na mapana
Bibi kweli meisema, urongo ndani hamuna
Toka mwanzo hadi tamma, kweli inaandamana

Tit for Tat • 239

60 The man supposed it was all just a joke
At first, he didn't believe what the woman said
He had no clue, Mr. So-and-So, that things had changed
He thought, as always, he'd get what he wanted

61 He didn't see the reason for the woman's denying him
How come my love has today gone on strike?
She hasn't done this before, in our whole lives
He thought quietly and spoke in his heart

62 He didn't remember even a single day
When he'd struggled to fulfill his desire
When he wanted something, he'd be given it without a hassle
He'd be served without being told to wait

63 When he realized he wouldn't succeed
She has stood her ground, the lady won't budge
He became feeble; his legs became weak
He's ailing, and the one with the cure has refused him

64 When he weighed what the woman told him
He examined it carefully, the length and breadth,
The lady had spoken the truth, there was no lie there
From start to finish, there was only truth

240 • *Kutendana*

65 Mate yakamkauka, akakosa la kunena
Angaa la kujibika, akatafuta hakuna
Hasira zikamshika, akakasirika sana
Moyoni akatamka: *leo n'napatikana!*

66 Kwenenda pasi kujibu, maneno aloambiwa
Akaona kubwa tabu, japo yote ni ya sawa
Kuondoka ni aibu, bila jawabu kutowa
Kwamba limpe jawabu, bongo akalisumbuwa

67 Bongo likamfunziya, maneno ya kujibisha
Ukavu akajitiya, na mato kuyakausha
Akajikosesha haya, tembe hakuzibakisha
Bibi akamlekeya, hayano akampasha

68 Mwanamume:
Vyema n'nayasikiya, yote uliyoyanena
Orodha 'menipangiya, ya mambo kila namna
Yote 'menihisabiya, ulobakisha hakuna
Ni kweli 'menifanyiya, moja siwezi likana

69 Basi kwa kutenda wema, ndiyo sasa wauimba?
Hayo usingeyasema, ela kwamba wajigamba
Sikuja n'kasimama, mlango wa yako nyumba
Kama 'masikini mama', na kuanza kukuomba

Tit for Tat • 241

65 His mouth dried up, he had nothing to say
He looked for a response and found none
His anger rose, he became very angry
He said in his heart: *today I'm cornered!*

66 To go along without responding to the words spoken to him
He found difficult—though all the words were correct
It's shameful to walk away without answering
He racked his brain in search of an answer

67 His brain taught him words to say in response
He gathered his nerve and fixed his eyes firmly on her
He did away with shame, every last bit of it
He approached the woman and had this to say

68 HE:
I've heard you loud and clear, everything you said
You've presented a list, items of all sorts
You've enumerated them, sparing none
It's true you did all that for me; I can't deny it

69 So then, because you did good, you have to sing about it now?
You wouldn't say that except in bragging
I didn't come to the door of your house
Like a beggar and beg you for help

242 • Kutendana

70   Bure silete utesi, kwa hayo uyanenayo
      Sikukushika kikosi, unitimiziye hayo
      Ni yako mwenye nafusi, na pendo la wako moyo
      Mayowe nda nini basi, hayo unipipigiyayo?

71   Mwanamke:
      Katika uhai wangu, sijapata kumuona
      Mwenginewe mlimwengu, ambaye fadhila hana
      Wewe ndiye mosi kwangu, wala sitaona tena
      Naapa haki ya M'ngu! Kamawe sitamuona

72   Ni kweli hukunijiya, ukaomba n'kufae
      Ni kweli hikufanyiya, kwa hiyari yangu mie
      Na wewe ukipokeya, kusudi tumbo lijae
      Nilipo hikwegesheya, kwa nini usikatae?

      Maelezo

73   Dume hivyo kusikiya, Bibi aloyatamka
      'Kaona sana vibaya, kooni yalimfika
      Uso ukangiya haya, tini akauwinika
      Akatamani kuliya, kwa aibu kumfika

74   Akangiwa na kidaka, mdomo kutofunguwa
      Moyo ukampasuka, vipandepande ukawa
      Akadangana hakika, kwa jawabu alopawa
      Amma aliaibika, mpenda kuegeshewa

Tit for Tat • 243

70   Don't needlessly cause a quarrel with the words you say
I didn't grab you at the neck, forcing you to do my wish
It was out of your own volition and your own heart's choice
What, then, is this din you're making?

71   SHE:
In all my life I have never seen
Any other person who is such an ingrate
You are the very first one, neither shall I ever see another
I swear to God! I've never seen someone like you

72   True, you never came to me begging me for help
True, I did what I did out of my own choice
And you received it, making your tummy full
When I pushed it towards you, why didn't you decline?

Explanation

73   When the man heard what the woman said
He felt terrible, terrible beyond compare
He was filled with shame and couldn't show his face
He felt like weeping out of shame

74   He was struck dumb; he couldn't open his mouth
His heart was broken into many pieces
He felt dazed because of the response he got
He was surely ashamed, this man who liked being served

244 • *Kutendana*

75 Vyema mupate elewa, dume lilivyohizika
Ni kama alovuliwa, nguo zikamuanguka
Yu tuputupu akawa, na hali anainuka
"...Huotama" twaambiwa, bali ye aliinuka

76 Ikamjiya akili, ya kubadili msemo
Akaona afadhali, ni kuipiga horomo
Kwani wake ufidhuli, un'shatiwa kikomo
Ili kusudi anali, akatengeza mdomo

77 Kumrai akaanza, na huku akimsifu
Mno akamtukuza, kwa kila la utukufu
Ulingoni kamkweza, juu palipo parefu
Kusudi apate weza, kupawa kwa ukundufu

78 Si kwamba 'kimdanganya, la! Sivyo! Hata nusu
Maradhi yalimpenya, akawa yu mahabusu
Alobakisha kufanya, ni maguu kumbusu
Moyo asingeukanya, 'ngejitiya hata kisu

79 Halafu akangiliya, mno kujisikitisha
Lau ungemsikiya, alivyo 'kijisemesha
Ungemsikitikiya, sikitiko lisokwisha
Naye akiyatiliya, mahanjamu ya kutosha

Tit for Tat • 245

75 You should understand well how the man was shamed
It was as if he'd been undressed, his clothes falling right off him
Like being naked while standing up straight
"A person crouches" then, we're told, but he remained standing

76 The thought crossed his mind to change his speech
He decided it was better to let the matter rest awhile
Because of his arrogance, he'd been crushed
To succeed in getting what he wanted, he readied his mouth

77 He began persuading her and praising her
He glorified her with all kinds of honor
He put her on a pedestal, hoisting her really high
To get whatever he could, to be given it willingly

78 He wasn't lying to her, not at all!
Sickness pierced him, making him a prisoner
What was left to do was to kiss her feet
Had he not checked himself, he would even have stabbed himself

79 Then he entered the phase of feeling too much self-pity
If you'd heard the way he was speaking
You'd have pitied him with endless pity
He made his delivery very expressive

246 • *Kutendana*

80   Hakubakisha kusema, kila la kutamkika
Na hapo akalalama, mwisho wa kulalamika
Kumweleza mwana-mama, tabu iliyomfika
Amuonee huruma, ampe analotaka

81   Akasema: "'Mejaribu, kutafuta usingizi
Kusudi hii adhabu, ngaa inipe pumzi
Bali ikawa ni tabu, kufumbika langu ozi
Nipoza wangu tabibu, ni mgonjwa sijiwezi"

82   Mwanamume:
'Mejaribu kila ndiya, halikutaka fumbika
Kila nikiliambiya, yangu halikuyataka
Mwenzangu nisaidiya, siniwate hateseka
Tabu yangu yakweleya, sivyo n'livyoshikika

83   N'nagaagaa mno, kitanda changu shahidi
Lau chasema maneno, ningefanya jitihadi
N'kakileta hapano, kikueleze zaidi
N'ondosheya tabu hino, nana usinikaidi

84   N'nahisabu boriti, moja baada ya moja
Kwamba nivute wakati, usingizi kuungoja
Sikuona tafauti, wala ishara ya kuja
Yomi n'siye bahati, n'saidiya mbeja

Tit for Tat • 247

80   He didn't spare a word that needed to be spoken
Then he lamented with much lamentation
Explaining to the woman how he had suffered
So she could sympathize and grant him his wish

81   He said: "I've tried to get some sleep
So I could gain some relief from the agony
Yet it was difficult to close my eyes
Cure me, my medic, I'm ailing very badly"

82   HE:
I've tried every way; my eyes didn't want to close
Each time I told them, they refused to heed
Help me, my friend; don't abandon me in my suffering
You know my hardship and how I'm overwhelmed

83   I'm always tossing in my bed, my bed is my witness
If only it could speak, I'd have been sure
To bring it right here so it could tell you more
Remove this hardship for me, my lady, don't refuse

84   I keep counting the rafters one after another
To occupy myself as I wait for sleep
But I find no difference, no sign of its coming
I'm the luckless one; help me, handsome woman

248 • *Kutendana*

85 La kutenda n'kakosa, 'ngetendani? Nambiya
Aseme kwa kugigisa, na sauti ya kuliya
Na mato kuyapepesa, yakawa kutotuliya
Shingo utadhani sasa, tini itaangukiya

86 "Ela," akazidi sema, "wewe kukufikiriya
Hainuka hasimama, na kuiandama ndiya
N'liona ni lazima, mwenzangu kukwandamiya
Basi huoni huruma, langu ukakubaliya?

87 Itizame inyeshavyo, hebu itizame mvuwa
Hisi kitetemeshavyo, kibaridi cha kuuwa
Piya haja vivyo hivyo, kwa kuwa nimelemewa
Basi nana hivi ndivyo, nenende bila kupawa?"

Maelezo

88 Una mambo ukosefu, ukitokusubiriwa
Hupa mtu kuwa pofu, kadhalika zuzu kuwa
Akajiona yu dufu, hafai kuthaminiwa
Akawa mtu dhaifu, hajiwezi 'ngaonewa

89 Na hupa mtu kusema, yasiyofaa kusemwa
Za upuuzi kalima, zake na za kuazimwa
Akaziona ni njema, kwamba zafaa ungamwa
Na kutojali hishima, yu radhi awe mtumwa

Tit for Tat • 249

85   There's nothing I could do, what could I have done? Tell me
He said while quaking, with a mournful voice
And blinking eyes; his eyes were restless
And if you saw his neck, you'd expect it to collapse

86   "Yet"—he continued speaking—"when I thought about you
I stood up straight and began my journey
For me it's a compulsion to come to you
So don't you sympathize, and won't you grant my wish?

87   Look at how it's raining, look at the rain
Feel how it makes one shake, the fatal chill
Despite that I came, because I'm overwhelmed
So, lady, is it right that I should go without receiving anything?"

Explanation

88   In conditions of deprivation, and when patience runs out
This makes a person blind, and a simpleton as well
He sees himself as valueless, absolutely worthless
He becomes weak and completely helpless

89   And it makes a person say unsuitable things
He makes foolish remarks, his own and borrowed ones
He views them as good, as needing to be spoken
Throwing honor to the wind, he's ready to be a slave

250 • *Kutendana*

90   Bibi kusikiya haya, akalianguwa teko
       Teko akamtekeya, lile lile la kimeko
       Lililojaa kinaya, na sitihizai fuko
       Ni mfano kumwambiya: kwangu mimi huna lako

91   Mwanamke:
       M'ngu akuzidishiye, uhodari wa uneni
       Ili ukusaidiye, kwa maisha ya mbeleni
       Elakini kwangu miye, hauna tena thamani
       Hata lipi unambiye, kweli yake siioni

92   Licha maneno matamu, ambayo waniambiya
       Hata matozi ya damu, lau hayo utaliya
       Hayawezi n'lazimu, wewe kukuhurumiya
       Uombe wako ugumu, upate kusaidiya

93   N'nani aliyeanza, kufanya mwende mjinga?
       Si wewe? Hebu nambiza, au urongo natunga?
       'Mepata ulichoweza, nacho ushakibananga
       Basi sikae 'kiwaza, kwamba kwangu utaunga

Maelezo

94   *Ni kama jiwe moyowe, mgumu kulainika*
       Hata lipi uambiwe, hauwi kubadilika
       Afadhali hilo jiwe, lipondwapo hupondeka
       Mwanamume ki mwenyewe, moyoni akatamka

90   When the woman heard this, she burst into laughter
       She laughed at him uproariously
       Laughter full of irony and endless ridicule
       It was the same as saying: with me you stand no chance

91   SHE:
       May God increase your powers of eloquence
       That they may help you in your future life
       But as far as I'm concerned, you have no more value
       No matter what you tell me, I can't believe you

92   Despite the sweet words you've spoken to me
       Even if you shed tears of blood
       That won't make me sympathize with you
       Ask your stinginess to help you

93   Who was first to make the other partner a fool?
       Wasn't it you? Tell me, please, or am I lying?
       You got what you wanted, and you've squandered it
       So stop imagining that you'll get more from me

       Explanation

94   *Her heart is like a rock: it can never be softened*
       No matter what you tell it, that heart won't change
       In fact a rock is much better, because if you pound it breaks
       The man spoke to himself, silently in his heart

252 • *Kutendana*

95   Tamaa hakuikata, akazidi bembeleza
Akasema "Yalopita, ni bora kuyanyamaza
Kuliko kuyafuwata, na kisasi kulipiza
Yalopita yashapita, si vyema kuyaregeza"

96   Mwanamume:
Nayakubali makosa, niswamehe wangu nyonda
Nayatubu hivi sasa, kwa ambavyo nakupenda
Kwa hakika n'nakosa, uaminifu kuvunda
Nadhani hutaniwasa, mswamaha kuuonda

97   Mwenziyo radhi niwiya, nipa nafasi nyengine
Nitakudhihirishiya, wewe mwenyewe uwone
Kwamba sitaendeleya, kutenda baya jengine
Kamwe sitakutendeya, tuketi tusikizane

98   Ni radhi kukufanyiya, lolote ulisemalo
Piya kukutimiziya, kila lile utakalo
Haya na mfano haya, sitakataa liwalo
Na wewe niangaliya, sendi kinyume na hilo

99   Kumbuka tulivyokuwa, tukipendana zamani
Piya sasa kwangu iwa, ulivyokuwa mwanzoni
Natusiyatiye dowa, mahaba yetu mwendani
Ni mgonjwa niaguwa, nioneleya imani

95   Yet he didn't give up; he continued wooing her
     He said, "As for the past, it's better to keep quiet about it
     Than to bring it up and seek revenge
     The past has gone by, it's no good bringing it back"

96   HE:
     I admit my mistakes, pardon me, my love
     I repent right now, because I love you
     I have truly erred in betraying your trust
     I hope you won't deny me the chance to taste forgiveness

97   Forgive me, my friend, give me another chance
     I will prove to you, you'll see for yourself
     That I won't ever again do anything bad
     Never shall I do you wrong, let's be together in harmony

98   I'm ready to do for you anything you say
     And also to fulfill for you anything you wish
     I won't decline to do so, whatever it may be
     And just you watch, I won't do otherwise

99   Remember how we were in love long ago
     Let it be with me now the way you were in the beginning
     Let's not blemish our love, my dear
     I'm ailing badly; feel pity for me

254 • *Kutendana*

100 Mwanamke:
Moyoni mwako nitowa, unifute n'siwemo
Mahaba n'shayatuwa, moyoni mwangu hayamo
Siwi wala sitakuwa, kama zamani; horomo!
Niwapo hivyo 'takuwa, najitiya kwenye shimo

101 Sasa nihisabu kwamba, n'shakufa kwako wewe
Na kaburi ukatimba, nimo ndani nifukiwe
Siwe na haja kuomba, kurudiyana mi nawe
Kama wawaza kuumba, umba mimi mwenginewe

102 Mimi nawe tuagane, wenende huko wendako
Wende kwa huyo mwengine, abebe mahaba yako
Asaa musikizane, ukapata farijiko
Sitakubeba vyengine, n'shafunguwa mbeleko

103 Labda si mimi tena, hili fahamu ujuwe
Sinite kwa langu jina, hirudiyana mi nawe
Na lau utaniona, mauti yanitukuwe
Kurudi huna namna, bure usijizuzuwe

Maelezo

104 Kila ye akiambiwa, *wimbo huo siuwimbe*
Yeye hujibu ya kuwa, *n'taubakiza tembe*
Hana la kumtopowa, ela huba za mpambe
Ndwee hii kuuguwa, binadamu usiombe

Tit for Tat · 255

100   SHE:
     Remove me from your heart, erase me completely
     I'm done with love—there's no room for it in my heart
     I am not, and will not be, like before; that's impossible!
     Becoming so would be like burying myself in a hole

101   Now consider me dead to you
     And you've dug the grave; I lie in it buried
     There's no need to beseech me to be together with you again
     If you can create, create another me

102   Let's bid each other farewell, and you go your own way
     Go to that other woman, and let her bear your love's burden
     Perhaps you'll get along well with her, you'll find comfort there
     I won't carry you farther, I've untied the knot

103   Perhaps I'm not me anymore; this you need to know
     Don't call me by name if we get back together
     And if you see me, may death take me away
     There's no way you can come back; don't waste your time

Explanation

104   Each time he is told, *don't sing this song*
     This is how he responds: *I will sing a tiny bit of it*
     Nothing can satiate him except the woman's love
     No one should pray for this kind of ailment

256 • *Kutendana*

105   Juu ya jawabu hizo, si kwamba aliondoka
      Hakutoshelezwa nazo, hakuona 'mejibika
      Ile ile yakwe nguzo, akazidi kuishika
      Mfano wa hamnazo, akarudi kuropoka

106   Maneno yayo kwa yayo, akawa kuyarudiya
      Tokeya maneno hayo, mtu 'kiona nda ndiya
      Hata mwisho masikiyo, yakachoshwa kusikiya
      Mwanamume ana payo, hawezi kujizuwiya

107   Akamtajiya pesa, mwanamume kazitaja
      Kwamba ati toka sasa, na siku ambazo zaja
      Hatakuwa akikosa, kumtimiziya haja
      Tena kila la anasa, atampa bila hoja

108   Mwanamume:
      Zozote uzitakazo, 'takuwa radhi kutowa
      Zote 'tazokuwanazo, kibindoni 'tafunguwa
      Kila muda hipatazo, peni sitalinyotowa
      Kwako nitakuja nazo, sitangoja kuambiwa

109   Mwanamke:
      Ituze yako akili, ituze kama unayo
      Si mali Bwana si mali, niliyo na haja nayo
      Mahaba yangu ni ghali, na bei yake si hiyo
      Kwangu tena huyanali, hata kwa bei iwayo

Tit for Tat • 257

105   Despite those answers, he didn't leave
       He wasn't convinced; he didn't feel he had been answered
       He stuck to his guns and refused to budge
       Like one who has lost his mind, he went back to speaking nonsense

106   He kept repeating those very same words
       In the beginning those words seemed to make sense
       Until the ears in the end became tired of hearing them
       The man is a chatterbox; he couldn't stop himself

107   He mentioned money to her, the man mentioned money
       That from then, and for all the days ahead
       He would never fail to meet her needs
       Also, he would readily give her every sort of leisure

108   HE:
       Anything you want, I'll be glad to give you
       Everything that I have, I'll open my purse
       Every time I get money, I won't pinch a penny
       I'll come to you with all of it; I won't wait to be told

109   SHE:
       Calm your mind, calm it if you have it
       It isn't wealth, Mister, it isn't wealth that I want
       My love is costly, and that isn't its price
       You won't buy it from me for any price

258 • *Kutendana*

110   Hata lau yangekuwa, kwa pesa yanunulika
Na kwamba wewe ukawa, kuyanunuwa wataka
Yasingelinunuliwa, na mtu wewe hakika
Kwani 'ngeliradhiwa, kaburini kuyazika

Maelezo

111   Zilikuwa zishapita, saa tano za usiku
Ni hapo alipokata, shauri la kuja huku
Dirisha akaligota, Ku! Ku! Ku! Ku! Ku! Ku! Ku! Ku!
Ili Bibiye kumwita, kwa kubwa mno shauku

112   Bibi ali mejinyosha, kitanda cha ukumbini
Taa aliirudisha, utambi ukawa tini
Kusudi kuliepusha, joto lisizidi ndani
Na piya halikutosha, kipepeo mkononi

113   Manukato muwilini, vyema yalifukizika
Ni nyudi za Arabuni, ambari na kadhalika
Ambao wavibaini, wajuwa vinavyonuka
Msojuwa ulizani, kwa ambao vyatumika

114   Isitoshe; muwilini, leso mbili 'mejivika
Mpya ambazo dukani, leo leo zin'toka
Nazo piya chetezoni, alikuwa 'meziweka
Zafurahisha puani, harufu njema zanuka

Even if it could be bought with money
And it happened that you wanted to buy it
It couldn't be bought by you, man, that's for sure
I'd prefer to bury it in the grave

Explanation

111 The night had worn on: it was well past eleven
That's when he decided to come this way
He knocked at the window, Ku! Ku! Ku! Ku!
And called to the Lady with tremendous enthusiasm

112 The Lady was in the living room, stretched out on the bed
She had lowered the wick on the lantern
To prevent its growing too hot inside
And in addition to that, she fanned herself

113 Her body was exuding a sweet-smelling fragrance
Arabian incense, ambergris, so forth and so on
All scents known by those who know their perfumes
Those of you who don't know, ask those who use them

114 Moreover, around her body, she had wrapped two wrappers
Brand-new wrappers, just come today from the shop
These she had put in the censer as well
They were a delight to the nose, sweet-smelling items

260 • *Kutendana*

115   'Kimtizama kitwani, nyele zilivyotanika
      Uzitizame na pini, jinsi alivyotomeka
      Na shada la asumini, alivyo kulipatika
      Lazima utatamani, ngaa upate zishika

116   Basi uje na shingoni, shingo mfano ya ninga
      Ni mjuzi kwa yakini, huyo aliyeitonga
      Ukitizame kidani, shingoni alojifunga
      Sijuwi ni fundi gani, ambaye alikitunga

117   Liwa jembamba usoni, alikuwa am'paka
      Akatinda na sikini, vizuri ikatindika
      Nacho kijembe nyushini, hakikusahaulika
      Umwonapo utadhani, si mja ni malaika

118   Na humo mwake matoni, ni wanda ameupaka
      Ule wanda wa Mangani, mno unaosifika
      Namo mwake midomoni, wekundu un'zunguka
      Si wa rangi Ulayani, ni mdaa kutumika

119   Vya dhahabu viungoni, vyombo am'vipambiza
      Kipini kimo puwani, kilipo kimpendeza
      Vipuli masikiyoni, vyandani pete ongeza
      Na bangili mikononi, kiyasi hakuzijaza

Tit for Tat • 261

115 If you saw her head, how she had combed her hair
  If you saw her hairpins, how they had been inserted
  And the wreath of jasmine, how she had arranged it
  You'd surely desire to touch her hair

116 Then come to the neck, like the neck of a green pigeon
  He's an expert indeed, the one who curved it
  If you look at the necklace that dangles on her neck
  I don't know which genius put it all together

117 To her face she'd applied a thin layer of sandalwood
  She parted her hair, and it is expertly parted
  Also, how she trimmed her brows, it's unforgettable
  If you saw her you'd think she is an angel, not human

118 And around her eyes she has applied liner
  Arabian eyeliner, that very famous kind
  And on her lips, the color red all around
  Not the color from Europe, but from the *mdaa*[4] plant

119 And with golden items she has adorned herself
  A stud in her nose, gorgeous in its place
  Earrings in her ears, plus rings on her fingers
  Bangles on her hands, just enough, for she didn't overdo it

---

4. *Mdaa* is a plant that produces a black dye (and that may also be used as a toothbrush). —*Ed.*

262 • *Kutendana*

120 Kwa ufupi hakubaki, kwa mapambo kujiunda
Mpita hiyo twariki, angataka kujipinda
Moyo utataharaki, uwe ni mbiyo kumwenda
Na bila shaka ashiki, zitazidi kumpanda

121 Ndipo hapo kusikiya, dirishale la chumbani
Hakuwa yakimweleya, aligotaye ni nani
Papale akabakiya, hakutukutika sini
Wala kusema ngojeya, au hivyo mathalani

122 Alipoona kwazidi, kugogotwa dirishani
Ikawa itambidi, kumuuliza n'nani
Agotaye kwa juhudi, huyuno ni mtu gani?
Jawabu haikurudi, ya kusema ni fulani

123 Basi alipoinuka, kwenenda kujioneya
Jito likamdirika, aliyemfahamiya
Baada ya shaka shaka, na vyema kutunguliya
Akaipata hakika, ndiye alemdhaniya

124 Kabla kumuuliza, aseme alilojiya
Naye kabla kuweza, kunena alofwatiya
Kila mtu akaganza, mwenziwe kumngojeya
Na kila mato kuanza, yenze kuyakodoleya

Tit for Tat • 263

120   In short, there was no adornment with which she didn't adorn herself
Any passerby on the road would turn to look
Excitement would seize his heart, making it beat fast
And no doubt lust would afflict him

121   That is when she heard her bedroom window
She couldn't make out who was knocking
She remained still and didn't move an inch
Not even saying wait, or something like that

122   When she realized that the knocking continued
She was forced to ask, who is it?
Knocking ceaselessly, who this person?
There was no response saying this is so-and-so

123   So when she rose to go and look
Her eye saw at once a person she knew
After some doubting, and looking intently
She became sure he was the one she thought

124   Before her asking him what had brought him
And before his saying why he had come
Each one was silent, waiting for the other
Each pair of eyes gazing at the other

264 • Kutendana

125   Lilompa kungojeya, Bibi 'kawa kutonena
      Alistaajabiya, Bwana kujizusha tena
      Nyezi nyingi zimesiya, tangu walipokutana
      Aligura hata ndiya, hakuwa 'kionekana

126   Akatafuta ni lipi, leo lilomrudisha?
      Au yuwatoka wapi, hapo akajipitisha?
      Na siku zote yu kupi, mbona alijihamisha?
      Leo yankwenda vipi, kuja kwake akabisha?

127   Bibi alivyo 'mepanga, ndani mwa akili yake
      Alitaka kulifunga, hilino dirisha lake
      Kusudi mwenye kugonga, hapo pake aondoke
      Ende pasi na kuzinga, atokomee na zake

128   Naye mume saa hiyo, akaona ni lazima
      Haja yake alonayo, asifite kuisema
      Aukaze wake moyo, amweleze mwana-mama
      Na tumbi visingiziyo, vilivyompa kuhama

129   Ndipo hapo mvutano, ulipoanza mwanzowe
      Utadhani mashindano, ya malenga mfanowe
      Kila atowaye neno, 'kijibiwa na mwenziwe
      Ukawa ule mfano, wa *Twaa* na *Twaa wewe*

Tit for Tat • 265

125   What made the woman wait and remain speechless
       Was her shock at seeing the man emerge again
       It had been many months since they'd last met
       He'd been gone a long time and hadn't been seen

126   She wondered, today what is it that brought him back?
       Or where is he coming from, that he would pass by here?
       And where was he, why did he disappear?
       What has happened today that he would come knocking?

127   What the Lady planned in her mind
       Was to close it, this her window
       So the person knocking would leave his post
       So he'd go roaming away and get out of sight

128   As for the man, he felt a compulsion
       Not to hide the need that plagued him
       He would embolden himself to explain to the Lady
       And offer his many excuses for disappearing

129   There and then a tussle began
       You'd think it was a contest between poets
       Each speaker being answered by the other
       In the pattern of *Take that* and *Take that*

266 • Kutendana

130 Hebu msomaji wangu, ulipofika simama
Kaa tupige mafungu, haya mambo kuyapima
Tujuwe tamu na tungu, la kumiza na kutema
Ukiyakubali yangu, kidogo turudi nyuma

131 Kwamba upate fahamu, na vizuri kuyashika
Mwanzo twangaliye hamu, mume ilokumshika
Yuli na kuu hamumu, kuu isokadirika
Ulibakiya wazimu, nusura ungemshika!

132 Pili twangaliye saa, yalipotukiya hayo
Giza lali mesambaa, kwa mvuwa kuu inyayo
Hata zile nyingi taa, mbingu ziing'arishayo
Hata mojapo angaa, haikujitokezayo

133 Katika huu ubeti, nataka kukwelezeya
Giza ndiye afiriti, wa kukuza maasiya
Lingiyapo huzatiti, nyoyo zikayaendeya
Lenyewe halijifiti, kila mtu yamweleya

134 Ongeza na kibaridi, kilicho cha kuviviya
Hicho kinaposhitadi, na mfupani kungiya
Rafiki hukosi budi, pa joto kukimbiliya
Basi hapo si zaidi, kwa mwenye huu udhiya?

Tit for Tat · 267

130   May you, my reader, stop where you've reached
Have a seat so we can dissect these issues and weigh them
Discern between sweetness and bitterness, what is for swallowing
    and for spitting
If you agree to my request, then let us go back

131   So you may understand and properly grasp things
First let's look at the desire that seized the man
He had tremendous longing, intense beyond compare
He was quite close to losing his mind

132   Second, let's look at the time when these events occurred
Pitch darkness everywhere as it rained torrentially
Even the countless lights that brighten the skies —
Not even one appeared

133   In this verse, I want to explain to you
How darkness is the devil that feeds evil
When it enters it aims to afflict the heart
It doesn't hide itself; every person knows that

134   Add the chill, the creeping chill
When it intensifies and enters the bones
Friend, you have no choice but to run somewhere warm
So isn't it all the more daunting for someone with this affliction?

268 • *Kutendana*

135   Tatu hebu kumbukiya, manukato nilotaja
Bibi aliyojitiya, kuikusudiya haja
Nuka yanavyonukiya, nuka tena mara moja
Halafuye niambiya, baadaye; sasa ngoja

136   Nne tizama mapambo, bibi alojipambiya
Fikiri vipi mrembo, ambavyo alitokeya
Lau angekuwa chambo, samaki angeshikiya
Yaswawiri haya mambo, n'nayokudondoleya

137   Fikiri wewe mwenyewe, zi vipi ashiki zake
Sasa hayo yatukuwe, kwa la kwanza uyapeke
Yaweke pamoja yawe, pamoja yakutanike
Ili kwamba uijuwe, mwanamume hali yake

138   Bila shaka taabani, haliye ilivyokuwa
Mbaya isiyo kifani, vigumu kuhadithiwa
Pima mwako akilini, huna haja kuambiwa
Kwani sitaweza sini, 'ngataka fafanuwa

139   Sasa naturudi nyuma, pale twalipowatiya
Mke alipo kinena, ya pesa kuyajibiya
Tumsikize na Bwana, vipi aliendeleya
Msikize vyema sana, 'endeleyavyo kuliya

Tit for Tat • 269

135 Third, do remember the fragrances I mentioned
That the lady applied to herself with an intention
Smell these fragrances, smell them once more
Then tell me afterwards—not yet

136 Fourth, look at the adornments she wore
Imagine how beautiful she appeared
If she were bait, a fish would bite
Picture these elements that I'm listing for you

137 Just imagine yourself how lustful he felt!
Now add that to the longing first mentioned
Put them together, let them converge
So you can understand the man's condition

138 No doubt his condition was deplorable
It was bad beyond compare; it's hard to explain
Weigh it in your mind—you need no one to tell you
Because I can't do it, even if I wanted to explain

139 Now let's go back to where we left off
When the woman was talking, responding about money
Let's listen to the man, how he proceeded
Listen to him carefully as he continues to lament

270 • *Kutendana*

140 Mwanamume:
Un'tendavyo si vyema, wala si haki mwendani
Na kweli n'kiisema, haya sikutumaini
'Mejikosesha huruma, chache hunayo moyoni
Toba! Yaa Rabbi salama, kiumbe n'nakosani?

141 Natoseka kwa mvuwa, ni chapachapa mwilini
Au hivi ni muruwa, kusema kwa dirishani?
Mlango hebu funguwa, uwate ningiye ndani
Ngaa nipate pumuwa, japo hutaniauni

142 Mwanamke:
Bwana jishikiye ndiya, rudi kuko utokako
Siwezi kufunguliya, siijali tabu yako
Wakatiwo ushasiya, kwangu hupati mashiko
Sina 'talokutendeya, rudi ulikokuwako

143 Na hili n'kueleze, lipate kukueleya
Hapa sijicheleweze, hivi sasa n'ondokeya
Nina mtu n'kwambize, na miyadi 'metimiya
Bwana usinivundize, usoweza nijengeya

Maelezo

144 *N'na mtu* ni tamko, Bibi alilotumiya
Lali kama mripuko, wa kombora nakwambiya
Tena kuripuka huko, lilipokuripukiya
Liliripuka ambako, kwa asolitarajiya

Tit for Tat · 271

140   HE:
The way you're acting isn't good, and it isn't right, my friend
And truly, I didn't expect this
You have rid yourself of pity, not an iota of it in your heart
God forgive me, what wrong did I do?

141   I'm being rained on, I am thoroughly soaked
Or is this all right, for me to speak through the window?
Please open the door and let me in
So I can have some relief, even if you don't help me out

142   SHE:
Mister, go away, go back where you came from
I won't open it for you, I don't care about your hardship
Your time is over, you'll get no hold here
There's nothing I can do, go back where you came from

143   And let me tell you this so you understand
Don't waste your time here, go away right now
I have someone else with whom I have a date
Mister, don't wreck for me what you can't build for me

Explanation

144   *I have someone else* is the phrase the woman spoke
It was like the explosion of a missile, I tell you
Moreover, in that exploding, when it exploded at him
It exploded in a way he didn't anticipate

272 • *Kutendana*

145 Sivyo ambavyo aruke! Kwa kombora kuripuka
     Mwanamume moyo wake, jinsi ulivyogutuka
     Lau si bahati yake, kwenye kiguzo kushika
     Angeona kazi yake! Lazima angeanguka

146 Mke kwisha kuyasema, hayano maneno yake
     Zaidi hakusimama, kutupa wakati wake
     Ela alilisukuma, 'kafunga dirisha lake
     Akakomeleya hima, na tumbuu juu yake

147 Kitendo hicho baada, kilipokwisha tukiya
     Akasimama kwa muda, akizidi kungojeya
     Akifikiri labuda, Mwana 'tabadili niya
     Hakuiona shahada, ya alotumainiya

148 Kisha 'kakata kauli, hapo kujiondokeya
     Mchofu kama hamali, mbebaji maguniya
     Enda huku kwenye mwili, mvuwa yamnyesheya
     Guu mosi guu pili, huyo akashika ndiya

149 Ndiya aliyoishika, nikueleze mwendani
     Ni ndiya ya kumpeka, hadi kwa Mishi nyumbani
     Kwa huyu ndiko kumbuka, Bwana kipeka mapeni
     Ndipo sasa akataka, ende akalipwe deni

145 Oh! Boy, how he leapt! With the missile's explosion
The man's heart was so shocked
If not for his luck in gripping a post
He'd have been in trouble, he'd have fallen

146 After the woman had spoken these words
She didn't linger any longer, she didn't want to waste more time
She instead pushed the window closed
She locked it fast and fastened the latch

147 After that act of closing the window had happened
He stood for a while, continuing to wait
He hoped that perhaps the lady would change her heart
There was no indication that his wish would be fulfilled

148 Then he decided to go away
Tired like a porter who carries gunny sacks
He went away with the rain beating on his body
One step after another, he followed the path

149 The path he followed, let me tell you, my friend
It was the path that would take him up to Mishi's residence
You may recall that here is where the man would take his money
So now he wanted to be paid what was owed him

274 • *Kutendana*

150   Akenda kwa kujikita, kupata ana yakini
     Ya kwamba atakipata, cha kumtibu moyoni
     Lakini alipogota, kama ilivyo kanuni
     Huko nako akakuta, hakuingiliki ndani!

151   Akambwa "Nasikitika, nafasi sinayo Bwana
     Na ambalo nakutaka, ni kutenda kiungwana
     Anza sasa kugeuka, ndiya i swafi na pana
     Mi nawe tulipofika, mbele hatwenendi tena"

152   Bwana hata hakuweza, kusema neno liwalo
     Akabaki kunyamaza, kama hakusikiyalo
     Jambo alilofanyiza, ni kulitimiza hilo
     Uso'we akageuza, lipi tena jenginelo?

153   Furifuri mijitozi, ende huku yamtoka
     Ndiya mbili mitilizi, 'kawa yammiminika
     Sababu vyake vipenzi, vyote vishamgeuka
     Yuwaliya kwa simanzi, aliya asikitika

154   Akazurura na ndiya, badala kwenda nyumbani
     Ovyo akajirangiya, kote mabarabarani
     Ni kama alopoteya, au yuko ugenini
     Kuliche ilipongiya, bado yu kuzururani

Tit for Tat • 275

150   He walked straight ahead, with certainty that he'd get it
       That he'd get what would heal his heart
       Yet when he knocked, as is often the case
       There too, he realized, it was impossible to get in

151   He was told "I'm sorry, I don't have time, Sir
       What I want from you is that you should act gentlemanly
       Turn around now, the path is clean and wide
       Where you and I reached, we can go no farther"

152   The man was unable to speak any word at all
       He remained silent, as if he'd not heard
       The only thing he could do was to remain silent
       He turned back; what else could he do?

153   Copious tears he shed as he walked
       He wept, tears trickling down his cheeks
       Because his beloveds had turned their backs on him
       He wept in sorrow; he wept and anguished

154   He roamed on the way, instead of going home
       He sauntered aimlessly on the road
       He was like someone lost or in a strange land
       When the sun rose, he was still wandering here and there

276 • *Kutendana*

Mnong'ono kwa Msomaji

155 Ndoo n'kunong'oneze, au tunong'onezane
Nilonayo n'kweleze, ya maana tupanane
Ndoo kwangu jijongeze, sitaki tusilikane
Jifite sijitokeze, kwamba tusionekane

156 Hebu kweli niambiya, mi nawe tusifitane
Hivi ukiy'angaliya, haya waja watendene
Yupi alotenda baya, kumtendeya mwengine?
Ni yupi mwenye hatiya? Usinifite mnene

157 Ni mwanamke wa kwanza, alejitweka ulezi?
Mwanamume 'kamtunza, wakati hanayo kazi
Hilino alilofanza, lali ni la upuuzi?
Sidhani litakutanza, lenyewe li waziwazi

158 Ingawa sote twajuwa, mambo haya hutokeya
Lakini tukitunguwa, kwa za kiutu tabiya
Alifanya sawasawa, dume kuliangaliya
Na hali huyo hakuwa, mwenzi wake wa shariya?

159 Na hilino neno zima, piya nalo n'julisha
Tushamwona mwana-mama, a'vyomsitarehesha
Je alifanya vyema, mwendo kuubadilisha
Mwenziwe kuja mnyima, alichomzowezesha?

A Whisper to the Reader

155   Come, let me whisper to you, or let's whisper to each other
      Let me tell you what I see, let's exchange something meaningful
      Come close to me, I don't want us to be heard
      Hide yourself: don't come out, so we won't be seen

156   Tell me the truth; you and I shouldn't hide it from each other
      When you examine how these people treated one other
      Which treated the other badly?
      Who bears guilt? Don't hide it, tell me

157   Is it the first woman, who took to pampering the man?
      She took care of the man when he was jobless
      Was what she did foolish?
      I don't think it will confound you—the matter is crystal clear

158   Although we all know that these things happen
      Yet when we examine the ways of virtuous conduct
      Did she act rightly in caring for the man
      When he wasn't her legal life partner?

159   In this whole matter, also let me know
      We have seen the woman, how she indulged him
      Did she do right to change her disposition
      By denying her partner what she had made him used to?

278 • *Kutendana*

160   Kisha tizama na hili, mwanamume alotenda
Ni sawa huyu fahali, kwa bibi huyo kwenenda?
Akapąwa maakuli, nguo pamwe na kitanda?
Na yeye akakubali, moja pasi kulikinda?

161   Je hivi ndivyo kiume, Bwana alivyofanyiza?
Ni sawa kwa mwanamume, hivino kujilegeza?
Badalaye ajitume, japo kunazi kuuza
Kwa maguuye akwime, asipate kurombeza

162   Na hili liangaliye, unipe hukumu yake
Kati yao afaaye, kumuweka mwenzi wake
Ni mke awekwe yeye, aula yeye aweke?
Angaliya unambiye, lifunuwe lifunuke

163   Lifuwatalo lipime, tena vizuri kabisa
Waona ni mwanamume, ambaye ana makosa
Kwa kurudi amuume, aliye akijiasa
Ajili amtizame, tabu 'siwe kumgusa?

164   Wakati alipokuwa, hana mbele hana nyuma
Sote piya tushajuwa, alionewa huruma
Vyema akapokelewa, na huyuno mwana-mama
Kwa kila kitu kupawa, na vyema kumtizama

Tit for Tat • 279

160   Now look at what the man did
Was it fair for this ox to go to this woman?
To be given food, clothes, and a place to sleep?
And he accepted all that, without refusing any of them?

161   Is that really manly, the way this man acted?
Is it fair for a man to just laze around?
Instead he could have tried even selling berries
To stand on his own feet, rather than waiting for handouts

162   And look at this, and give me your judgment
Who between them is supposed to care for the other
Is the woman to be cared for, or is she to take care of him?
Consider, then tell me; explain it to me clearly

163   Now weigh the following, weigh it very well
Do you think that it is the man who is guilty
For coming back to bite the one denying herself
In order to care for him so he'd be untouched by hardship?

164   When he was utterly destitute
All of us have come to know he was pitied
He was well received by this very same lady
Who gave him everything and took care of him

280 • *Kutendana*

165 Aliponafasikiwa, kuanza kuwa na chake
Alivyofanya ni sawa, kumpiga mwende teke?
Na kusahau ya kuwa, ndiye mfadhili wake?
Afaa kuhukumiwa, kumuhuni mwanamke?

166 Na mwisho ni huyu Mishi, alotenda tushaona
Kwa kumuiza bilashi, alipomwendeya Bwana
Uweke kando ubishi, alitenda kiungwana?
Usiwe mlalamishi, sitaki lalamishana

167 Alitenda kiungwana, kumkataa ghafula?
Na hali vya huyu bwana, ni yeye alo 'kivila?
Halafu vilije tena, kuzisahau fadhila?
Tafuta yakwe maana, uyajibu masuala

168 Mwisho wa hayano yote, nitowe yangu maoni
Singetaka n'kufite, yaliyo mwangu moyoni
Kwa hivyo sasa niwate, n'kupe wangu undani
Kwangu mimi hao wote, nawatiya makosani

169 Si huyu Mishi baini, mkukutaji mwenzake
Wala si la samahani, hili jenginewe jike
Na wala dume 'sidhani, tamuwata aondoke
Wote wamo makosani, kila mtu kosa lake

165 When he prospered and began to have means
Was it right for him to abandon his partner?
And to forget that she had been his benefactor?
Should he be judged for abandoning the woman?

166 Finally, there is this Mishi, we have seen what she did
She rejected the man for nothing when he went to her
Leave disputes aside; did she act humanely?
Don't be a bickerer: I don't want us to bicker

167 Did she act nobly in rejecting him suddenly?
And wasn't she enjoying this man's wealth?
How come, then, she forgot his kindness to her?
Look for the answers to give to these questions

168 After all this, let me give my opinion
I don't want to conceal from you what's in my heart
Therefore let me now give you my take
For my part, I see all of them as culpable

169 This Mishi, you should know, who distressed her partner —
This can't be forgiven, also the other woman
Nor will the man be left to go free
All of them have erred, each has done wrong

282 • *Kutendana*

170   Na ambavyo nawaona, watendaji hivi visa
      Wantafautiyana, kwa kadiri ya makosa
      Yuko aliyekazana, kidogo akayagusa
      Wako walozidiyana, na alozidi kabisa

171   Sasa palipobakiya, ni pako si pangu tena
      Kazi n'takuwatiya, tuwe kusaidiyana
      Hili ukiliridhiya, anza bongo kulikuna
      Upate kunifanyiya, hii kazi 'tayonena

172   Hawano watu watatu, walopatwa na hatiya
      Muhukumu kila mtu, kulingana na shariya
      Siwe kuogopa kitu, na wala kupendeleya
      Wala 'sidhulumu mtu, wala kumhurumiya

173   Sisemi kadiri gani, ya makosa walonayo
      Sitakwambiya "Fulani, afaa hukumu hiyo"
      Sikwambii aswilani, haya ya makadiriyo
      Tafuta yako mizani, ya kuyapimiya hayo

174   Patosha n'lipofika, hapa ndipo 'tapokoma
      Kalamu tini naweka, kusema kwingi si kwema
      Kitu n'nachokutaka, shairi wishapo soma
      Jaribu kuyaepuka, haya ulosoma nyuma

—*6 Juni mpaka 27 Novemba 1971*

170 And looking at them, the things they've done
They differ somewhat in their magnitude of guilt
There's one who was firm but was tainted a little
There are more guilty ones and a most guilty one

171 Now what remains is your task, not mine
I'll let you perform it so we can assist one another
If you accede to this, start flexing your brain
So you can undertake for me the task I'll name

172 These three people who were found guilty
Judge each of them according to the law
Don't fear anything or show favor toward anyone
Treat no one unjustly, nor display pity

173 I won't mention the degree of guilt each one has
I don't tell you, "So-and-so deserves such and such judgment"
I don't instruct you at all in these matters of degree
Find your own scales for weighing that

174 It's enough where I've reached; here is where I'll stop
I'm putting down the pen—it's not good to say too much
The thing I wish of you after you've finished this poem:
Try to avoid what you've read in here

—*6 June to 27 November 1971*

N'sharudi

1 Si mwengine ni yuyule, wa ki-Mvita kijana
Mzawa mji wa kale, mtaa Kuze kwa jina
Huwo ndiwo mzi mle, tipuzi ya langu shina
Basi n'sharudi tena, alo na lake nanene

2 Nijile tena nijile, mneni nijile tena
Zangu tomi zinyemele, zinyemele kwa maana
Tangu siku n'toshile, hi' leyo ndiyo nanena
Basi n'sharudi tena, alo na lake nanene

3 Si kwamba nali nilele, ndipo hawa sikunena
Wala kwamba n'choshile, hahitajiya kusona
Wala sikucha sichile, kunena n'taloona
Basi n'sharudi tena, alo na lake nanene

4 Maozi yangu mbonile, yatizama na kuona
Na masikizi vivile, nayasikiziya sana
Ili kwamba yaningile, yaliyonipita jana
Basi n'sharudi tena, alo na lake nanene

5 Sitatongowa tongole, leo niya hiyo sina
Leo sikukusudile, kungali mapema sana
Mwanzo n'atani niole, mambo nipate yaona
Basi n'sharudi tena, alo na lake na'nene

—*22 Julai 1972*

I'm Back

1   It's none other than the selfsame young man from Mvita
Born in Old Town, a neighborhood called Kuze
That's the deep root over which my tree trunk sprouted
So I've come back, and let anyone who will, speak

2   I've come again, I've come; I the speaker have come back
My pains have quieted, they've quieted for a reason
Of all the days since my release, today is when I speak
So I've come back, and let anyone who will, speak

3   It's not that I've been slumbering and that's why I didn't speak out
Or that I grew tired and needed a rest
Nor did I fear—I didn't fear—speaking of things as I see them
So I've come back, and let anyone who will, speak

4   My eyes are wide open; they look and see
And my ears also: I hear with them very well
So I can comprehend what I missed yesterday
So I've come back, and let anyone who will, speak

5   I won't talk in detail, I don't intend to do so today
Today I have no such intentions, it's still too soon
First let me look around so I can see things
So I've come back, and let anyone who will, speak

—*22 July 1972*

Critical Perspectives

Sauti ya Dhiki

Its Place in Swahili Literature and East African Literature

Ann Biersteker

ni Utetezi
ni Maombolezo
ni Sauti ya shime
ni Mjadala wa nafsi
ni Kitulizo na kiliwaza[1]

Abdilatif Abdalla's *Sauti ya Dhiki* is likely the most influential work in the history of East African literature as well as in the history of Swahili literature. When it was published, this volume of poetry established Swahili as the language of young, highly educated, politically progressive writers in East Africa and connected their work to the long history of politically engaged writing in Swahili. While there were earlier literary works written in Swahili by post-independence authors, including Ebrahim Hussein's *Kinjeketile*,[2] Euphrase Kezilahabi's *Rosa Mistika*,[3] and Penina Muhando's *Hatia*,[4] and while writing in Swahili had been encouraged by the works of Julius Nyerere and many others, *Sauti ya Dhiki* was more widely read, praised, and cited as an influence by post-independence Kenyan and Tanzanian authors than any other

---

1. May Ndyanao Balisidya Matteru, of *Sauti ya Dhiki* in her 1975 review, p. 28 as quoted by Chacha Nyaigotti-Chacha in *Ushairi wa Abdilatif Abdalla: Sauti ya Utetezi* (Dar es Salaam: Dar es Salaam University Press, 1992) (p. 65). Capitalization is that of Matteru. The following translation is mine:

    It is a statement
    It is a lament
    It is a voice of encouragement
    It is an internal debate
    It is soothing and calming

2. Ebrahim Hussein, *Kinjeketile* (Dar es Salaam: Oxford University Press, 1969).
3. Euphrase Kezilahabi, *Rosa Mistika* (Nairobi: East African Literature Bureau, 1971).
4. Penina Muhando, *Hatia* (Nairobi: East African Publishing House, 1972).

work of literature from East Africa. This is not to deny the impact of Ngũgĩ wa Thiong'o's early novels in English, *Weep Not, Child* and *The River Between*, or Okot p'Bitek's *Song of Lawino*.[5] These works also had a profound effect on many East African readers, but perhaps not the impact that *Sauti ya Dhiki* had on a key generation of university-educated East African writers who were bilingual in Swahili and English and chose to write in Kiswahili. Swahili might have become the dominant language of East African literature without *Sauti ya Dhiki*, but this poetry collection did far more than contribute to a trend in progress to establish Swahili as the language of East African literature.

Young East African scholars and writers engaged with *Sauti ya Dhiki* even before it was published. In 1973, when Abdalla and the Tanzanian novelist, poet, and scholar Euphrase Kezilahabi were both working at the University of Dar es Salaam, Kezilahabi read the manuscript for *Sauti ya Dhiki*. Because he wanted to use it in his Swahili literature courses, Kezilahabi convinced Oxford University Press to publish the book within three months. *Sauti ya Dhiki* was first taught at the University of Dar es Salaam in the year of its publication[6] and was taught at the University of Nairobi and at Kenyatta University within the next year or two. May Ndyanao Balisidya Matteru, a novelist, short story writer, and the first woman to teach Swahili at the University of Dar es Salaam, wrote one of the earliest reviews of *Sauti ya Dhiki* in the University of Dar es Salaam journal for Swahili teachers, *Mulika*. In her review Matteru stated:

> Katika kuutoa msimamo wake na kuutetea; katika kueleza wazi wazi dosari za walio juu yake, Abdilatif amefanya jambo moja kubwa sana ambalo linai-kanganya Fasihi ya Kiswahili leo, nalo ni kutoa mijadala na mazungumzo ya kisiasa katika fasihi. [7]

> In putting forth his position and speaking out; in explaining openly the faults of those ruling over him, Abdilatif has done something very significant which is to jolt Swahili literature today, into incorporating opposing viewpoints and political conversations.

---

5. Ngũgĩ wa Thiong'o, *Weep Not, Child* (Nairobi: Heinemann, 1964); Ngũgĩ wa Thiong'o, *The River Between* (Nairobi: Heinemann, 1965); Okot p'Bitek, *Song of Lawino: A Lament*. Nairobi: East African Publishing House, 1966.

6. Abdilatif Abdalla, personal communication, October 2018.

7. May Ndyanao Matteru Balisidya, "Mapitio ya *Sauti ya Dhiki*," *Mulika* 7 (1975): 32, capitalization that of the author; my translation follows. Raymond Ohly's "A Review of Abdilatif Abdalla's Sauti ya Dhiki," *Kiswahili* 44, no. 2 (1974): 82–91 and M.M. Mulokozi's "Mapitio ya Sauti ya Dhiki," *Umma* 4, no. 1 (1974), had been published earlier.

Sauti ya Dhiki • 291

Many leading East African poets, novelists, playwrights, and scholars have described the effect that reading *Sauti ya Dhiki* had on them. For example, the Pemban/Zanzibari poet, playwright, and novelist Said Ahmed Khamis has stated:

> I read *Sauti ya Dhiki* for the first time in a poetry class at the University of Dar es Salaam in 1976. Abdalla's revolutionary spirit made an impact on me. I quickly absorbed and digested what I considered the poet's naked truth, his advocacy and appeal to Kenyan people to fight for their rights, which was by implication the appeal to all African people and all oppressed people in the world. I therefore started to draw parallels between Kenyan and Tanzanian political situations and their ramifications. At that time Kenya and Tanzania were two different countries separated politically and ideologically at least on the surface, though at the underlying level, they were two countries whose citizens were disillusioned with how their governments were running the countries as (neo)colonies. It was as if some of us were blinded and tongue-tied, and *Sauti ya Dhiki* immediately opened our eyes and made us not to be afraid to speak out our plights and predicaments.[8]

Khamis also notes that his volume of poetry *'Sikate Tamaa* was inspired by *Sauti ya Dhiki* and by his realization of the causes that he shared with Abdalla.[9] As the poet and playwright Alamin Mazrui relates in his essay in this volume, his reading of Abdalla was instrumental in his own detainment and creative processes. The playwright and scholar Kimani Njogu has similarly remarked on the formative influence of Abdalla's poems:

> I recall reading the book around 1974 when I was a student of Kiswahili, Literature and Education at Kenyatta College. Our lecturer then was Said Hilal Bualy, originally from Zanzibar and Oman. At the time, I was also reading Walter Rodney, Frantz Fanon, Ngũgĩ wa Thiong'o and Mwalimu Julius Nyerere and I must say I found *Sauti* to be absolutely irresistible! I was impressed by his use of Kimvita and the power of his symbolism and imagery.

---

8. Said Ahmed Khamis, "Whither Swahili Literature? Translation and World Recognition of Abdilatif Abdalla's *Sauti ya Dhiki*," in *Abdilatif Abdalla: Poet in Politics*, edited by Rose Marie Beck and Kai Kresse (Dar es Salaam: Mkuki na Nyota, 2016), 37–38.

9. Khamis, 37–38.

His unambiguous call to the spirit of resistance to the excesses of state power spoke to me in a special way. As a young man who had grown up in a "Shauri Yako" home, a home that could be demolished because it belonged to the state and we were squatters, I understood clearly that the political class had betrayed ordinary citizens.[10]

As these testaments suggest, Abdalla's collection, in its political stance, its poetic craft, and its underlying courage, transformed how fellow writers understood the potential of their art.

By 1976–1977 *Sauti ya Dhiki* was being taught as a required text in secondary schools in Tanzania.[11] The anthology was also required reading in Kenyan secondary schools for more than ten years during the last years of Jomo Kenyatta's rule and the early years of Daniel Arap Moi's presidency, even though many of the poems are highly critical of Kenyatta, his party, and of Kenyan crony-capitalism. As Ahmed Rajab observes, "It is a measure of Abdilatif's influence on Kenyans … that his *Sauti ya Dhiki* is still in print over 35 years since it was published."[12] The same, of course, could also be said of the impact of *Sauti ya Dhiki* on Tanzanians, and on Swahili readers worldwide.

IMPACT ON POETRY

As noted above, *Sauti ya Dhiki* had a profound impact on the younger generation of Swahili poets, particularly Said Ahmed Mohamed [Khamis], especially in his *'Sikate Tamaa*, and on Alamin Mazrui and his *Chembe cha Moyo*. An important aspect of its influence lies in its strong affiliations with Swahili poetic and political tradition. As noted by Mazrui:

At the artistic level, obviously, no modern collection of Swahili poetry can be placed in the same league with *Sauti ya Dhiki*. After all, Abdilatif's mastery of Swahili poetic diction and idiom is one that is unmatched and sets him apart

---

10. Kimani Njogu, personal communication, October 2018. He added that, "Later, I was to teach it and translate a few verses into Gikuyu for the *Mutiiri* journal."

11. Deo Ngonyani, personal communication, October 2018.

12. Ahmed Rajab, "The Urgency of Memory in an Age of Greed," in *Abdilatif Abdalla: Poet in Politics*, edited by Rose Marie Beck and Kai Kresse (Dar es Salaam: Mkuki na Nyota, 2016), 68.

from all his contemporaries. His poetry is truly unique in that it is classical, but also inventive and creative, without being stilted.[13]

The poems in *Sauti ya Dhiki* draw upon classic genres of Swahili poetry, especially those composed in Northern dialects of Swahili; and most specifically upon the poetry of Muyaka bin Haji, the famous early nineteenth-century poet of Mombasa. The volume's epigraph, "Ngome intuumiza, naswi tu mumo ngomeni," draws upon a poem by Muyaka. The poems also draw upon the Abdalla family history of poetic genius, especially that of Abdalla's half-brother, Ahmad Nassir, the author of poetry collections including *Malenga wa Mvita*, and his maternal great uncle, Ahmad Basheikh bin Hussein,[14] and the family history of political activism, notably that of his brother Sheikh Abdilahi Nassir. According to Clarissa Vierke:

> His great-uncle Ahmad Basheikh Hussein, a poet and respected scholar, started to take care of him when he was three and sensitized him to language variability by taking him to various parts of the coast …. At an early age, Abdalla was exposed to various Swahili dialects as well as poetic traditions …. Later, Ahmad Basheikh gave him his poetry to read before he performed it on Sauti ya Mvita [The Voice of Mombasa], the local radio station and an important mouthpiece for coastal Muslims from the 1940s until the 1960s.[15]

Vierke also discusses echoes of Ahmad Nassir's poetry in *Sauti ya Dhiki*, especially the topoi of "dunia"/ "worldliness" and "subira"/ "patience."[16] She argues that: "In his poem 'Kichu Hakiwi ni Uchu' ['Material Goods Do Not Make a Human Being'], Abdalla explores his brother's concept of *utu* (humanity) as a counter-concept to moral corruption."[17]

---

13. Alamin Mazrui, "Abdilatif and I: Reflections on Comparative Experiences," Paper presented at a roundtable on "The Imaginative Vision of Abdilatif Abdalla: Kenyan Poet and Activist," Princeton University, 9 November 2017, 5.

14. Rajab, 72. The collection by Ahmad Nassir mentioned here is *Malenga wa Mvita* (Nairobi: Oxford University Press, 1971).

15. Clarissa Vierke, "'What Is There in My Speaking': Re-Explorations of Language in Abdilatif Abdalla's Anthology of Prison Poetry, *Sauti Ya Dhiki*," *Research in African Literatures* 48, no. 1, (Spring 2017): 141. See also: Kai Kresse, *Swahili Muslim Publics and Postcolonial Experience* (Bloomington, Ind.: Indiana University Press, 2018).

16. Vierke, 149–152.

17. Vierke, 152.

In his *Ushairi wa Abdilatif Abdalla: Sauti ya Utetezi*, Chacha Nyaigotti-Chacha compares the styles of classic meter and rhyme scheme patterns that Abdalla and Ahmad Nassir, as well as other poets including Amri Abedi and Shaaban Robert, use in their poems.[18] Chacha argues:

> Abdilatif kwa kutumia miundo hii yote anadhihirisha uwezo wake kama mshairi shupavu wa lugha ya Kiswahili. Huu siyo uwezo mdogo na ni ukweli kudai kwamba unamweka katika kijopo cha pekee cha washairi wa Uswahilini.[19]

> Abdilatif by using all these styles proves his ability as a talented Swahili language poet. This is not an insignificant ability and it is true to claim that it puts him in a unique category among Swahili poets.

Kimvita and, to a lesser extent, Kiamu, the dialects of Mombasa and Lamu, are used in many of the poems, but Abdalla also draws upon various dialects of Swahili, and the poems in *Sauti ya Dhiki* are of varying levels of accessibility. For example, poems such as "Wasafiri Tuamkeni" (here, "Travelers, Let's Wake Up") and "Usiniuwe!" ("Don't Kill Me!") are written almost entirely in Standard Swahili and, with a brief explanation of orthographic variation, even learners of Swahili are able to read and understand them. Chacha Nyaigotti-Chacha has written a guide for teaching "Mnazi: Vuta N'kuvute" ("The Coconut Palm: A Tug of War") in a college classroom.[20] Another poem, "Kichu Hakiwi ni Uchu" ("Things Can't be Human"), as pointed out by Chacha, is written partially in Kitikuu, one of the northernmost dialects of Kiswahili.[21]

Abdalla clearly demonstrates unique mastery of classic Swahili poetic genres and of Swahili poetic language and dialects in *Sauti ya Dhiki* but his poems are also inventive in a number of ways. One example is his use of alliteration in the highly original poem "Kuno Kunena" ("This Speaking Out"). Although there is natural alliteration in Swahili because of its noun class system, few poets writing in Swahili have employed alliteration, but Abdalla

---

18. Chacha Nyaigotti-Chacha, *Ushairi wa Abdilatif Abdalla: Sauti ya Utetezi* (Dar es Salaam: Dar es Salaam University Press, 1992), 112–126.

19. Nyaigotti-Chacha, *Ushairi wa Abdilatif Abdalla*, 126. My translation follows.

20. Chacha Nyaigotti-Chacha, "The Teaching of Kiswahili Poetry: A Thematic Analysis in a College Class," *Journal of Proceedings: A Workshop on Swahili Instruction*, edited by Philip T.K. Daniel, Ann Biersteker, and Victoria Moreland (DeKalb, Illinois: Northern Illinois University, Center for Minority Studies, 1983), 91–109.

21. Nyaigotti-Chacha, *Ushairi wa Abdilatif Abdalla: Sauti ya Utetezi*, 127.

does so effectively in this poem that literally calls for answers and sonically reverberates with his plea for speaking out.

The poems in *Sauti ya Dhiki* also demonstrate a wide range of experimentation with voice. Many of the anthology's most powerful poems, such as "N'shishiyelo ni Lilo" ("I Won't Compromise") and "Siwati" ("I'll Never Let Go"), are written in the first person and seem to be in the voice of the author and addressed to a general audience. Others such as "Usiniuwe!" ("Don't Kill Me!") are written in the first person, but the speaker is defined as a fetus and the explicit addressee is the mother of the fetus. Vierke notes that the poem "Kamliwaze" ("Go and Console Him") begins with an address to a fictive messenger and, in this way, "[t]he poet inscribes himself into the genre tradition of the letter poem, often a love letter, which comes with a well-established repertoire of forms, such as, for instance, the request to the messenger at the beginning."[22] Vierke also demonstrates how an intricate system of parallels transforms the rhythm of the poem "Siwati" ("I'll Never Let Go") into a "rhythm of thought."[23]

As Said Ahmed Khamis points out, "In Abdalla's anthology words of everyday usage are beaten into new shapes, images, and symbols for a number of meanings and nuances." He gives the examples of "mnazi" (a coconut tree, a traditional symbol of wealth in Swahili that becomes nation/national wealth in "Mnazi: Vuta N'kuvute") and "mamba" (a crocodile who becomes "a leader who rules with an iron fist" in "Mamba"), among other examples.[24]

IMPACT ON FICTION

In addition to its impact on East African poetry, *Sauti ya Dhiki* also influenced East African novels and short stories. Mugyabuso Mulokozi cites *Sauti ya Dhiki* as the first example of proletarian literature in East Africa and notes the impact of the volume on subsequent explicitly socialist works, including the novels of Shafi Adam Shafi and Said Ahmed Mohamed [Khamis].[25] Certainly the novels of Katama Mkangi[26] should also be included among the socialist novels

---

22. Vierke, 148.

23. Vierke, 144.

24. Khamis, 39.

25. Mugyabuso M. Mulokozi, "A Survey of Kiswahili Literature: 1970–1988," *Afrika Focus* 8, no. 1: 55.

26. Mkangi's clearly socialist works are *Walenisi* (Nairobi: East Africa Educational Publishers, 1995) and *Mafuta* (Nairobi: Heinemann Educational Books, 1984).

296 • THE IMAGINATIVE VISION OF ABDILATIF ABDALLA'S *VOICE OF AGONY*

influenced by *Sauti ya Dhiki*. Furthermore, *Sauti ya Dhiki* was among the first literary works in East Africa that explicitly critiqued the post-colonial state. While works such as Penina Muhando's plays *Hatia* and *Tambueni Haki Zetu*[27] criticized corrupt officials and exploitive practices, poems such as "Mnazi: Vuta N'kuvute" ("The Coconut Palm: A Tug of War") and "Mamba" ("Crocodile") in *Sauti ya Dhiki* directly challenged the Kenyatta regime and other unjust and dictatorial regimes. It is also likely that Abdalla's poem "La Mjini na la Shamba" ("The Town Cockerel and the Country One"), about the interdependence of urban and rural peoples, which is built on the proverb "Jogoo la shamba haliwiki mjini"/ "The country rooster doesn't crow in the city," inspired Eddie Ganzel's popular socialist detective novel *Jogoo la Shamba*.[28]

IMPACT ON DRAMA

The impact of *Sauti ya Dhiki* on subsequent poetry is perhaps obvious, but it is also apparent that *Sauti ya Dhiki* has had an impact on drama in Kiswahili. Abdalla had demonstrated his capacity for creating dramatic dialogue in his earlier narrative poem, *Utenzi wa Adam na Hawaa*. Farouk Topan recognized this and argued:

> Kila ukiusoma utenzi huu unazidi kupata utamu wa kisa hicho, hata unahisi 'drama' yenyewe inavyotendeka. Inakuwa hapana haja ya jukwaa. Mtu mwe- nyewe huwa anavisawiri vitendo hivyo moyoni mwake.

> Every time you read this narrative poem you are more attracted to this story, you even feel the drama itself that is taking place. It doesn't need to take place on a stage. An individual is able to draw the actions in his/her heart.[29]

The dialogue poems in *Sauti ya Dhiki* ("Mnazi: Vuta N'kuvute" and "Kutendana") are particularly dramatic, especially "Mnazi: Vuta N'kuvute," which has been dramatized and performed in a number of different contexts.[30] Vierke observes:

---

27. Penina Muhando, *Hatia* (Nairobi: East African Publishing House, 1972) and *Tambueni Haki Zetu* (Dar es Salaam: Tanzanian Publishing House, 1973).

28. Eddie Ganzel, *Jogoo la Shamba* (Arusha, Tanzania: Eastern Africa Publications, 1978).

29. As quoted by Chacha, *Ushairi wa Abdilatif Abdalla* (p. 115), from Farouk Topan, *Uchambuzi wa Maandishi ya Kiswahili* (Nairobi: Oxford University Press, 1972), 67. My translation.

30. A performance is available on YouTube at: https://www.youtube.com/watch?v=C2TJZrs4GoQ.

Sauti ya Dhiki • 297

In September 2009, during the performance festival Jukwaani in Nairobi, for instance, one of the poems composed in 1970, "Mnazi, Vuta N'kuvute" ["The Tug of War for the Coconut Tree"], was performed on stage by Musa Adam and Alai Kai, members of the prolific hip-hop project Ukoo Flani Maumau. I observed young Kenyans attending the performance with great enthusiasm. For those youngsters, roughly a year after the post-election violence in Kenya, the dispute between the two brothers over a coconut tree depicted in the poem did not merely refer back to the conflict between the government and the opposition right after independence, but also presented an inspiring commentary on the present situation of Kenyan politics, spelled out in lively scenes.[31]

As Ngũgĩ wa Thiong'o has pointed out, "In conceiving it, Abdilatif may have had Kenyatta and Odinga in mind, but here, in the poem, Badi and Alii become representatives of class social forces and not of biological ethnic entities."[32] Chacha wrote a study of "Mnazi: Vuta N'kuvute,"[33] and his plays, especially the more explicitly Marxist *Wingu Jeusi*[34] and *Hukumu*,[35] clearly show the impact of his study of Abdalla's *Sauti ya Dhiki* and *Utenzi wa Adam na Hawaa*. The same can be said of Kimani Njogu's *Zilizala*[36] as well as other, more recent Swahili plays.

Of course, Abdalla was not the first Swahili poet to write dialogue poems. This had become a convention well before *Sauti ya Dhiki* was published, and Abdalla's dialogue poems draw upon earlier traditions of exchanges of poetry in Swahili. Swahili poets for centuries have exchanged poetry in times of conflict and of celebration. The most well-known historical exchanges are those that took place between Muyaka bin Haji of Mombasa and Zahidi Mngumi of Lamu during the early nineteenth century,[37] but there are also many additional examples from this period and earlier. Poetry has also long been exchanged at Swahili weddings and between romantically involved couples. As Kelly Askew has described in detail, East African musical groups performing sung

---

31. Vierke, 136.

32. Ngũgĩ wa Thiong'o, "Abdilatif Abdalla and the Voice of Prophecy," *Abdilatif Abdalla: Poet in Politics*, edited by Rose Marie Beck and Kai Kresse (Dar es Salaam: Mkuki na Nyota, 2016), 12.

33. Nyaigotti-Chacha, "The Teaching of Kiswahili Poetry," 91–109.

34. Chacha Nyaigotti-Chacha, *Wingu Jeusi* (Nairobi: Heinemann, 1987).

35. Chacha Nyaigotti-Chacha, *Hukumu* (Nairobi: Longman Kenya, 1992).

36. Kimani Njogu, *Zilizala* (Nairobi: Longman Kenya, 2006).

37. See Mohamed H. Abdulaziz, *Muyaka: 19th Century Swahili Popular Poetry* (Nairobi: Kenya Literature Bureau, 1979) and Ann Biersteker and Ibrahim Noor Shariff, *Mashairi ya Vita vya Kuduhu* (East Lansing: Michigan State University Press, 1995).

298 • THE IMAGINATIVE VISION OF ABDILATIF ABDALLA'S *VOICE OF AGONY*

poetry have long debated political and social issues.[38] Abdalla himself edited a collection of poems from the island of Pemba that includes several early twentieth-century dialogue poems.[39]

The impact of *Sauti ya Dhiki* is evident even in criticism of Swahili literature. For example, in his conclusion to *Ushairi wa Abdilatif Abdalla: Sauti ya Utetezi*, Chacha explicitly draws upon the metaphors of the poem "Wasafiri Tuamkeni" ("Travelers, Let's Wake Up") when he says:

> Huu umekuwa ni mwanzo wa safari ndefu. Safari hii ni ya muhimu kwa wataalam wa lugha na fasihi. Ni safari ambayo itazaa vitabu vingi vya kitaaluma, kama vile uhakiki na ufafanuzi, ili kwamba vizazi vijavyo vije viipate ghala iliyojaa amana ambayo watajivunia.[40]

> This has been the beginning of a long journey. This journey is important for scholars of language and literature. It is a journey that will bring forth many scholarly works, and likewise certainty and clarity, so that future generations will gain secure stores of which they may be proud.[41]

Similarly, even in its title *Sauti ya Dhiki* refers to earlier cultural texts. It draws upon Sheikh Muhammad Kassim's Islamic periodical *Sauti ya Haki*, as well as the independent radio program from Mombasa, "Sauti ya Mvita."[42]

CONCLUSION

Sauti ya Dhiki is a central text in the history of Swahili literature and in the history of East African literature. It should also be a key text in the study of socialist and global political literature in the late twentieth century. For example, if a history were written of socialist poetry worldwide published

---

38. See Kelly M. Askew, *Performing the Nation* (Chicago: University of Chicago Press, 2002).

39. Abdurrahman Saggaf Alawy and Ali Abdalla El-Maawy, *Kale ya Washairi wa Pemba: Kamange na Sarahani*, ed. Abdilatif Abdalla (Dar es Salaam: Mkuki na Nyota, 2011).

40. *Ushairi wa Abdilatif Abdalla*, 141.

41. My translation.

42. For more information on these publications, see Kai Kresse, *Swahili Muslim Publics and Postcolonial Experience* (Bloomington, Ind.: Indiana University Press, 2018) and Alamin Mazrui, *Swahili Beyond the Boundaries: Literature, Language, and Identity* (Athens, Ohio: Ohio University Press, 2007), pp. 80 and 102.

in 1973, it might compare *Sauti ya Dhiki* with Allen Ginsberg's *The Fall of America: Poems of These States, 1965–1971*, Audre Lorde's *From a Land Where Other People Live*, and Victor Jara's poem "Estadio Chile," to name just a few examples. As Vierke notes, Abdalla credits Fidel Castro's speech "History Will Absolve Me" as one of the main sources of his moral and political inspiration.[43] It should be obvious but must be pointed out: socialist poets writing in the 1970s, in a wide range of languages, shared texts among themselves and with their readers.

Even more obviously, *Sauti ya Dhiki* should be an essential text in the study of East African political and cultural history. This is a shared text that has inspired nearly all contemporary Swahili writers as well as millions of East Africans and other readers of Swahili since the 1970s. The poems in *Sauti ya Dhiki* draw upon the rich history of Swahili poetry and prose as well as upon a wide range of Islamic and socialist texts. It is hoped that this translation will encourage further study of the poems in *Sauti ya Dhiki* and inspire and inform a diverse range of new audiences.

---

43. Vierke, 136.

Abdilatif and I

Reflections on Comparative Experiences

Alamin Mazrui[1]

The first time I became cognizant of the political power of Abdilatif Abdalla's poetry was in 1982. The realization came soon after I had begun my teaching career at Kenyatta University in Nairobi, Kenya. As someone familiar with Abdilatif's poetry, I had of course always known that his eloquently compelling collection *Sauti ya Dhiki* (*Voice of Agony*) is as militant as it is unrepentant in tone. The sense of isolation and the effects of confinement are vividly captured in the evocative imagery he employs—all amounting to a powerful indictment of the regime of the time of the Kenya African National Union (KANU). To a degree, the collection is reminiscent of some of the poems of Muyaka bin Haji, the nineteenth-century poet from Mombasa, in which he castigated the treasonable behavior of some of his compatriots. Perhaps it is not a coincidence that Abdilatif prefaces his anthology with the words of Muyaka: "Ngome intuumiza, Naswi tu mumo ngomeni" ("The fort has caused us much suffering, yet in it we continue to remain"). It was not until 1982, however, that I developed a sense of how sections of the Kenya government were reading the poems and that, in fact, the state regarded *Sauti ya Dhiki* as a text that bordered on sedition.

1982, of course, was the year I was arrested right on the Kenyatta University campus where I was working. I was subsequently held in police custody for some ten days or so under relentless interrogation. It was under these circumstances that Abdilatif's name surfaced as one of the state's "persons of interest." Given the ethnicized nature of Kenyan politics, my first group of interrogators was entirely Swahili. And these ethnic compatriots of mine used the ethnic card to try to persuade me into taking them into

---

1. I am very grateful to Alwi Shatry and Kimani Njogu for their comments on an earlier draft of this short essay.

THE IMAGINATIVE VISION OF ABDILATIF ABDALLA'S *VOICE OF AGONY*

their confidence with somewhat veiled promises of helping me out of my police custody and even impending imprisonment on charges of sedition. In fact, the first interrogator was none other than my own first cousin, Kasim Rashid,[2] who by then had become the Deputy Director of Intelligence, taking over from Stephen Muriithi, who had been terminated from the position and later detained by President Daniel Arap Moi. Rashid's appearance as the second highest-ranking officer in the intelligence apparatus in Kenya was intended to underscore both the gravity of my arrest and the possibility of freedom through his personal intervention with President Moi. He was then followed by more junior and younger officers—all of Swahili background.

It was clear from their line of interrogation that these Swahili officers were charged with the responsibility of unearthing a broader Swahili connection in what were regarded as my clandestine activities. Here, Abdilatif Abdalla became an important point of departure, even though he and I hardly knew each other. By then, of course, Abdilatif was in Britain working for the BBC. "Do you know Abdilatif Abdalla? How dare you claim not to know him well enough? What are you hiding? Wasn't he the person who drew you to this seditious conspiracy? Has he been in touch with you? What about you—have you been in touch with him in recent months?"

Then one morning, one of the Swahili officers walked in with a copy of Abdilatif's *Sauti ya Dhiki*. It turned out to be my copy of the book, one of the many items that the police had taken from my office at the university. "Why do you have a copy of Abdilatif's book?"

"Is it banned?" I asked.

"No, but why do you have it?"

"Because I teach some of his poems in my class on textual analysis," I responded.

"Why?"

"Is there any reason I should not?"

The officer then produced a photocopy of the poem "N'shishiyelo ni Lilo" ("I Won't Compromise"). Again, it was my photocopy with extensive markings and comments on it. "Why do you have a photocopy of this poem?"

---

2. Sheikh Abdilahi Nassir, Abdilatif's elder brother, was very appreciative of Kasim Rashid's efforts in the 1970s to alert him and a few other Muslim leaders about potential police visits and arrests as they continued to meet in one of their residences to discuss strategies of counteracting the newly proposed Law of Succession Act, which was deemed to be in contravention of Islamic law of inheritance.

It was the poem I was discussing in class last week; the photocopy allowed me to make more detailed notes about the poem without having to mess up the book itself. I remember having particularly extensive comments on the margins and around the third stanza of that poem:

> Kweli nnaifahamu, haipendwi aswilani
> Kwa mja hiyo ni sumu, mbaya iso kifani
> Mwenye kuitakalamu, hapendezi katwaani,
> Sasa n'shayaamini, ni kweli haya ni kweli.

> Truth is never valued, this I now understand
> To the mortal it's sheer poison, potent without measure
> Whoever utters it is permanently disavowed
> This I now accept, it's nothing but the truth.

So, why this particular poem—a *kichwa ngumu* (strong-headed) poem—a reference, I supposed, to the sense conveyed by the title of the poem. Well, I was exploring the theme of "truth" with my students—especially, comparing the notion of *kweli* (truth) and that of *haki,* which combines truth and justice. And I also wanted my students to think critically about whether there is, in fact, one kind of truth as well as the relationship between truth, justice, and power. Do the exploiter and the exploited share the same truth, for example? And so on and so forth as we continued to dance around Abdilatif and his poetry. It was after this Abdilatif phase of my interrogation by fellow Waswahili that the process shifted from the carrot phase to the more brutal stick phase with some senior non-Swahili officers taking over the interrogation.

After several days in special branch police custody, I was eventually hooded—in the dark of the night, ironically—and transferred to the Kamiti Maximum Security Prison. As the metal doors to the cell building where I would spend the next couple of years virtually in solitary confinement creaked open, my attention was immediately drawn to a middle-aged warden, whose name I later came to learn was Kariuki, because of his rather unusual remarks. Kariuki seemed astonished to see me—as if he had known me before and was not expecting to see me there. And he expressed his surprise in a Swahili with some measure of Gikuyu interference: "Ee! Muthwairi mwingine!" ("Oh! Yet another Mswahili!") I immediately sensed that my fellow Mswahili, the leftist-leaning Professor Ahmed Muhiddin (Taji, as he was popularly known) of the Department of Government at the University of Nairobi, had also been arrested and was probably now detained at Kamiti.

304 • THE IMAGINATIVE VISION OF ABDILATIF ABDALLA'S *VOICE OF AGONY*

It was not until about two days later, during my one-hour-a-day break out of my cell, that I saw Kariuki again. And in measured conversation with him, I came to understand that, in fact, by "Muthwairi mwingine," he meant the Mswahili who came after Abdilatif, not after Taji.

As it turned out, Kariuki's seeming bewilderment at seeing me at Kamiti had much to do with the fact that, like many other Kenyans at that time, he held a view of the Swahili that was somewhat in accord with Abdilatif's own opinion of his ethnic compatriots. This is the view we find in his poem "Zindukani" ("Come to Your Senses"), which, after condemning their attitude and behavior, calls on members of his community to choose a path of change. What is needed, he urges them:

> Ni nyendo kuzigeuza, ambazo 'metupotowa
> Na hatua kuz'ongeza, zaidi zipate kuwa
> Petu tupate pakuza, kwa jasho letu kutowa
> 'Kingoja kusaidiwa, tutakufa masikini.

> It requires changing the ways that have misdirected us
> And expediting our movement, increasing our steps
> To develop our home through the sweat of our labor
> We'll perish in poverty if we (just) wait to be assisted

For Kariuki, as a rule, the Waswahili were a lazy, timid, subdued, and complacent lot. He regarded Abdilatif as an exception to the rule. And even in his wildest imagination, he could not fathom that there would be more than one exception to that ethnic rule, that he would see yet another "Muthwairi" brought to Kamiti for political reasons during the tenure of his already long service.

More remarkable to me, however, was the fact that Kariuki still remembered Abdilatif even though it had been some ten years or so since he left Kamiti. And in my continued conversation with Kariuki over the course of the next few months, it was clear why: Abdilatif had left one hell of an impression, a record of an activist who had completed his prison term unbroken, unrepentant—embodying an inspirational force of political defiance—and all in his special polite and humble demeanor. Perhaps that is why the special branch police was so suspicious of my interest in Abdilatif's poem "N'shishiyelo ni Lilo"—afraid of the very idea of unwavering commitment to one's beliefs and principles.

After my release from Kamiti Maximum Security Prison, I discovered that I had lost my job at the university and no institution was willing to employ me without written permission from the Office of the President, which, needless to say, I was unwilling to seek. Nonetheless, there were sympathetic individuals who were prepared to take the risk of engaging my services on short contracts, but all behind the scenes. One of these was a certain Abdallah Ismaily, who was then the Managing Director of Oxford University Press of Nairobi, Kenya, a position previously held by Abdilatif's own elder brother, Sheikh Abdilahi Nassir. Abdallah Ismaily had sent me a message through a third party requesting me to meet him in his office on a specified day and time. And so I went.

When I arrived, Abdallah Ismaily was escorting someone—I believe his marketing manager—out of his office. Abdallah then introduced me to the gentleman in Kiswahili: "This is Alamin Mazrui." Instantly the man added, "Oh yes, the author of *Sauti ya Dhiki* [*Voice of Agony*]." "No, of *Kilio cha Haki* [*Cry for Justice*] actually," Abdallah quickly corrected him. And without hesitation or acknowledging his mistake, the gentleman continued, "That's right. First there was the voice of agony. Then the voice of agony became a cry for justice. *Sivyo* [Isn't that the case]?!"

It is true, of course, that my play *Kilio cha Haki* came after Abdilatif's *Sauti ya Dhiki*. To be precise, *Sauti ya Dhiki* was published in 1973, the year after Abdilatif's release from prison. My *Kilio cha Haki* was published in 1981, the year before my imprisonment. And if Abdilatif's *Sauti ya Dhiki* was a product of his confinement, my *Kilio cha Haki* is widely believed to have been the cause of my own incarceration. So, perhaps the marketing manager was not altogether wrong to suggest that *Sauti ya Dhiki* and *Kilio cha Haki* were texts that were somehow in dialogue with each other.

But, like Abdilatif, I too ended up producing my own collection of prison poems, *Chembe cha Moyo* (*Arrow in My Heart*), published in 1988.[3] Was it a coincidence that, unlike fellow Kenyans like Josiah Mwangi Kariuki and Ngũgĩ wa Thiong'o, Abdilatif and I elected to capture our respective experiences of incarceration in verse rather than in prose? Or did the choice have something to do with our Swahiliness? Some of you might be aware that when two of the sons of the late Professor Ali Mazrui suddenly lost their eyesight, both he and his relatives in Mombasa turned to poetry as one of the strategies for dealing with the trauma. In the process, Mazrui produced his own Swahili poem "Mshipa wa Jito," which he then translated into English as "Ode to the Optic Nerve." When Derek Robinson later interviewed Mazrui on the BBC about why he decided to express his pain and distress in verse,

---

3. Alamin Mazrui, *Chembe cha Moyo* (Nairobi: Heinemann, 1988).

Mazrui explained that it was "influenced by the Swahili part of my background, because there is a good deal of composition of verse in moments of great significance in one's life."[4] Similarly, in the case of Abdilatif and me, it is quite possible that, searching for an artistic "safety-valve" in our moments of confinement, our shared Swahili heritage impelled us towards poetry rather than prose. Partly inspired by Ngũgĩ's *Devil on the Cross*, I had in fact started writing a novel in my initial weeks at Kamiti Maximum Security Prison.[5] In no time, however, I had succumbed to the Swahili muse of poetic expression. This is not to suggest, of course, that people in confinement who are not ethnically Swahili would not turn to poetry under conditions of incarceration. We know too many who have done so to accord such a suggestion any degree of validity. The point here, rather, is that the Swahili would have somewhat of a "natural" cultural propensity towards poetry in such moments of personal suffering and inner challenges.

The relationship between poetic expression and the state of incarceration is, of course, quite evident in the titles of the two collections themselves—*Sauti ya Dhiki* and *Chembe cha Moyo*. Abdilatif's choice of the title of his anthology is made clear in his "Dibaji" (Preface): "Kwa kuwa maisha ya kifungoni si ya raha, mashairi haya nimeyapa jina la *Sauti ya Dhiki*" ("Because life in prison is not easy, I have given these poems the title of *Sauti ya Dhiki* [*Voice of Agony*])."[6] My *Chembe cha Moyo* (*Arrow in My Heart*), however, has a dual symbolism. Pierced by an arrow, the heart is in pain, evincing its own, my own, voice of agony. But the "arrow in my heart" is also a Cupid's arrow, an arrow of love, the love of the many cherished dimensions of that reality from which one is now cut off, completely detached. Even in their variation, then, the two titles point to that common experience of anguish.

A remarkable thing, however, is that I never took another look at this collection of my poems again until 2017—that is, after a period of almost 30 years! In April 2017, a certain Maryam Ali Hamad, a graduate student at the University of Dodoma, Tanzania, contacted me by email, indicating that she was writing her thesis on Kiswahili prison literature, focusing exclusively on

---

4. As quoted in Ibrahim Noor Shariff, "The Function of Dialogue Poetry in Swahili Society," EdD dissertation (Rutgers University, 1983), 248.

5. Early in his imprisonment, Abdilatif Abdalla began writing a novel, "Ni Haki Yangu" ("It's My Right"), that he never finished. See Kimani wa Wanjiru, "Abdilatif Abdalla: My Poems Gave Me Company," Pambazuka News, 14 October 2010. https://www.pambazuka.org/arts/abdilatif-abdalla-my-poems-gave-me-company. —*Ed.*

6. Abdilatif Abdalla, *Sauti ya Dhiki* (Nairobi: Oxford University Press, 1973), xiii.

Abdilatif's *Sauti ya Dhiki* and my *Chembe cha Moyo*. Hamad's thesis finally appeared in October 2017, and in it she analyses the many senses in which the two anthologies articulate the idea of confinement. She also looks at how the specific contexts and conditions under which the two poets were imprisoned—one (Abdilatif) as a result of a court ruling with a sentence of a specific duration, and the other (Alamin) as a consequence of a presidential decree that indicated no definite period—might have influenced aspects of their prison poetry.

Unknown to Hamad at that time was that, in fact, she was following in the footsteps of Ken Walibora Waliaula, who included a comparative study of *Sauti ya Dhiki* and *Chembe cha Moyo* in his *Narrating Prison Experience: Human Rights, Self, Society, and Political Incarceration in Africa.*[7] Hamad lamented that she was able to find a wealth of information about Abdilatif and his life on the Internet, but found virtually nothing about me. So she wondered if there was any way she could have an interview with me about my personal history. As luck would have it, I had to make an unexpected trip to Kenya in May 2017, and Maryam traveled to Mombasa to interview me.

As it turned out, Maryam Hamad had numerous questions not only about my life, but also about many of the poems in my *Chembe cha Moyo*. Inadvertently, then, she forced me to reread and think about the poems in a way that I had never done since they were first published, after a lapse of some 30 years. And because of the comparative frame of her own thesis topic, and the fact that I was then well familiar with *Sauti ya Dhiki*, I could not help but look at *Chembe cha Moyo* in light of *Sauti ya Dhiki*.

On the surface of it, the most apparent divergence between the two collections may appear to be in form. Ken Walibora Waliaula suggested that "Abdalla and Mazrui's literary style are seemingly worlds apart."[8] And after some analysis of the two texts, Waliaula concluded that "while Abdalla comes across as a prisoner of prosodic style, Mazrui frees himself from the chains of convention without completely abandoning convention."[9] As much as Abdilatif may appear to be devoted to the long-established Swahili poetic norms of composition, however, there is no doubt that his poetry is truly unique in that it is classical and inventive at the same time; and it combines convention

---

7. Ken Walibora Waliaula, *Narrating Prison Experience: Human Rights, Self, Society, and Political Incarceration in Africa* (Champaign, IL: Common Ground), 2013.

8. Waliaula, 95.

9. Waliaula, 96.

308 • THE IMAGINATIVE VISION OF ABDILATIF ABDALLA'S *VOICE OF AGONY*

and creativity in very distinctive ways without being stilted. One can say with certainty that no modern collection of Swahili poetry can be placed in the same league as *Sauti ya Dhiki*. Abdilatif's mastery of Swahili poetic diction and idiom is unmatched and sets him apart from all his contemporaries.

At the thematic level, on the other hand, there were some convergences between the two collections. For one, both include poems that reveal the agony of imprisonment. Here again, it may be useful to quote Ken Walibora Waliaula, who suggests:

> there are striking resemblances in the thematic concerns in the two anthologies. In a sense both poets embark on a psychic journey and philosophical journey, which entail articulating a wide range of "voices" as a means of dealing with the reality of incarceration. The multivocality of the multiple "I"-s that inhabit the poetic universe of their collections of poems represent[s] multifarious conceptions and narrations of self and confinement. Both poets capture in the carceral imagination and experience the aporia and uncertainty of the revolutionary struggle ....[10]

As one might expect, we both also reflect on the theme of political exile once out of prison. And here I have to say that Abdilatif spoke for both of us in his moving poem "Naja" when he asked, "Kaa kwingine anapi, ela kwenye lakwe gando?" ('Where else can a crab run to, save its own shell?')

Hamad also explores the many recurrent themes that appear in the two anthologies—from feelings of dislocation to those of intellectual suffocation, from the surreal sense of double-imprisonment to incarceration as an embodied experience. She draws our attention to moments of self-doubt that both Abdilatif and Alamin seem to have undergone, sometimes leading them to seek for help from others.[11] In his "Ndiya Panda" ("Crossroads"), for example, Abdilatif writes in earnest:

> Shauri jema munipe, enyi binadamu wenda
> Nipani musinitupe, musiwe wa kunivunda
> Nipate juwa kweupe, ndiya ipi ya kwenenda
>   Kwenye hii ndiya panda

---

10. Waliaula, 96.

11. Maryam Ali Hamad, "Suala la Ufungwa katika Ushairi wa Kiswahili: Mifano kutoka Diwani za *Sauti ya Dhiki* na *Chembe cha Moyo*," MA thesis (University of Dodoma, Tanzania, 2017), 105–106.

Abdilatif and I • 309

Give me some sound counsel, ye people of mine
Give me, abandon me not, do not let me down
Clearly I need to know which path to trail
    At this forked road (1973, 80)

A similar moment of uncertainty and searching for help and guidance is evident in my poem "Nishike Mkono" ("Hold Me by the Hand"):

...basi,
   hebu nishike nami mkono
   unambie safari ndiyo hino
     matata yajapo
     zinduko lijapo
     faraja ijapo
       niwe pamoja nawe
       pamoja tu
       mkono kwa mkono.

Come hold my hand
and tell me the journey has begun
   when trouble begins to approach
   when consciousness surges forth
   when redemption finally arrives
     let me be with you
     just together, you and I
       hand in hand (1988, 56)

Central to both poems, of course, is the journey motif. Along the way, questions begin to arise: Am I still on the right path? Or have I lost my way? The inner poetic dialogue is sometimes a quest for self-validation.

But what I found particularly striking in the contrast between the two collections is the extent to which a number of my poems betray a sense of alienation from the Swahili existential self in a way that Abdilatif's poems do not. For example, Islam is virtually an accompanying attribute of Swahili culture and identity. Throughout *Sauti ya Dhiki*, Abdilatif expresses his political radicalism and leftist leanings in ways that are not in conflict with his Islamic faith and identity. He has even been able to translate radical ideas from the West in ways that make them organic to the African body politic. In his "Tuza Moyo" ("Worry Not"), for example, Abdilatif writes:

> Akhi tuliza mtima, uwate kusononeka
> Hakuna lisilokoma, siku 'kifika 'tatoka
> Kusubiri ni lazima, na kumuomba Rabbuka
> Wasiya wako 'meshika
>
> Brother take heart, and stop grieving
> Nothing is endless, my release day'll come
> Patience is needed here, as are prayers to your Lord
> I have heeded your advice. (1973: 6)

Throughout his collection, Abdilatif leaves no room for doubt about his continued faith in God's powers of intervention in human affairs.

In my *Chembe cha Moyo*, on the other hand, I could see a clear disconnect between my political position and my religious background. At one point, I was even shocked at the audacity of my younger self, of my days of rabid Marxism, to conclude my poem "Risala" by declaring:

> Lakini enyi mafukara wa dunia
> Hofu yangu kubwa nawambia
> Mungu huenda ikatukia
> hajui kusoma...hili nachelea
>
> But ye, wretched of the earth
> My biggest fear, let me tell you
> It may just happen that God
> Is in fact illiterate...This I worry (1988: 24)

In spite of the fact that it was intended to be read metaphorically, this is a kind of statement that would certainly make my ancestors turn in their graves. In other words, that sense of Islamic belonging—in terms other than cultural affiliation and identity—that continues to frame Abdilatif's poems has somewhat receded both in my writings and personal life.

This contrast between Abdilatif and me may appear surprising at first, given the similarities in our backgrounds—both Mombasa, Old Town boys of the transcolonial generation. Our respective families are well known for being deeply religious and politically radical at the same time. Indeed, Abdilatif's brother, Sheikh Abdilahi Nassir, and my father, Sheikh Muhammad Kasim, were comrades-in-arms, fully devoted to each other in the campaign for a reformed Islam. And the two met periodically to discuss possible political strategies in dealing with the government of Jomo Kenyatta and later of Daniel Arap Moi in matters affecting the Muslims of Kenya.

With this background in mind, it is possible to argue that, from the beginning, Abdilatif was inspired by both the religious and the political experiences of his background, and to this day continues to embody this family tradition to varying degrees in his life, thinking and writing. Though Abdilatif is by no means your typical Mswahili, perhaps the fact that he did not get the opportunity to pursue higher education in Africa—brilliant as the man is—may have shielded him from its alienating effects. As Ali Mazrui once put it, by design the African academy has been the greatest purveyor of cultural alienation and intellectual dependency partly because it has been planted in the African space with few if any concessions to African cultures.[12] It is true that Abdilatif was introduced to Che Guevara, to V.I. Lenin, to Mao Dze Dong, in a European language, English. But that entire process of learning about these revolutionaries and their revolutionary ideas took place outside the confines of the Western-style academy and within the cultural and epistemological milieu of his Swahili-Islamic society.

In my case, on the other hand, I seem to have been inspired by neither the religious nor the political orientation of my family history, even though I continued to be a devoted practicing Muslim well into my early adulthood. In fact, my interest in politics did not begin until the mid-1970s, when I was in my mid-20s (and, coincidentally, it all started at Princeton University, where I first presented these reflections in 2017 at a symposium on Abdilatif Abdalla). Two of my friends at that time, Apollo Njonjo of Kenya and Waldon Bello of the Philippines, were die-hard Marxists struggling to complete their PhD dissertations in political science at Princeton. In time, I was drawn to many hours of discussing and debating the political goings-on in the world with the two, a process that set in quick motion my own politicization and radicalization, which ultimately led me to Kamiti Maximum Security Prison some seven years or so later.

The point here is that even though my process of learning about Marxist ideas was somewhat informal, I think that because it took place within the structures of the American academy, it had a more profoundly alienating effect on me than I had realized before rereading *Chembe cha Moyo*. And the more I came to appreciate Marxism, the more I became estranged from Islam as an integral part of my Swahiliness. My journey here could be compared quite closely with that of Samba Diallo, the main character in Cheikh Hamidou

---

12. Ali A. Mazrui, "The African University as a Multinational Corporation: Problems of Penetration and Dependency," *Harvard Educational Review* 45, no. 2 (1975): 191–210.

312 • THE IMAGINATIVE VISION OF ABDILATIF ABDALLA'S *VOICE OF AGONY*

Kane's *Ambiguous Adventure* (*L'aventure ambiguë* 1961; English translation 1962). Perhaps like Samba Diallo in that colonially framed encounter between my Islamic background and the Western impact, "I have become the two."[13]

In the final analysis, then, some of the contrasts between *Sauti ya Dhiki* and *Chembe cha Moyo* once again raise the problematic role of Western-style formal education in Africa as one of the primary agents of cultural alienation. The pressure now is for some readjustment towards a greater balance between the continuities of African cultures and new forces that have developed on the continent. And I believe Abdilatif is one great example of this possibility—the possibility of a balance between the old and the new, between tradition and modernity in their various articulations. The challenge now is to discover a systemic formula towards that end.

---

13. Cheikh Hamidou Kane, *Ambiguous Adventure*, translated by Katherine Woods (London: Heinemann, 1972), 150.

Rhymed, Metrical Translations of Four Poems

Meg Arenberg

This Is What I Hold Fast | N'shishiyelo ni Lilo

1　My brother, listen, what I'm saying you should hear
　Put your ear to my heart; let me tell you what's there
　You should know my belief, the one thing I hold dear
　I will not let it go; this is what I hold fast

2　Our shrewd ancestors said so; it's nothing new
　The truth can be bitter when it's given to you
　I've come to believe them; the old sayings are true
　If you don't know it yet, listen well and you will

3　I now understand that truth is despised;
　It's like poison to men, the taste undisguised
　And Truthsayers then, are rejected not prized
　I've come to accept the truth of these truths

4　I spoke the truth, and for speaking I paid
　I told them the truth and by them was betrayed
　My wickedness rivals the Pharaoh, they said
　Truly, I believe: there are few who love truth

5　I spoke the truth to those in control
　What became of the ones who challenged their rule
　To the people of this country, I told it in full
　My present affliction is my only reward

6   When Truth came to cut them—as it always does
     My innocent words became adequate cause
     To arrest me at once, shut me behind bars
     Punished by prison, they thought I'd regret

7   And brother, believe me, Truth became pain
     The vengeance on body and heart I've sustained
     Simply for stating the acts that I'd seen
     I no longer question the bitterness of truth

8   It's Truth that removed me, and holds me apart
     Severs me from home and those dear to my heart
     Why am I punished, why kept under guard?
     Simply for speaking what I knew to be true

9   Truth has me captive from noon until night
     Dawn never breaks, I can't feel the sun's light
     And the guard never lets my cell door from his sight
     You'd think I'm a beast, the way I'm restrained

10   Truth has me sleeping on the floor, in the cold
     Despite the blanket, once the shivering takes hold
     The agony in my limbs is relentless, uncontrolled
     This is the torture of sleeping on cement

11   And though towering walls imprison me inside
     Conversation between prisoners is strictly proscribed
     For fear words will spread, all contact's denied
     Lest I stir something up with the things that I know

12   Truth has revoked all the rights I am due
     Letters are forbidden; no visitors let through
     I swear every word that I've told you is true
     I'm refused correspondence with anyone outside

Rhymed, Metrical Translations of Four Poems • 315

13   But I'll stop; I won't name every grim play of force
Let me turn back instead to my opening verse
Tell you the nature of the faith that I nurse
So you can know fully the will of my heart

14   The day I stood up, to speak what I knew
I assumed there's no wrong in saying what's true
I had no notion of what I'd be put through
That they'd clamp my mouth shut, so I'd never be heard

15   Even if their torture goes on without end
Employs every tactic to debase and torment
It will never be enough to make me relent
Where I see truth I'll speak it, I won't be gagged

16   Their abuse may wound me, but my heart is unmoved
My will to speak is strong; truth can't be disproved
They're wasting their time. I will not be moved
I'll only go forward, only toward truth

17   Those with worthy hearts, unbound by fear
When the pain they are destined to suffer draws near
Look to Merciful God, give thanks, and persevere
I too stand firm, take strength for what comes

18   Torture can cause unsteady hearts to withdraw
Without strength of will, vows quickly dissolve
A man may feel it's best to loosen resolve
But I won't let it go; this is what I hold fast

19   Many have been victims, I'm not the first
Many have been killed who had strength in their hearts
I'm willing also; I follow their course
I'll walk in their footsteps; this is what I hold fast

316 • THE IMAGINATIVE VISION OF ABDILATIF ABDALLA'S *VOICE OF AGONY*

20   The Prophet Mohamed, cherished by the Lord
       Told us: speak truth, however harsh your reward
       It's the core of my faith, it cannot be stirred
       These beliefs of a lifetime, I won't let them go

21   Truth is where I'll end; brother, goodbye
       Truth won't go unspoken while I'm standing by
       Truth! In my lifetime, I won't cease my cry
       And for my own part, I'll accept what is true

    —September 1969

    —Translated by Meg Arenberg

TRANSLATOR'S REFLECTION

I first began work on this poem over a decade ago; I have returned to it again and again, producing many versions. Less playful than the other poems I have translated from the collection, it was much harder to translate. The gravity of the poem's content seemed to resist my attempts at rhyme in the English. Ultimately, however, I found the independence of the fourth line in each stanza could act as a kind of anchor, pulling back the other lines from too breezy a cadence. I allowed these repeated interruptions in the rhyme to also loosen somewhat the hold of the poem's meter, effectively slowing down the reader, and inviting each stanza to be savored on its own. Taken together, these final lines also constitute the moral center of the poem, offering repeated formal representation of the poet's spiritual immovability.

Rhymed, Metrical Translations of Four Poems • 317

Crocodile | Mamba

I too have words; I'll join those already speaking
I'll gild my verse so it pleases those who're reading
Untwist these words, for their sense may be misleading

There's a croc gliding smugly down the river
A boastful sop who believes he's brave and clever
He loves to talk, tells the world he'll live forever

With fool's conceit he strings himself along
Sustains belief that he'll always be this strong
But self-deceit and pride can only last so long

He should know, someday he'll breathe his last
He too will go, once his die's been cast
Time will show his power finally passed

What lies ahead none of us can comprehend
What fate has set, no show of fierceness can transcend
Don't forget: what has a start must have an end

—23 March 1970

—Translated by Meg Arenberg

TRANSLATOR'S REFLECTION

"Mamba," perhaps Abdalla's most famous poem, was the first of his that I attempted to translate. I love how the poem seems to steal power from its untouchable subject, how, even as it ridicules the crocodile's boastfulness, it performs a boast of its own. The poem's mocking quality lends itself to rhyme in the English, but it was important to me not to let a rollicking tone undermine the dexterity and moral authority of the poetic voice. Some of this is accomplished in diction. But a mix of full and slant rhymes (at both end and midlines) also helped retain some of the formal qualities of the original without giving way to sing-song in English.

THE IMAGINATIVE VISION OF ABDILATIF ABDALLA'S *VOICE OF AGONY*

I Remember You | *Nakukumbuka*

Though we are parted you and I, I remember you
And if I had feathers, I would fly
It's for the impossible that I pine

Though we are parted you and I, my beloved
My love shall not subside
Rest assured, you are mine

Though we are parted you and I, persevere
I'll again be by your side
Let's pray to God for healthy lives

　　—*1 May 1970*

　　—*Translated by Meg Arenberg*

TRANSLATOR'S REFLECTION

As with many of the poems in *Sauti ya Dhiki*, repetition is essential to "Nakukumbuka." The hemistich which opens the poem, "Mi nawe mbali tungawa," acts as a kind of gravitational force, repeatedly drawing the listener back to the poem's immutable center: the stark reality of the poet's separation from his beloved. This repeated return offers a secondary wave of motion, not incompatible with, but distinct from, the poem's line-by-line prosody. Retaining this repetition was thus essential. Knowing I could not reproduce the poem's formal elements exactly, I chose to make the first line in each stanza a bit longer in the English, drawing out the repetition of that first hemistich, and introducing the "I" sound which I then sought to weave through the other lines.

Rhymed, Metrical Translations of Four Poems • 319

Which Will It Be? | Lipi Litakalokuwa?

Which will it be? Let it be then, and let it be known
Let it be that we may know, let us know and let us see
Let it happen that we might let go, let it be so that we may speak
We can't have it another way, it will be so or it will not be

Let it be and make itself known; let it not remain concealed
If light then let it pour in, into every corner let it flow
Is it darkness? Then let it shroud the ground before our feet
We can't have it another way, it will be so or it will not be

Let our hearts not thump in fear, let it be so they might rest
Uncertainty has clung too long, knitted to our breasts
What they carry is enough; let this not be an added weight
We can't have it another way, it will be so or it will not be

If it wants then let it be so, and thus let the truth be known
Let it not unduly vex us, why should we be discomposed?
It won't if it does not want, let us not try to coax and plead
We can't have it another way, it will be so or it will not be

—*14 January 1971*

—*Translated by Meg Arenberg*

TRANSLATOR'S REFLECTION

"Lipi Litakalokuwa" is at once grave and playful. The poet moves deftly between the torment of obfuscation and the lightness of equanimity. The unspecified subject ("li") that dances through the poem teases us with its ambiguity even as it gestures to the darker side of not knowing. While the poem never names this unknown thing around which it circles, the grammar of Bantu noun class allows the poet to designate a narrower set of possibilities than the fully ambiguous English "it." The affix "li" suggests the class of words and ideas—more likely a spoken thing than a physical one. This presents a special challenge to translation. From the perspective of sound alone, however, the poem's frequent use of subjunctive forms and the verb "kuwa" (to be) offers the opportunity to use the English "let" and "be" as partial sonic replacements for "li."

Textual Backgrounds:
Voice of Agony *in Its Historical Moment*

Kenya: Twendapi?

Kenya: Where Are We Heading?[1]

Abdilatif Abdalla

Translated by Kai Kresse

For a period of three months—since July 1968 when we released our pamphlet that we called *Turuuu* [*See, I told you so!*] until today—we have remained silent. Everyone interpreted this silence of ours in the way they wanted. One of the many interpretations given for our silence is, we have been told, "How come you are silent—is it that you've already been intimidated?" To those who thought this, we say YOU ARE SLEEPING!! Not us. An intimidation is not something that makes one keep away from doing what one thinks is right. On the contrary, we believe that an intimidation will only increase a person's courage to continue what they[2] are doing, provided they truly believe in it. Therefore even if, let's say, we were to be intimidated again this time, we still will not be silent. Twice before we have been intimidated. But since that day, instead of instilling us with fear, those threats have increased, and will continue to increase, our determination that what we are doing is right. For if it were not right, those with the power to intimidate people would not have

---

1. English translation of Abdilatif Abdalla's *Kenya: Twendapi?* (Mombasa, November 1968), by Kai Kresse in consultation with Abdilatif Abdalla. For the original Swahili text, see *Abdilatif Abdalla: Poet in Politics*, edited by Rose Marie Beck and Kai Kresse (Dar es Salaam: Mkuki na Nyota, 2016), 76–80. For discussion of the context of the pamphlet's creation and of Abdalla's arrest and trial, see Kai Kresse, "*Kenya: Twendapi?*: Re-Reading Abdilatif Abdalla's Pamphlet Fifty Years after Independence," *Africa* 86, no. 1 (February 2016): 1–32. We reprint the English translation from that article with the permission of Cambridge University Press and the kind assistance of Kai Kresse. Subsequent footnotes belong to him.

2. *Mtu* (a person), with its singular references in the original, can appropriately be rendered as "they" here, which is widely accepted as the gender neutral third person singular pronoun in colloquial English.

324 • THE IMAGINATIVE VISION OF ABDILATIF ABDALLA'S *VOICE OF AGONY*

gone to such trouble. Thus we say again, ONE NEVER ABANDONS WHAT ONE BELIEVES IN.[3]

In this month's pamphlet, we will talk about the very shameful action carried out by the KANU government all over Kenya, in August 1968. We have no choice but to speak out about it. They did as they pleased because of the governmental powers they wield. Now, what can we, who are denied our rights and who do not have these governmental powers, do, so that we can reclaim our rights? What other means shall we employ to attain those rights when the appropriate and democratic means have been discarded and disregarded by those in governmental power? What should we do since KANU wants to "rule" by force—"forever"[4]—without the consent of us Citizens?[5] Which path should we take in order to remove this KANU government and its dictatorial rulers, who have become increasingly more dictatorial than those who began with it? Which path could that be, fellow Citizens? What is to be done? These are the questions that a person must ask themselves. We do not know which answers you will give to these questions. But from our side we have an answer that is accepted everywhere else [in the world] where such injustices have occurred. Also, an answer like the one we are going to give you has helped all of those who have been ruled by dictators such as those in the KANU government We will explain this answer to you later, since first we want to explain to you what brought us to the point where we will no longer consider any other way to get rid of this dictatorial KANU government, apart from the one that we will tell you about now.

Without doubt, our comrades, you have not yet forgotten those absurdities[6] that were perpetrated by the government in August—absurdities which have not been perpetrated anywhere else in the whole history of politics! Those absurdities were the trickery and treachery that the KANU government used against the opposition party of the KPU—a legally registered party just like KANU. And it is a party with more followers than KANU. These treacherous acts were committed in order that KPU not be given the opportunity to put forward their candidates in the municipal elections. What was done (as you

---

3. Literally: A RIGHTFUL OWNER DOES NOT LET GO OF HIS POSSESSION (Swahili saying).

4. Literally: for life.

5. The capitalization of "Citizen(s)" (*Mwa/Wa-nanchi* in the original) is one of the idiosyncrasies of the text, highlighting the importance of the agents of democratic participation.

6. Literally: unbelievable things.

have heard and seen) was to reject the papers of the KPU candidates because they—TAKE NOTE—"were not filled out correctly as required by the law"!!! Here we have a few questions that you might consider for your own judgement. Does it fit into your heads, fellow Citizens, that among the "submitted 1,800" KPU papers there was not even one that was filled out correctly "as the law required"? Can your minds accept that among all the KANU papers there was not even a single one that had a mistake? (Or maybe theirs were filled out by demi-gods.) Such reasoning cannot be accepted even by a madman!! Or was it that the KPU leaders did not know this law about how to fill out these forms? Not possible! As we know all laws are made in parliament. Therefore, it cannot be that the representatives of KPU, who are members of parliament, did not know this law. And it also cannot be that after KPU came to know this law that they did not follow it, as their intention was to beat KANU [in the elections]. And this was open and obvious to all! We are saying that KPU followed the law as required. And this we will prove to you when we tell you what happened in Machakos.

This indeed is the treachery of the KANU government. After the KANU government saw that those who were always in charge of accepting the submitted papers for municipal elections perhaps would not be able to unjustly reject the papers of KPU candidates, they instead put the DCs[7] in charge of receiving such papers. We are saying this based on the evidence we have, that a *Town Clerk*[8] of Nairobi was forced to reject the KPU papers in Nairobi, but he refused. Thereupon the local DC was put in charge. We also have evidence that the *Town Clerk* of Mombasa was forced to do so, as well. As he did not have the guts to do so,[9] he could not decline and show courage by refusing, like his colleague in Nairobi. And you see the result of this, dear comrades. Here we need to remind each other about one thing regarding those DCs who were appointed to receive the election papers. On 27 July 1968, there was a big meeting of all KANU leaders that took place in Nakuru. All DCs and PCs[10] of Kenya were ordered [by the government] to attend. Also, we want to explain that the DCs and PCs are actually "Servants of the Citizens" (*Civil Servants*[11]).

---

7. DC: District Commissioner.
8. English in the original.
9. Literally: he "had a small heart."
10. PC: Provincial Commissioner.
11. English in the original.

326 • THE IMAGINATIVE VISION OF ABDILATIF ABDALLA'S *VOICE OF AGONY*

And any Civil Servant is prohibited from engaging in political matters, and also from assisting any political party. Even if it is the one that formed the government. This is a democratic tradition in every country that has more than one political party. If a country has only one political party, then it becomes imperative to assist this party in any possible way. So, how come that the KANU government, which claims to follow democracy, uses Civil Servants to serve the interests of their party, KANU? Without doubt, you have seen how the Coast PC and the DC of Mombasa have actively involved themselves in politics these days. Now they are behaving like the *Organizing Secretary*[12] of KANU and his assistant. What a travesty!![13] What kind of democracy is this? Can't you be honest?!

Therefore, it was in Nakuru [at that meeting] that the DCs were ordered to "fail"[14] the KPU papers by any means possible. To substantiate that the DCs were indeed given such orders in Nakuru, we will give you just one example, from the many others that we have. For example: the papers of the contestants for the election in Machakos were received before that meeting in Nakuru took place. Since the meeting had not been held yet, 32 papers of KPU candidates were accepted. So these were filled in "as required by law," as they would otherwise not have been accepted. After the Machakos DC returned from the meeting in Nakuru, he failed all these same 32 papers that he himself had passed earlier, before going to Nakuru. When it comes to this, what more is there to say? Do you see the ways in which injustice was committed?

Comrades. This is indeed what was done by the KANU government which—TAKE NOTE—is led by an African. And those to whom this was done are also Africans just like those running the government. There is nothing lacking in their Africanness.[15] When matters reach this stage, then people are inclined to say things that in their hearts they do not like to say. Comrades, we have seen the Brit[on][16] when he was ruling us. The Brit is not an African like us. Yet on top of all the evil he has done to us, and the ways he showed his contempt and humiliated us beyond limits, still he did not dare to do what our African peers have done to us. During those [colonial] times of the

---

12. English in the original.

13. Literally: what causes of alarm (or horror)!!

14. To invalidate. *Wazifelishe* is literally "they should cause to fail," appropriating the English verb "fail" into Swahili.

15. Literally: they are not diminished by anything in their Africanness.

16. *Muingereza* (in the original) comes from and relates to "the English," but with reference to people the term is used generically to refer to the British.

British, the election papers were not failed for not being properly filled. And if you made mistakes, you were shown them and you were allowed to correct them. And on top of all this, thereafter this same paper would be accepted. What caused your election paper to be rejected was when you submitted it after the deadline. If this is how things are, well then we "prefer Pharaoh to Moses." Indeed, at this point people say, about something that they preferred not to be there, that "the times of the colonial ruler were better." (Give the devil his due.)[17] And when things reach this level, it feels more painful: to see an African committing such evil deeds to his fellow African, things that even the Brit, who neither cared for us nor respected us, did not do to us. But THE END OF ALL RIPE FRUIT IS TO ROT. Nothing else.

The KANU government brought this injustice upon the KPU party, since without a doubt KANU would otherwise "have had to eat dry rice."[18] The KANU government knows that the people have become tired of this government. The people are tired of the barbaric[19] acts committed by this government. And for the KANU government, bringing such injustice upon KPU has in effect denied the Citizens their right to choose. This right gives the Citizen the power to elect the one who he thinks will be useful to him. (This is not how things have actually been done—somebody coming and ordering that so-and-so and so-and-so should be elected.) Also, this right to vote gives the Citizen the power to reject a government he does not want—peacefully— without using any force. But today you will see that the Citizens have been denied this right, and the KANU government has appropriated it, in order to forcefully give itself the authorization to impose on the Citizens representatives whom they do not want. Representatives who have been put in place in order to work for a certain tribe so that other tribes would be oppressed more and more. This is indeed the democracy of the Boerish[20] KANU government.

Earlier on in this pamphlet, the second question we asked was: "What other means shall we employ to attain those rights when the appropriate and democratic means have been discarded and disregarded by those in

---

17. *Mgala muuweni na haki mpeni*, a historical Swahili saying. Literally: "kill the Galla and give him his right."

18. An idiomatic expression, meaning it would have been in a difficult situation; it would have lost the elections.

19. The application of this term to someone (*mshenzi*) and/or their acts (*kishenzi*, as here) is commonly seen as the strongest possible insult to the opposite party.

20. *Kikaburu*, a neologism coined by Abdalla here, is used as an adjective meaning "like the (South African) Boers."

328 • THE IMAGINATIVE VISION OF ABDILATIF ABDALLA'S *VOICE OF AGONY*

governmental power?" We promised you that we would answer this question. [But] First we would like to clarify the following:—if it is true, seriously in your hearts, that you care[21] for Kenya and you love this country with all your heart (if someone feels that this is indeed their home and has nowhere else to go), and if you want equality and humanity to be realized in Kenya and the injustices to go away (since we believe that there is no one who likes to be harassed or oppressed), well then, listen carefully to what we are telling you and keep it in your minds. We (THE DISCONTENTED) we understand that we are always under surveillance. And we understand that this time especially, because of what we have just said, all possible means to silence us will be employed so that we will not continue to enlighten[22] the people any more. Also, we do understand that this time there will be another plan to make us disappear (this plan has already been tried twice in the past), but our hearts will not relent[23] even one little bit[24] because we believe that what we do and say is just and right. Also, we understand that anyone who agrees with what we are saying will be in trouble. But when the hearts of the people unite in order to do what they are determined to do, there is nothing that can defeat them. Neither imprisonment, nor even death. This is indeed common everywhere in the world where there are people who are ready to sacrifice themselves and endure all the troubles for the sake of saving their fellow human beings, who will live on after them. When unified in heart, thought and belief,[25] we will succeed without a doubt. Not even once will we agree to keep quiet for fear of being persecuted, since the KANU government continues to oppress people in such unjust ways. Also, we ask our fellow Citizens not to fold their arms behind their backs, expecting that things will change without us ourselves putting effort into changing them. Nor should we agree with attitudes like those of other people, saying "God will remove this for us." It is true that it is not difficult for God to do this; but God himself has told human beings he will not change their situation for them unless they first put some effort into changing it themselves.

Fellow Citizens. The answer to the question we have been asking above is the following. Since peaceful means of removing the government—namely,

---

21. Literally: feel the pain.
22. Literally: open the eyes of.
23. Literally: step back.
24. Literally: grain.
25. Literally: with one heart, one thought, and one belief.

by the ballot—are already being choked off[26] by the KANU government ahead of the big[27] elections in 1970, and since the KANU government has committed such dirty acts as those we have seen, well then, there is no remedy or alternative peaceful way to remove this government. But before we can have the ability to take this path that is not peaceful, it is necessary that we first of all have a belief (not in terms of taking pity on anyone), that is, a BELIEF [conviction] that what we are doing is right and proper. This kind of belief indeed gave the Kikuyus ("Mau Mau") the courage[28] to enter the forest and fight against the British, to fight for the lands and fields which they were robbed of. It was the same kind of belief that helped the people of North Vietnam. Belief of this kind helped our brothers in Zanzibar until they were successful. And such a belief indeed gave strength and courage to the people of Biafra in Nigeria—so that they keep on fighting until today. And such a belief will indeed give us the strength, and the courage, to get rid of these dictatorial rulers of the KANU government. Rulers whose skin and whose faces are African, but whose hearts and actions are like those of the Boers. We did not expel those white Boers in order to put black Boers in their place. The time of "leaders in name alone" is now up. Now we want "leaders in deed."

It is true that taking this path is no mean task nor is it easy. It is a matter that requires us to give our sweat[29] if we want to succeed. There is nothing that can save human beings from death. Everywhere where there is protest and liberation struggle there will necessarily be deaths. All human beings have to die, but there are two types of death. As one famous activist once said, "even though death will reach every human being, there is a death as heavy as a rock and one as light as a feather."[30] There are still some days left. Let's wait for 1970 and see what happens. If things turn out to be as they were in August this year, or as they were in 1966, well then that will be it….![31]

---

26. Literally: killed.

27. That is, the general, parliamentary and presidential elections.

28. Literally: (mental) strength/determination.

29. That is, our dedication.

30. This is Mao Zedong (1893–1976), and the quote is from his famous "Serve the people" speech delivered in September 1944 at the funeral of the soldier Zhang Side, a former participant in the Long March (1934–1935) who had died in an accident and who was taken to represent communist virtues as endorsed by Mao in his speech. Mao quotes the ancient Chinese writer Sima Qian (d. 86 BCE) to coin a new anti-fascist statement. It is from this speech that Mao's "serve the people" slogan arose.

31. Meaning that the time has come to take the necessary action.

330 • THE IMAGINATIVE VISION OF ABDILATIF ABDALLA'S *VOICE OF AGONY*

"LONG DELAYED JUSTICE OR LONG CONTINUED INJUSTICE PROVOKES THE EMPLOYMENT OF FORCE TO OBTAIN REDRESS"

–J.B.[32]

NOVEMBER 1968   *THE DISCONTENTED*
                       MOMBASA

---

32. John Bright (1811–1889), British radical reformer, member of parliament, and a brilliant orator. Abdalla is likely to have taken this quote from Tom Mboya's book *Freedom and After*, which was first published in 1963, where a longer version (attributed to a speech from 1866) is cited by Mboya on page 52. However, Abdalla remembers that he encountered it in his reading of Gandhi's autobiography, *The Story of My Experiments with Truth*. I have not been able to verify this.

Introduction to the 1973 Edition

Shihabuddin Chiraghdin

Translated by Ann Biersteker

After reading *Sauti ya Dhiki*, I am convinced that this is a courageous young man who is outraged because of the pain that he has experienced. If someone is in agony, there is nothing better than to express those feelings. And for a Swahili person, the best way is to voice them in a captivating manner in poetry and song, if he knows how—something that Abdilatif, thank God, had no difficulty in doing.

The late Amri Abedi Kaluta said of Swahili poets that many are "people who did not receive a great deal of modern education [that is, they were not completely consumed by foreign thoughts], and because of this, the thoughts that they speak poetically are ideas and philosophies that come from their life experience [in their cultural environment]."[1]

It would not be true to say that Abdilatif was not influenced by the foreign education he received. Many of us have been affected by this, being influenced by foreign cultures and customs in our writings and thought. But Abdilatif did not succumb to the control of these influences. As a result, his poems do not show any influence from foreign forms, and his thoughts are in accord with Swahiliness and with Africanness in general. That's not an easy task. Take, for example, the way he describes how a woman puts on her make-up in the poem "Tit for Tat" (p. 215). There is nothing European at all. Even the lip color is not "lipstick"; it is *mdaa*.[2] He is able to talk about issues which are controversial today, like ending a pregnancy, abortion, and he doesn't go

---

1. Mathias E. Mnyampala, *Waadhi wa Ushairi* (Dar es Salaam: East African Literature Bureau, 1965), v. (The bracketed remarks are Chiraghdin's addition. —*Ed.*)

2. Tree, *Euclea fructuosa*, of the East African coast, the sticks of which deposit red color. —*Ed.*

THE IMAGINATIVE VISION OF ABDILATIF ABDALLA'S *VOICE OF AGONY*

looking for foreign ideas; for example, the embryo that has yet to take on human form tells its mother (p. 127):

> I won't lack someone to clean me after birth

> Whenever I wail ng'aa! ng'aa! she will comfort me quickly

Or when it pleads for justice and, speaking of life and death, says to its mother that she shouldn't kill it, or when it debates with its mother, saying to her (p. 127), "The world isn't full, there's still plenty of space."

This is indeed what the late Shaaban Robert said: "The language of poetry is of the most carefully chosen words ... the beauty of poetry is enduring beauty ... Poems with the intensive thought, the moral integrity, and the righteousness in actions which people of any century will be unable to reject or forget are the kind of poetry that is wanted."[3] I am hopeful that Abdilatif fits the bill. A few examples will suffice:

> ... Like a dog that sees a bone and is scared to gnaw it, Mama
>
> ("Our Mother Africa")

> What belongs to yesterday dies with it and becomes departed
> You won't see it again, even if you live forever
> Perhaps things that resemble it may come in turns
> But the real thing —never ...

> Focus your eyes well so today won't escape you
> Leading you to complain after it's disappeared
> Leaving you saying, why didn't I grab it?
> Grab it now, grab it ...

> Tomorrow is a telescope that peers far ahead
> And it is the apple of our eye; look there so you may see
> Tomorrow is full of promise, that you may hope for this and that
> Tomorrow is forever ahead
>
> ("Yesterday and Today and Tomorrow" [stanzas 7, 15, 28—*Ed.*])

---

3. *Swahili* 1, no. 32 [1961], part III: 32.

Introduction to the 1973 Edition • 333

... Trouble and anxiety are ways of knowing the world
One not beset by these is not yet a worldling

("Don't Cling to Silence")

... Until you used it all up and made yourselves nothing

("Come to Your Senses")

... One plus one isn't one, yet for us it's so

("Goodbye")

... What makes someone human is his humaneness towards others

("A Thing Can't Be Human")

... If you can create, create another me

("Tit for Tat")

And now I want to use *Voice of Agony* to expound upon my own anguish, and this anguish is something we all share: the way Kiswahili has suffered historically and politically. When the Europeans arrived, it was in their interest to use a local language which had spread more than others. That is why they studied Kiswahili; experts emerged to teach it to their fellow Europeans, they compiled dictionaries, they wrote grammar books in their languages, and they collected, preserved, and studied Swahili literature. They certainly did a great deal, and we should thank them—in other words, give the Devil his due.[4]

Their expertise, though, was not much concerned with the culture or structure of the Swahili language. For this reason they left a large gap and were in other ways misguided in their research. And among the things about which they were uncertain is the origin of those whose language it is—the Swahili people.

They brought us this "Standard Swahili." The idea behind "Standard Swahili" is very good. But its shortcoming is that it denies itself the span and the broad horizons of the language by choosing only one or two dialects of Swahili when there are more than ten; and some of these are more widespread and have longer histories than those which they chose.

Now our current difficulty is that some of us have persisted in following in the footsteps of the foreigners who colonized us; we miss no chance to do

---

4. The Swahili expression here, "Mgala muue na haki umpe," more literally translated "Although we are at war with the Mgala, still we have to give him his rights," connects historically to attacks by the Oromo people on Swahili city-states and contains a dated term, now considered derogatory, for an Oromo person. —*Ed.*

so. We want all of our Swahili language instruction to depend entirely on European books. For such people, anyone who comes forward and shows the flaws of those dictionaries and grammars, it is as if that person has blasphemed.

We have been running from ourselves, and we have hidden facts from ourselves under the guise of politics by denying that there are indigenous Swahili people. When we call the dialects of Swahili "lesser languages,"[5] we show that this "standard" language established for us by our colonizers is the most esteemed, and all other dialects are less worthy. We tend to forget that these dialects are the roots of language; if these roots dry up, the tree will fall, or even if it continues to stand, it will be simply a shell of itself, lifeless.

We should not be afraid to say that Swahili has indigenous speakers, because the good thing about it is that it can also belong to whoever claims it. For Swahili and other regional languages are like cousins; they are kin. So if we Africans are able to study Arabic, French, and English to the extent that these languages become ours, it is not surprising that Swahili, for Africans of this region and even others, if they engage with it, becomes theirs as if they were born with it. But we should not try to uproot it from its natural environment, because as Abdilatif says in another context (p. 183), "What place does the crab have besides its own shell?"

So "this is what I hold fast"—that is, we should develop the language by including all regional varieties of Swahili; we should not impair it by persisting in that same colonial arrogance and laziness, compelled by that heritage.[6] One way of developing, revering, and revitalizing the Swahili language is to obtain writings like this one of Abdilatif—originating from different regions. Therefore, I say congratulations, or as we say in another region, offer him felicitations (for positive reasons, no others), for dancing to our own beat, not to other people's.[7] I also congratulate him for teaching us (p. 183) that we should resist oppression: "I'll die where I was born, I'm not running away."

---

5. Swahili *vilugha*: Chiraghdin argues against use of this word, then the accepted terminology, with its derogatory implications, preferring *lahaja*, "dialects." —*Ed.*

6. Chiraghdin quotes the title phrase of the poem "N'shishiyelo ni Lilo," in this volume rendered "I Won't Compromise" in the translation of Ken Walibora Waliaula (p. 5) and more literally in the translation of Meg Arenberg (p. 313). —*Ed.*

7. Chiraghdin uses two Swahili terms for congratulations, *heko* and *hongera*. The parenthetical (in Swahili, "ya haki salama, si ya mengineyo") separates his celebration of Abdilatif's poems from outright embrace of the political position they articulate, a precaution important at the time of his writing. —*Ed.*

Abdilatif says (p. 5) that he will not abandon his conviction, and since he says this, it is not for me to tell him he should abandon it. But I will tell him to calm his heart, as he has said in his poem "Worry Not" (p. 15).

SHIHABUDDIN CHIRAGHDIN
Mombasa, May 1973

Author's Preface to the 1973 Edition

Abdilatif Abdalla

Translated by Ann Biersteker

All the poems here except "I'm Back" (p. 285), which I composed after being released, are poems that I wrote while imprisoned in Kenya, from March 1969 through March 1972. Because life in prison is not pleasant, I gave these poems the title "Voice of Agony."

Although this is not the place to explain the reason why I was jailed, I feel mentioning it is essential, because perhaps I would not have written these poems had I not been imprisoned.

The reason for my imprisonment was that I was found guilty of "inciting people to overthrow violently the Government of Kenya," after writing, publishing, and distributing in several towns of Coast Province, Kenya, a pamphlet I called "Kenya: Where Are We Heading?"

The poems included here deal with the reasons why I was imprisoned; the imprisonment itself; what I felt in my heart; my convictions, and my views concerning what was taking place outside the prison walls.

Although I don't want to explain every poem in this book, there are a few I would like to elucidate:

The first is "Worry Not" (p. 15). I composed this poem to respond to the following verse written by someone who sympathized with me:

> Patience brings solace, better that you persevere
> Keep on with it and raise your hands to the heavens
> Pray to the Almighty: God willing you will be rewarded
> Heed this advice[1]

---

1. In Swahili, the stanza reads:
   Subira huvuta kheri, ukisubiri ni mno
   Nawe zidi kusubiri, wekeze mbingu mikono
   Uombe alo Qahari, inshallah hukosi neno
   Ushike wasiya huno —*Ed.*

The second is "Be Patient, My Heart" (p. 115). The purpose of composing this was to comfort myself. I wrote this poem on October 20, 1971, as a response to not having been released on October 19 as I had expected.

The third is "Don't Cling to Silence" (p. 155) which I composed for my brother, Ahmad Nassir (Ustadh Bhalo), wanting to know why I was not receiving his letters.

The fourth is "Come to Your Senses" (p. 165). I wrote this for my compatriots on the Kenyan coast.

The fifth is "Goodbye" (p. 175). I composed this to bid farewell to my fellow prisoner Israel Otieno. This was a young man with whom I got along very well. I wrote this poem when I was transferred from Kamiti Prison to Shimo la Tewa Prison.

The sixth is "I'm Coming" (p. 183). When I composed this, I still had three months of my sentence to serve. I wrote this to tell myself that I was approaching the end of my time, alerting my well-wishers of my impending return and warning those who awaited me with hostility.

Before finishing my preface, I wish to thank very much Mr. Shihabuddin Chiraghdin for writing the introduction for this collection of mine. This, for me, is a great honor.

ABDILATIF ABDALLA
Dar es Salaam,
22 February 1973

BIBLIOGRAPHY

Abdalla, Abdilatif. "Matatizo ya Mwandishi wa Jamii katika Afrika Huru" ("Problems of a People's Writer in Independent Africa"). 1978. In *Abdilatif Abdalla: Poet in Politics*. Edited by Rose Marie Beck and Kai Kresse. Dar es Salaam: Mkuki na Nyota, 2016, 87–95.

Abdalla, Abdilatif. *Sauti ya Dhiki*. Nairobi: Oxford University Press, 1973.

Abdalla, Abdilatif. *Utenzi wa Adamu na Hawa*. Nairobi: Oxford University Press, 1971.

Abdalla, Abdilatif. "Wajibu wa Mshairi katika Jamii Yake" ("The Obligations of a Poet within His/Her Society"). 1976. In *Abdilatif Abdalla: Poet in Politics*. Edited by Rose Marie Beck and Kai Kresse. Dar es Salaam: Mkuki na Nyota, 2016, 81–86.

Abdulaziz, Mohamed H. *Muyaka: 19th Century Swahili Popular Poetry*. Nairobi: Kenya Literature Bureau, 1979.

Agweule, Augustine. "Practice of Historical Linguistics and Language Codification in Africa." *History Compass* 6, no. 1 (2008): 1–24.

Alawy, Abdurrahman Saggaf and Ali Abdalla El-Maawy. *Kale ya Washairi wa Pemba: Kamange na Sarahani*. Edited by Abdilatif Abdalla. Dar es Salaam: Mkuki na Nyota, 2011.

Armah, Ayi Kwei. *Wema Hawajazaliwa*. Translated by Abdilatif Abdalla. Nairobi: Heinemann, 1975.

Askew, Kelly M. *Performing the Nation: Swahili Music and Cultural Politics in Tanzania*. Chicago: University of Chicago Press, 2002.

Balisidya, May Ndyanao Matteru. "Mapitio ya *Sauti ya Dhiki*." *Mulika* 7 (1975): 24–32.

Beck, Rose Marie and Kai Kresse, eds. *Abdilatif Abdalla: Poet in Politics*. Dar es Salaam: Mkuki na Nyota, 2016.

Biersteker, Ann and Ibrahim Shariff. *Mashairi ya Vita vya Kuduhu*. East Lansing: Michigan State University Press, 1995.

Chiraghdin, Shihabuddin. "Utangulizi." In *Sauti ya Dhiki*. By Abdilatif Abdalla. Nairobi: Oxford University Press, 1973, ix–xii.

Ganzel, Eddie. *Jogoo la Shamba*. Arusha, Tanzania: Eastern Africa Publications, 1978.

Hamad, Maryam Ali. "Suala la Ufungwa katika Ushairi wa Kiswahili: Mifano kutoka Diwani za Sauti ya Dhiki na Chembe cha Moyo." MA Thesis. University of Dodoma, Tanzania, 2017.

Havel, Vaclav. *Uzinduzi*. Translated into Swahili by Abdilatif Abdalla and Alena Rettová. Prague: Zdeněk Susa, 2005.

340 • *Bibliography*

Hussein, Ebrahim. *At the Edge of Thim*. Translated by Kimani Njogu. Oxford: Oxford University Press, 2000.

Hussein, Ebrahim. *Kinjeketile*. Dar es Salaam: Oxford University Press, 1969.

Hussein, Ebrahim N. *Kinjeketile* [English version]. Dar es Salaam: Oxford University Press, 1970.

Hussein Ebrahim N. *Kwenye Ukingo wa Thim*. Nairobi: Oxford University Press, 1988.

Kane, Cheikh Hamidou. *Ambiguous Adventure*. Translated by Katherine Woods. London: Heinemann, 1972.

Kezilahabi, Euphrase. *Rosa Mistika*. Nairobi: East African Literature Bureau, 1971. .

Khamis, Said Ahmed. "Whither Swahili Literature? Translation and World Recognition of Abdilatif Abdalla's *Sauti ya Dhiki*." In *Abdilatif Abdalla: Poet in Politics*. Edited by Rose Marie Beck and Kai Kresse. Dar es Salaam: Mkuki na Nyota, 2016, 35–43.

Kresse, Kai. "*Kenya: Twendapi?*: Re-Reading Abdilatif Abdalla's Pamphlet Fifty Years after Independence." *Africa* 86, no. 1 (February 2016): 1–32.

Kresse, Kai. *Swahili Muslim Publics and Postcolonial Experience*. Bloomington, Ind.: Indiana University Press, 2018.

Madumulla, Joshua, Elena Bertoncini, and Jan Blommaert. "Politics, Ideology and Poetic Form: the Literary Debate in Tanzania." In *Language Ideological Debates*. Edited by Jan Blommaert. New York: Mouton de Gruyter, 1999, 307–341.

Mazrui, Alamin. "Abdilatif and I: Reflections on Comparative Experiences." Paper presented at a roundtable on "The Imaginative Vision of Abdilatif Abdalla: Kenyan Poet and Activist." Princeton University, 9 November 2017.

Mazrui, Alamin. *Chembe cha Moyo*. Nairobi: Heinemann, 1988.

Mazrui, Alamin. *Swahili Beyond the Boundaries: Literature, Language, and Identity*. Athens, Ohio: Ohio University Press, 2007.

Mazrui, Ali A. "The African University as a Multinational Corporation: Problems of Penetration and Dependency." *Harvard Educational Review* 45, no. 2 (1975): 191–210.

Miehe, Gudrun, Abdilatif Abdalla and Liyongo Working Group, eds. *Liyongo Songs: Poems Attributed to Fumo Liyongo*. Cologne: Rüdiger Köppe Verlag, 2004.

Mkangi, Katama. *Mafuta*. Nairobi: Heinemann Educational Books, 1984.

Mkangi, Katama. *Walenisi*. Nairobi: East Africa Educational Publishers, 1995.

Mnyampala, Mathias E. *Waadhi wa Ushairi*. Dar es Salaam: East African Literature Bureau, 1965.

Mohamed, Said Ahmed. '*Sikate Tamaa*. Edited by Abdilatif Abdalla. Nairobi: Longman, 1980.

Muhando, Penina. *Hatia*. Nairobi: East African Publishing House, 1972.

Muhando, Penina. *Tambueni Haki Zetu*. Dar es Salaam: Tanzanian Publishing House, 1973.

Mulokozi, Mugyabuso M. "A Survey of Kiswahili Literature: 1970–1988." *Afrika Focus* 8, no. 1 (1992): 49–61. DOI https://doi.org/10.21825/af.v8i1.5850

Mulokozi, M[ugyabuso]. M. "Mapitio ya *Sauti ya Dhiki*." *Umma* 4, no. 1 (1974).

Nassir, Ahmad. (Juma Bhalo). *Malenga wa Mvita*. Nairobi: Oxford University Press, 1971.

Njogu, Kimani. *Zilizala*. Nairobi: Longman Kenya, 2006.

Nyaigotti-Chacha, Chacha. *Hukumu*. Nairobi: Longman Kenya, 1992.

Nyaigotti-Chacha, Chacha. "The Teaching of Kiswahili Poetry: A Thematic Analysis in a College Class." In *Journal of Proceedings: A Workshop on Swahili Instruction*. Edited by Philip T.K. Daniel, Ann Biersteker, and Victoria Moreland. DeKalb, Illinois: Northern Illinois University, Center for Minority Studies, 1983, 91–109.

Nyaigotti-Chacha, Chacha. *Ushairi wa Abdilatif Abdalla: Sauti ya Utetezi*. Dar es Salaam: Dar es Salaam University Press, 1992.

Nyaigotti-Chacha, Chacha. *Wingu Jeusi*. Nairobi: Heinemann Kenya, 1987.

Nyamaume, K.A. *Diwani ya Ustadh Nyamaume*. Poems collected by S.C. Gonga. Edited by Abdilatif Abdalla. Nairobi: Shungwaya Publishers, 1976.

Ohly, Rajmund. "A Review of Abdilatif Abdalla's *Sauti ya Dhiki*." *Kiswahili* 44, no. 2 (1974): 82–91.

p'Bitek, Okot. *Song of Lawino: A Lament*. Nairobi: East African Publishing House, 1966.

Rajab, Ahmed. "The Urgency of Memory in an Age of Greed." In *Abdilatif Abdalla: Poet in Politics*. Edited by Rose Marie Beck and Kai Kresse. Dar es Salaam: Mkuki na Nyota, 2016, 65–73.

Rettová, Alena. "Swahili and Swahili Poetry in Lubumbashi: The Language and Lyrics of Sando Marteau." *Archiv Orientální* 86, no. 3 (2018): 333–362.

Reynolds, Matthew. Introduction to *Prismatic Translation*. Edited by Matthew Reynolds. Cambridge: Legenda, 2019, 1–18.

Scheub, Harold. *The Uncoiling Python: South African Storytellers and Resistance*. Athens, Ohio: Swallow Press, 2010.

Shariff, Ibrahim Noor. "The Function of Dialogue Poetry in Swahili Society." EdD dissertation. Rutgers University, 1983.

Talento, Serena. "Consecration, Deconsecration, and Reconsecration: The Shifting Role of Literary Translation into Swahili." In *Translators Have Their Say?: Translation and the Power of Agency*. Edited by Abdel-Wahab Khalifa. Zürich: LIT, 2014, 42–64.

Thiong'o, Ngũgĩ wa. "Abdilatif Abdalla and the Voice of Prophecy." In *Abdilatif Abdalla: Poet in Politics*. Edited by Rose Marie Beck and Kai Kresse. Dar es Salaam: Mkuki na Nyota, 2016, 11–18.

Thiong'o, Ngũgĩ wa. *The River Between*. Nairobi: Heinemann, 1965.

Thiong'o, Ngũgĩ wa. *Weep Not, Child*. Nairobi: Heinemann, 1964.

Topan, Farouk. *Uchambuzi wa Maandishi ya Kiswahili*. Nairobi: Oxford University Press, 1972.

Venuti, Lawrence. *Contra Instrumentalism: A Translation Polemic*. Lincoln: University of Nebraska Press, 2019.

Vierke, Clarissa. "'What Is There in My Speaking': Re-Explorations of Language in Abdilatif Abdalla's Anthology of Prison Poetry, *Sauti Ya Dhiki*." *Research in African Literatures* 48, no. 1 (2017): 135–157.

342 • Bibliography

Waliaula, Ken Walibora. "Doing Things with Words in Prison Poetry." In *Abdilatif Abdalla: Poet in Politics*. Edited by Rose Marie Beck and Kai Kresse. Dar es Salaam: Mkuki na Nyota, 2016, 55–63.

Waliaula, Ken Walibora. *Narrating Prison Experience: Human Rights, Self, Society, and Political Incarceration in Africa*. Champaign, IL: Common Ground, 2013.

Waliaula, Ken Walibora. "Prison, Poetry, and Polyphony in Abdilatif Abdalla's *Sauti ya Dhiki*." *Research in African Literatures* 40, no. 3 (2009): 129–148.

Wanjiru, Kimani wa. "Abdilatif Abdalla: My Poems Gave Me Company." *Pambazuka News*, 14 October 2010. https://www.pambazuka.org/arts/abdilatif-abdalla-my-poems-gave-me-company.

CONTRIBUTORS

Meg Arenberg is a scholar of African literary and cultural studies and a literary translator. Her translations from Kiswahili have been published in *Words Without Borders* and *The Black Anthology: Language* from 1010 Press. Having completed a postdoctoral research fellowship in the AMESALL Department at Rutgers University, she is now Assistant Professor of Comparative Literature at the Africa Institute in Sharjah, UAE.

Ann Biersteker co-edited *Mashairi ya Vita vya Kuduhu* (1995) and is the author of *Kujibizana: Questions of Language and Power in Nineteenth- and Twentieth-Century Poetry in Kiswahili* (1996) and *Masomo ya Kisasa* (1990). She recently co-authored a study of the Dhaiso language, *Kidaiso: Sarufi na Msamiati* (2019), and she has published numerous articles on African literatures and languages.

Annmarie Drury is the translator and editor of *Stray Truths: Selected Poems of Euphrase Kezilahabi* (2015) and the author of *Translation as Transformation in Victorian Poetry* (2015), as well as of many articles and poems. She is Associate Professor of English at Queens College, City University of New York.

Kai Kresse is the author of *Swahili Muslim Publics and Postcolonial Experience in Coastal Kenya* (2018) and of *Philosophising in Mombasa: Knowledge, Islam, and Intellectual Practice on the Swahili Coast* (2007), as well as articles about knowledge cultures in coastal East Africa, and on African philosophers. Among his co-edited volumes are *Abdilatif Abdalla: Poet in Politics* (2016). He is Vice Director for research at Leibniz-Zentrum Moderner Orient, Berlin, and Professor of Social and Cultural Anthropology at the Free University of Berlin.

Alamin Mazrui teaches in the Department of African, Middle Eastern and South Asian Languages and Literatures at Rutgers University. He has (co-)authored or (co-)edited several books, including *Cultural Politics of Translation: East Africa in a Global Context* (2016), and his essays have

344 • Contributors

appeared in various journals and edited collections. He has also published poems and plays in Kiswahili.

Ngũgĩ wa Thiong'o is the author, in Gĩkũyũ and English, of internationally acclaimed fiction, plays, memoirs, and literary essays. He was held as a political prisoner in Kenya from 1977 to 1978, an experience he details in *Detained: A Writer's Prison Diary* (1982) and *Wrestling with the Devil: A Prison Memoir* (2018). He is Distinguished Professor of English and Comparative Literature at the University of California, Irvine.

Ken Walibora Waliaula, who died in 2020, held a PhD in Comparative Studies from The Ohio State University and authored articles and a monograph, *Narrating Prison Experience: Human Rights, Self, Society, and Political Incarceration in Africa* (2013), on the prison literature of Africa. He worked for the Nation Media Group in Kenya and was celebrated for his novels—including, in Swahili, *Siku Njema* (1996) and *Ndoto ya Amerika* (2003), which was awarded the Jomo Kenyatta Prize for Literature—and a memoir, *Nasikia Sauti ya Mama* (2014), also awarded the Jomo Kenyatta Prize.